LOOK AT IT MY WAY SIR

Bits of a Life, 1946 – 2016

Lance St John Butler

Printed and Published by
For The Right Reasons
fortherightreasons@rocketmail.com
60 Grant Street Inverness IV3 8BS
2016

CONTENTS

4

NOTE

There is an immodesty about memoirs, a genre which risks seeming like an intolerably extended version of that already-intolerable genre the Round-Robin Letter. You must have had one, probably at Christmas, a tedious and densely-printed two-sides-of-A4 in which some middle-distance friend lets you know that 'in February, after much thought, Geoffrey decided it was time for him to buy a new computer' and 'in October we felt we deserved a short break in Tuscany.'

In the summer of 2012 however, on a holiday in Brittany (there seems no escape from the register) a friend suggested that since I had 'a lot of stories which should be written down' I ought to set about it at once, clearly suppressing the logical addendum 'before it is too late.' This was too flattering to be resisted. I was reading Lord Chesterfield's *Letters* at the time and received three body-blows from the old poseur ('great and good' according to Beckett, rather astonishingly) while I considered my enterprise. First, he says, Do Not Speak About Yourself; second, Never Laugh. Then he weighs in with the knockout: third, Never Tell Stories. Dear God, what's left?

CHAPTER ONE.   DORSET (1946 – 1966)

1. FIRST

My first memory is of sunshine. I sprang out of oblivion, like Athene fully-armed from the head of Zeus, at about the age of three, rounding a corner at Silton House and pushing a bear on wheels. The bear was on all fours and faced forwards. Behind him a metal bar steadied my gait and in front of us, beyond the corner of the house and beyond the gravel, stretched a sunlit lawn. I have never forgotten the moment. Like many others I have a special place in my heart for bears. Sunshine also.

The grown-ups were behind me, darkly present. They were of course the post-Victorians who had to cope with the fact that Britain (more usually just 'England' then) was not what it had been. At the time of Queen Victoria's Diamond Jubilee in 1897 Britain owned or ran most of the world, being legally in charge of a quarter of its land area and a third of its people, was possessed of a hundred colonies and, in those places where its writ did not run, was the nation most admired or feared by the locals - I am thinking of the importance of the United Kingdom to say Argentina, China or even France in terms of influence and prestige. We were Top.

Fifty years later, in 1947 when I was one year old, things were very different. In spite of the fact that we had won two world wars we found ourselves handing India back to the Indians (I have in my lifetime met a number of Indians who didn't say Thank You for this - I don't mean that they had bad manners but rather that they wished we had never left), decolonising rapidly, declining economically and losing ground in terms of world leadership; 'British and Best', which I

7

remember as a catch phrase, was replaced by 'You don't want that car / machine / system; it's the British one. Try this German model.' The red on the map of the world that had adorned the walls of my earliest schools was disappearing and British influence was waning. So my parents' generation struggled between two worlds, one dying, the other only too stridently insisting on being born, and perhaps my generation has too.

I was born in 1946 at Silton, the northernmost parish in Dorset, where my mother Diana and my aunt Eleanor lived together and brought up their four children without benefit of very many husbands but with benefit of various servants and hangers-on. Eleanor's husband Dick Honnywill, a millionaire of sorts of whom more will be said later, had bought Silton House not long before. His own uncle Arthur had gone down in the *Lusitania*, torpedoed by a German U-Boat in 1915, leaving to Dick and his brother Jack the bulk of a fortune made in the cotton mills of Lancashire. Jack was a ne'er-do well who will feature very briefly in these memoirs, which is how he figured in my life *in propria persona*. But Uncle Dick was an Evangelical Anglican who joined the Navy and belonged to that species of naval officer which is equally interested in the message of Jesus Christ and the fortunes of the Senior Service, and he ended up for a few years as my substitute father *in loco parentis*.

My mother Diana and her sister Eleanor, who had been born in India (in 1920 and 1916 respectively), lived together at Silton after the war while their husbands, my father and my Uncle Dick, were away. My father was a Gunner (since these things are falling out of common parlance let me say that I mean he was an officer in the Royal Artillery) and like Dick was employed on military business in London clearing up

8

after the end of hostilities. Eleanor and Diana said later that this period was the happiest time of their lives. They were devoted to each other and both had that extreme self-abnegating spirit of many ladies of their generation (and it was made apparent to me that they were *ladies*) who had been brought up to get involved, to take responsibility, not to complain and generally to Do Their Best. I remember my mother telling me that she and Eleanor had it as a motto that You Hadn't Done Enough until you had Done As Much As You Possibly Could. There were still servants of various kinds in those days, who had not yet been re-named 'Help' by a guilty middle class, and Silton had several of them, but these were also the days before the labour-saving device and there were four children to bring up in the large house and garden and in the rural neighbourhood where they took the social lead.

I fear that this halcyon period for my mother and aunt was happy partly *because* their husbands were away. For these marriages, though decent enough, were not really marriages of love.

So, to resume, I was born in Dorset after World War Two. My grandparents had seen the light of day back in the later nineteenth century. All I ever knew of my paternal grandfather was that he was a soldier who during the First World War had received an uncomfortable amount of shrapnel in the head, which destabilised him a bit. He had been invalided out first to Ireland, whence like all good Butlers he originally came, and thence to Cornwall where according to current medical opinion the air was better for head wounds. He was accompanied, at His Majesty's expense, by a batman-for-life as well as by his long-suffering wife and two sons, one of them my father. The old boy's antics with his service revolver, wielded according to legend fairly freely at the time of the full moon, led to my father's leaving home forever at the age of eighteen, and as a result of that I never met the old man or, come to that, my grandmother on that side.

My mother's parents were a little clearer to me. My maternal grandfather had, it is true, died in 1932 at the age of 51 and I never knew him. He was born in India in 1881, educated at Winchester in the same house as Oscar Wilde's Bosie, and became a professional Indian Army soldier. Some fair diplomatic know-how led to his appointment in the 1920s to the Indian Civil Service and a post as Political Resident in various parts of what was then known as Persia: Meshed, Bushir and Bandar-Abbas spring to memory. In these places Lt Col Sir Hugh Vincent Biscoe, to give him the full mouthful, became an effective Resident if rumour over the years is to be believed. He was on faintly intimate terms with the eponymous founder of Saudi Arabia, King Abdulaziz Ibn Saud, with the Emir of Kuwait and with the Sultan of Muscat whom he was instrumental in putting on the throne after bringing about the removal of his father, the dreadful old tyrant who had preceded him. Such was British power in those days. Such also was my grandfather's command of Arabic, Farsi and the Indian languages normal for an officer of his background. The thought that this servant of empire was any kind of fascist bully, mistreater of natives or capitalist exploiter is nothing short of absurd. Out of a sense of duty, duty to the people he defended and administered as much as duty to the British Crown, he remained in the East where he was overworked and comparatively poorly-paid; he chose, instead of the early retirement strongly indicated by a heart condition, to soldier on to an early death when he left an impoverished widow and three children.[1]

This widow, my grandmother Lady Dorothy Biscoe or 'D', the only grandparent that I actually knew, who had also been born in India, returned to England in 1932 with these three children (my aunt Eleanor, my mother, and their older brother Dudley), more or less penniless. Like many of her class and time D saw her daughters' future as lying in marriage so she, and they, joined what was known as the Fishing Fleet which every year took eligible young ladies out to India where there were plenty of eligible bachelor officers. By 1937 my aunt Eleanor had married a naval lieutenant, the said Uncle Dick, and my mother Diana, aged only seventeen, had married a Gunner subaltern seven years her senior – my father, Lt George Alec Lawrence Butler, known to family and friends as Guy or sometimes Gay, the latter a soubriquet he might not have adopted so heartily after, say, 1970. Successful Fishing had occurred. That either my aunt Eleanor or her younger sister knew the first thing about love, sex, marriage or life may well be doubted.

Eleanor had been sent briefly to convent schools in Britain, living with vague semi-aunts of her own and being very miserable, like Rudyard Kipling under similar circumstances, until the age of eleven when my grandparents thought it best for her to join them in the Middle East. She then travelled overland to Baghdad with some British travellers in a Buick, feeling sick, hot and confused, to meet parents she only vaguely remembered. She never went back to school.

My mother, if you come to that, never went to school at all and was educated in the Political

---

[1] For further brief thoughts about the Empire, see the Appendix at the end of these Memoirs.

11

Residencies where my grandfather held sway, by English governesses. I have a book of hers, a present from a departing governess, which attests that she was Top in Everything. As we shall see, Diana was not an altogether happy woman and reacted with some sadness to her minimised status and her lack of education. I rarely saw her smile and never heard her laugh. She was, for all the teams of oriental servants she had known in Meshed or on the Trucial Coast, reduced as a married woman, especially after we left Silton, to the status of posh lonely skivvy. This was a *de facto* situation, not one brought about by any design or malice on the part of my father who, after he had left home in 1931, slamming the door behind him to avoid further confrontations with his father's service revolver, had inherited nothing from his parents and had only his army pay to live on. We never stayed anywhere long enough for my mother to make friends, there was little in the way of help and there were few labour-saving devices.

When my mother died of cancer in 1963 at the age of forty-two, more or less on the day I went up to Cambridge, it turned out that she had asked her sister Eleanor, 'Arnie', along with Uncle Dick, to take care of my brother Piers and me, both of us in our late teens by then. This was in some sense a ghostly revival of the best days of her life when the two sisters had worked, and sometimes allegedly even laughed, in Silton House after the war.

2. FOREHEAD

Early in life there is for all of us, conventionally, a
moment of vocation, of vision into our futures. In
Middlemarch George Eliot gives Tertius Lydgate a very
explicit moment of this kind when, standing on the
moveable steps in his uncle's library, he is transfixed by
a book he has stumbled on more or less by accident.
Without moving to a more comfortable position he
stands there, reading away for dear life. It is a medical
textbook, and it determines his vocation as a doctor, a
calling that in his case will come to so little after its
promising start. My friend Charlie Maclean, at a similar
age, had the same experience with a glass of whisky, a
drink he now sells for a living; he has had no regrets.
Here is my own moment.

At Silton in the late 1940s there were always
quite a lot of people about: children, visiting Canadians,
unspecified grown-ups, other Dutch Uncles and Aunts,
the odd domestic, nannies. I was always the smallest,
but no harm in that. The youngest can usually get away
with most because the juices of parental revenge have
run a bit thin by the time the older children have been
dealt with over the years. Punishment has turned to
sentiment. But then the youngest and smallest has a
certain amount of asserting to do if he is not to be
trampled underfoot in the mad rush of Egos of All Sizes
above him, and this he cannot, by definition, do with his
fists, feet or elbows.

I was a peculiarly dense baby, mind-wise, and
extraordinarily passive. If I could lie down I would lie
down, and if I couldn't lie I would sit. Only with
reluctance would I crawl or later walk. I had few
reactions and no expressed desires. When I went to
school in due course I was considered almost as a sort

13

of dumb pet, a hopeless backwardee. I remained in the same form at prep school (2B) more or less, without noticing it, until I was ten. For some odd reason I then jumped forward two years in as many months and was not only always thereafter the youngest in my class but also Second-in-Class at the end of each year. Second is not as good as Top, of course, but Top was a Polish genius called Krzanowski who could do Maths and Physics and the subjects where you can get 100% and other unfair numbers. He stayed Top and ended up a Lecturer in Maths at Reading University. I, though Second, managed a Professorship in English. Such is fate.

But I was Second *and* a year younger than my classmates. For a while I didn't notice this any more than I had noticed things when an infant blob, but then I realised, slowly and with much surprise, that some people thought me Clever. Naturally I knew, and certainly know now, that no one is *really* clever who can't do Maths and Science. So I didn't impress myself much and still don't. My denseness never altogether evaporated and to this day I have to imagine a map with the Americas on one side and China on the other before I can remember whether west is left or right.

Words, nonetheless, came jerkily towards me in my first years, offering ambiguous friendship. Things I said provoked laughter and that was very nice. People listened – often only to correct me or snigger of course - but they did listen. And so it came to pass that I Made a Funny, by accident, one spring morning in, well, in the Morning Room at Silton, scene of many a family conspiracy and drama. This was my Tertius Lydgate moment, though I was only three. A lot of people were there, perhaps having the coffee that had just come back on the market, though in a severely Rationed manner, after the end of the war. The discussion turned to the topic of baldness as I lolled densely in a corner, one day to be pretty bald myself. The word 'forehead' rang in the air (to rhyme with 'horrid' in that place and time and among those people.) I stirred and listened. There was a pause. My thinning father, back for the weekend from some piece of War Office bumf-shovelling in London, touched his hair. I squeaked to get attention and then said: 'Pa has got a lot of forrid in the corners.'

Hoots of derisive or appreciative laughter greeted this innocent observation; people banged the table, Uncle Dick had a coughing fit, my mother looked both pleased and embarrassed; the domestic slave Humpy Annie, who was stone deaf, shouted 'What? What did he say?' Whatever it was it clearly put me into a new and desirable position among the adults of the house, even among my cousins and my brother. Years later, when I had found out that losing one's hair, unlike say losing one's teeth, is a legitimate object of ridicule, I felt I understood better.

At all events this moment, in retrospect at least, set a pattern of wanting to entertain, of finding validation in the laughter of others. I grew up wanting to be a comic actor or, when I found out what it was, an academic with an amusing lecturing-style. For what it's worth, the only complaint I ever heard about my lectures at Stirling University was from a student who said that he was unable to take proper notes because he was so busy laughing – not an altogether complimentary reaction.

Getting a foothold in the only career where I could have been happy was a matter of luck, as we shall see, and luck has sometimes been my lot I think. At school, for instance, I was often in trouble, as we shall also see. I thought that the monks at Belmont rather

15

liked me, but perhaps they didn't. Father Illtyd seemed to like me rather a lot in the book cupboard one damp afternoon though it only came in the end to a hug, but the others may only have been pretending because, one day, extending their tonsures on the subject of my derelictions without my really knowing what it was all about, they made the decision to get rid of me. Expulsion came as a bit of a surprise as I think it went past me entirely unexplained and I was on a train home without really knowing how or why.

Without realising how important it was, I had applied, aged 16, to both Oxford and Cambridge. Pembroke College Cambridge and Lincoln College Oxford accepted me in spite of interviews in retrospect lamentable, and I wrote accepting Pembroke and rejecting Lincoln; unfortunately there must have been a resurgence of my old denseness because I put the letters in the wrong envelopes and, after a number of baffled phone-calls from the respective Admissions Tutors and a fair amount of fast footwork, secured the place at Cambridge. As I was so young and had not taken my A-levels this place, obtained by means of a scholarship exam, was dependent on my also obtaining some piffling A-level grades. To obtain these I had to return to Belmont Abbey, the school whence I had just been expelled (trying harder to remember, I now think that my expulsion was the result of an illicit visit to a pub and the collection on the way home of a number of trophies) and the school was willing for this to happen since they didn't get many boys into Oxbridge at all. But the school, I told my father, would not allow me back to live on the premises; and then my father, I told the school, would not allow me to sleep in the place whence I had been expelled. As a consequence I spent the fortnight of the exams in the Green Dragon Hotel in

Hereford, living the life of a small Reilly, taking a taxi up to the school most days and wearing a bow tie to emphasise the fact that I was not wearing uniform. Thus I dawdled my way through some A-levels and got enough to be let in to the hallowed halls of Cantabrigia.

As a result, at a time when you needed a good record and two or three A-grades at A-level to get into Oxbridge, I went up to Pembroke on an expulsion from school and, as far as A-levels went, a D, an E and a Fail. Lucky.

Similarly, at a time when there were a hundred applicants for every university lectureship in English, I happened to bump into a professor, one Tommy Dunn, who had a clutch of them in his briefcase, metaphorically, and who slipped me into his department at the new University of Stirling with barely an interview, partly of course because he always tried to get Oxbridge men (in those days this meant Oxbridge *men*) for his department and partly because, desperate for a drink during his official academic visit to dry Saudi Arabia, he had come upon me when I, needless to relate, Had A Supply. That was in 1970 when I was the first teacher of Eng Lit at the fledgling university in Jeddah and this professor-with-jobs-in-his-pocket was the first Head of English at Stirling and had been sent out to inspect the new English Department at Jeddah which meant inspecting, well, me. We got on famously over glasses of Medina (rots your liver, makes you laugh) and Mecca (rots your brain, makes you cry), the home-made 'wines' of the Saudi expatriates, as brewed. So Tommy offered me a post in Scotland that I held for thirty years, which was lucky enough and, as Tommy used to say, better than working for a living.

Thus did luck lead to a career in academia – almost the only career for which I was not unsuited –

one where I could indulge my intellectual tastes and my desire to make people laugh. Nowadays I have so extensive a forehead that you might as well leave out the 'fore'.

3. PARENTS

My father, who was born in 1913, had been educated in Devon at Blundell's School where his nickname had been King of the Underworld and where he kept two tame owls called Wednesday and Thursday and won the Open Mile in 1931. These and other vaguer talents clearly suited him for military life and on leaving home he went to 'the Shop' (Woolwich, the Royal Artillery's equivalent of Sandhurst) where they trained Gunner officers. He saw his parents and his brother Alec again only once, which meant that for my own brother and myself he was pretty much *sui generis*. For us, *family* was largely my mother's family.

 The army was quite busy between the 1930s when my father was commissioned and the early 1960s - if you remember, a world war intervened - when he went back into *mufti* (his Anglo-Indian expression, meaning 'civilian clothes'; we were brought up with a raft of these Indianisms and often used '*panee*' for water, '*dhobi*' for washing, '*dood*' for milk and 'the *khud*' for a bank or hillside). Military service sent him to India in 1936 where he rode about on nice horses, drank a lot like all subalterns, grew a moustache, met my mother and married her in Hong Kong Cathedral, spent the early years of the war in West Africa and then came back to serve gallantly in the defeat of Hitler (arriving in France with his guns in 1944 on D-plus-three and winning the Military Cross.) This was followed by service in Egypt and the inevitable

18

Germany. These overseas postings were interspersed with stints in Britain: Shrivenham, Colwyn Bay, Troon, Oswestry, other places. In twenty-six years of marriage my poor parents moved twenty-seven times. As a result my brother Piers (born a year before me in 1945) and I went home from boarding school most holidays to a different house, often to a different country. We had no 'home' friends. My mother tried to maintain continuity against considerable odds. We looked back at Silton, and occasionally went there, in a cloud of nostalgic insecurity.

Pa, though a jolly raconteur in public, was a sad, not to say a bitter man by the time I clocked him as a separate person in the 1950s. By then his hopes had been dashed all round and one has to feel sorry for his generation and class. In his case things had started badly; his relations with his own father, about whom he never spoke, were clearly of the worst and his schooldays pretty mixed. He never once mentioned his mother in my hearing, and at all events he left home at eighteen never to return. Without financial backing he couldn't go into a glamorous regiment and chose the Gunners, which was merely respectable. Things must have seemed all right for a few years in India, perhaps even in the war, but he must soon have worked out that his marriage wasn't much of a success, though perhaps not the disaster depicted in Ian McEwan's *Chesil Beach*, a novel about an unadjusted couple of the same generation as my parents'. And, of course, by the time I came to know my father, he felt that the country had betrayed him, as well as the whole officer class and everything it stood for, by voting against Winston Churchill and for a Labour government in 1945 and by handing India back to the Indians in 1947. In fact, unlike other career soldiers such as my uncle Dudley, Pa

19

managed to stay on in the rapidly-shrinking post-war army and was a Full Colonel by the time he retired.

Guy was by preference and nature a *bon-viveur* with memories of rags at the Trocadero and other such subalterns' delights in pre-war London (remember? '*We* had a rag at Monico's, *We* had a rag at the Cri...' John Betjeman I think) but his disastrous family background, his bitterness about marriage, his historical bad luck and several other things kept him at home when I knew him. He had literally no social life outside. Not only that; he didn't like visitors and would not have anyone in the house, not anyone *at all* besides the four of us, throughout my childhood. Once we had left Silton and were *à quatre* in our married quarters, Pa, Mutti, Piers and I, we were entirely without benefit of the Other. My parents never went out and nobody ever came in. It seemed normal of course, but I think it wasn't.

They also slept in separate beds for all the time that I knew them. There wasn't a great deal of Art or Intellect or bonhomie in the house, but in spite of all this my boyhood, well, the one-third of it that was not spent at boarding school at any rate, was reasonably happy. Nobody yelled at me and I have grown up with a profound distaste for screaming matches, arguments, indeed disagreements and violence of all kinds. My parents never argued and I have spent a lifetime resisting the people who tell you that 'it is good to clear the air once in a while' and that 'expressing your emotions' is the only way to go.

My father was allegedly a Protestant though you'd hardly have noticed, but one thing that was a constant in my mother's life was her Catholicism. Automatically Piers and I were christened, made to learn our Catechisms, taken to First Communion (in Egypt, at the garrison RC church, in white shorts and white shirts – quite a picture we made) and sent to Catholic schools back in Britain.

My mother was RC because her own mother, D, had surprisingly converted. Born into the Protestant Ascendancy in Ireland in 1888, D was naturally Church of Ireland. But one fine year in the 1920s in Kensington she was on furlough from India with my grandfather and their small children and saw the light shining from Rome. A *furlough* was a six month holiday granted to people in the imperial service every five years; my grandfather would rent a house for the whole period, often in London and once in Pau, a town where I would later work. That year in Kensington D was impressed by the conversion of her Hindu Aya, the nursemaid who was brought from India to help with the memsahib's children. This Aya, on asking the mem for the way to the nearest temple, had been offered a substitute, reasonably enough there being few Hindu temples in Kensington in the 1920s, in the shape of the Convent of the Sacred Heart. With her spirit of Hindu eclecticism this sounded good enough to the girl, so she took off her shoes and went to Mass. By the end of six months she was nestling in the bosom of the Pope. My grandmother liked this a lot, rather more I should imagine than her husband did, and she thought that if God could reach out to a pagan illiterate Aya like that and inveigle her into going to Mass then He must be a Catholic too. D herself converted and brought her three children over to Rome with her. My mother never regretted this, and on the whole, though no longer a believer, neither have I. At least it is better than having started life as a Methodist.

The longer-term result of this action of the Aya's was that Piers and I were sent to a brace of Catholic prep schools in the 1950s and subsequently to Belmont

Abbey, a Benedictine Public School of a couple of
hundred boys outside Hereford, closed by the year 2000
as a result of the trend against boarding schools (we had
few day-boys there on the Welsh marches.) More will
be heard of this establishment in what follows, as well
as more of several other things.

4. SILTON

The West Saxons were marginally less aggressive,
perhaps, than some of our other Germanic invaders of
the sixth century. King Alfred, at any rate, has the credit
of translating some of the Gospels into English. And
even today, by vague impression at least, people from
'the West Country' sound a little less fearsome than say
The Scots, or The Northumbrians. The Wessex accent
(when there is one) has a rounded burr to it, what Hardy
in *Tess* calls the richest sound known to be uttered by
the human voice, 'UR' as he puts it, unconsciously
nodding to his own heroine, possessor of all graces,
Tess of the D*'UR*bervilles. The sounds made by
Tynesiders and Glaswegians could not be characterised
in this way.

Once, returning to Dorset from Scotland after
twenty years in the bracing north, I was driving with my
brother through Sturminster Newton (that UR again)
and stopped for petrol. In my way on the forecourt was
a large tractor idling and unmanned, blocking all access
to the pumps. A moment's effort at patience gave way
to a mild expletive and a gesture towards getting out of
the car to 'see what was going on.' Piers, who had spent
nearly all his life in Dorset, put a hand on my arm, 'Not
down here Jim' (he has always called me Jim –
cherchez pas à comprendre) 'It'll be fine.' And so it
was. Within a few seconds a smiling young man

emerged from the petrol station, looked at me, waved, shouted an apology of the friendliest, climbed up into the considerable height of his cab and departed at speed. Being born in the county made me slightly abashed by this encounter, which I replayed several times with my brother to be sure that I had understood it. The merry Scots had never seemed so patient as this, and I had learnt how not to be patient myself, without knowing it. Piers understood this. He called on Hardy's workfolk to testify: 'You remember Joseph Poorgrass? Or the way they treat Christian Cantle in *Return of the Native*?' he asked. 'And Widow Edlin in the horrible *Jude*? 'Marriage' she says 'was a game 'o dibs' to her generation.' Yes. Yes of course. Something of an old-fashioned softness seemed to cling both to Hardy's anachronisms (as I fear they were) and to my nostalgic thoughts about old England, *a fortiori* the old West Country.

Silton was an old place to be born in. The house was a Queen Anne rectory much expanded by Victorian Rectors with large families, and starting life there taught me to focus on the instant pang generated by looking back across the hills and the years, a pang that never left me. My first memory, as we have seen, is of the lawn between the house and the walled garden. I came round a corner into the sunshine, popping out into memory from nowhere at all, pushing a horizontal bear on wheels. The bear was solid and furry, an entirely reliable friend who may have given me another impossibly high ideal, this time of loyalty, to drag forward through life.

The staff at Silton had been reduced in quantity, possibly also in quality, since the war. By 1950 they consisted of an under-gardener, later identified as 'Dungworth', a name which as a child I took to be

23

descriptive rather than onomastic though it was in truth the poor man's family appellation; my father used to refer to Dungworth bitterly and opaquely as 'a socialist.' Then there was Humpy Annie, the deaf kitchen help, who was about the same size as me when I finally left the house aged 5; in those days before deep-freezes she salted runner beans from the garden and put them in a large brown ceramic version of Ali-Baba's hiding place. Then there were the Brookses, a couple apparently both vigorous and highly antique, who were head-gardener and cleaner-cum-cook and who lived in a cottage my uncle had bought for them in the local town. Then there was a series of nursemaids who were brought in to look after my brother and me and to some degree our rather older cousins Celia and Hugh.

These nursemaids had an unfortunate Tess-ish tendency to indulge in what a million years later would be known as Unprotected Sex. With surprising regularity, once a year, the nursemaid-in-residence fell pregnant and had to be replaced; this was not, I think, because pregnancy would entail her being unable to deal with two annoying little boys so much as that her loose morals, of which the evidence was incontrovertible, might affect the souls and social standing of us children altogether.

Now, one of these nursemaids was called Iris Toogood, a name that was presumably a source of delight in the local pubs to the nice furry young men. When Iris had her baby she asked my father and uncle whether she could call her new son 'Piers' (my brother's name) because she found it romantic. Many years later, when my brother returned to Silton to get married and we took him to a pub for a pleasant if unextravagant Stag Night, we were approached by a large young man, indistinguishable in many respects from the tractor-driver who proved the temperamental superiority of the people of Wessex at about the same time. He smiled in the regulation manner and, cutting straight to the chase, said 'UR.' We looked at him. He put out his hand and, guessing correctly, said to my brother. 'You be Piers Butler!' Piers admitted it and took the hand. 'UR' said the young man again, 'Oi be Piers Toogood!' Within reasonable limits you could say that they then fell on each other's necks like long-lost clichés. We did not invite him to the wedding.

By the 1960s the Dorset tendency to procreation-without-licence had moved on. In one of the council houses down the lane was a family consisting of one mother, no father and six children. Without malice they were known in the village as 'The Illegits.' With such impeccably humble beginnings behind them several of them are probably now on the Bench, in the City or at least in the Cabinet.

Silton thinks itself to be famous for its Oak Tree. Contrary to the metaphorical tendency of many such antiquarian maunderings, this Oak Tree is, without any argument, an oak tree and not for instance a pub or a furniture warehouse. I played in its hollow trunk as a boy. In the vestry of the church is a facsimile of the page from Domesday Book where Silton is mentioned. Even then, in 1098, the oak figured as a noteworthy local object. Later Judge Jeffries or some other sadistic maniac dispensing Justice on the Western Circuit sat under the oak and dispensed; well, he smoked a pipe and talked in the evening let us say. All of which is to indicate that Silton Oak is, and was even when I was a child, bloody old. I mean consider: it was *already* a well-known landmark in the eleventh century. Nowadays it is reduced to several almost-independent trunks that rise no more than twenty feet into the air, in the middle of one of Farmer Harris's fields. They enclose a fairly substantial hollow space where sheep shelter from sun and rain and they are hedged about with green vegetation in the summer, including their own exiguous foliage. So the Titan lives still. In its last stages, surely, but not bad for a couple of thousand years old.

Silton was wiped out in the Black Death in the mid-14th century and has never really recovered. Because of its medieval importance the church is big – technically the parish has a Rector not a Vicar - and it was in the Rectory, become Silton House, that we lived.

Some twenty years later we sold Silton for a pittance, a few thousand pounds. Five years later, after the first great property-price hike of 1971, it was worth a million. It's a wonderful place. My uncle did not want to keep it up alone; Arnie had made it clear that she was staying in London, at the Knightsbridge flat they had had since the 1950s, *à tout prix*. She was working for the Antarctic explorer Sir Vivian Fuchs who, on the death of Uncle Dick in 1972, would become Arnie's second husband and thus my uncle as it were *en secondes noces*. She had held the fort for him in London as general factotum and administrator during the Trans-Antarctic Expedition of 1954-1956 while Fuchs, universally known as 'Bunny', ploughed across the least hospitable part of the planet to meet Sir Edmund Hillary at the South Pole and carry on to the other side. He wrote a book about it, with Arnie's help, called *The Crossing of Antarctica* and he became famous because this was the first time humans had crossed the whole continent overland. The Queen cabled Bunny his knighthood at the Pole – quite a cool gesture in several senses.

Arnie, anyway, went on to be Bunny's PA when he came home and took over the British Antarctic Survey which was first housed in Queen Victoria Street and then in Cambridge where, by a happy chance, Bunny lived with his wife Joyce. This was a less happy chance for Arnie because it meant that she only had her idol with her during the week; he returned to Cambridge at the weekends to garden with Joyce in their three acres on the Barton Road surrounding the nice house that is now a major part of Wolfson College. So Arnie only had to go to Silton at the weekends (to the Mews cottage we had kept behind the main house) to 'look after' Uncle Dick while Bunny returned to Joyce and the three acres of lawn.

Once poor old Uncle Dick had drunk and smoked himself to death in 1972 Joyce Fuchs hung on for a considerable time but she was eventually gathered to the great garden in the sky and Bunny and Arnie were free to marry, which they did at Chelsea Register Office in the early 1990s. The reception was held at the Cadogan Hotel in Pont Street, scene of various disasters and triumphs in my early life. Scene too, of course, of the Arrest of Oscar Wilde a hundred years earlier. So Silton was sold with the exception of the Mews Cottage and there in the mews my cousin Hugh still lives. He got the nine acres of land too, the old Glebe I suppose, where he has planted a grove of oaks, perhaps in anticipation of a couple more millennia. So I can still go there at times and wander about feeling confused and nostalgic in the regulation manner.

5. ROLLS

In the garage at Silton lurked Uncle Dick's Rolls-Royce, a monster landship that had been made for the

Duke of Sutherland in 1936. It had a custom-built body made to accommodate the enormous Duke and his obviously gnome-like chauffeur in two very unequal sections. In front of the glass panel that separated these sections was the small driver's cabin full of levers and dials; behind it there was about an acre of leather seating and wide carpeted floor. There we sat as children or, more accurately, lay about with our feet a foot off the floor, being swooshed round corners and feeling grand but sick. No seat-belts in those days of course, so we were hurled from one corner of the vast expanse of leather to the other with merry shrieks and occasional vomitious gurglings. Uncle Dick was himself a tall man and clearly His Grace's Man of Business had seen him coming because I distinctly remember being told that it was 'lucky' that Dick was 'almost the same height' as Sutherland. It didn't occur to anyone that as he, Dick, had bought the car in order to drive it he would be confined to the gnomish chauffeur's compartment where, tightly squeezed-in and hunched against the wide wheel among the levers and dials, he would be unable to converse with his passengers in the back (because of the glass screen) and would pass the whole journey in acute discomfort.

But so it was. To gymkhanas and garden parties we went, or to the local town for supplies, down the tiny lanes that surrounded Silton, the Rolls ('Rosalind' to my uncle) filling the entire available space for vehicular passage, at considerable speed. The few locals who owned cars in those days would creep slowly around the corners, peering nervously at the hedgerows, usually with their windows open so that they could hear Dick's approach before it was too late. As we rounded bends I was often surprised to see a small car clinging onto the bank or half-tipped into the ditch with an ashen-faced native behind the wheel, opening and closing his mouth in fear and orotund imprecation. 'Bloody fellow!' or 'Bloody woman!' Dick would say as we shot past an inch from the opposition bodywork 'Won't they *learn*?' Alternatively, locals strolling about (rare when it was known Uncle Dick was down from town) would plunge into the undergrowth with cries of 'It's the Captain!' and we would see their indignant glares peering out of the dark green spaces while their children clung to their knees.

There were sometimes difficulties with owning so vast a car. It took, for instance, thirty-three gallons of petrol - this in the days when a full tank for a more normal car never exceeded ten. At the garage in a nearby village the owner always sent his boy out to fill up the Rolls, not least because he did not have an electric plump; like all the early garages his was equipped with a pumping-handle and to fill the Rolls someone had to put in a manual performance roughly analogous to keeping a leaky organ going through the whole of *The Messiah* with nothing but Armstrong's Patent to help him. The boy would sigh and roll his eyes and eventually break into an impressive sweat before asking, at about the 25 gallon mark, for a breather. Uncle Dick used to give him a tip. We seemed to go to the garage pretty often since the car only did eleven miles to the gallon.

But, as Uncle Dick used to complain, the main difficulty with having the car was that all sorts of people felt free to ask straight out whether Dick could take them to places such as weddings (these were bride's fathers), Stag Nights or even the ruridecanal conference at Salisbury Cathedral (general meetings with the Rural Dean). His answers were respectively: No (he hated weddings), Yes (he liked exuberant young men and a fair old snifter of gin) and Yes, when he himself got some position in the local rural deanery. But when the *Great Britain*, the huge iron ship designed by Brunel, was taken off the sea-bed in the Falkland Islands and towed back to Bristol it became apparent that Dick was himself proposing an expedition in Rosalind to go and look at her rusting hull at Clifton or Avonmouth or somewhere. A naval man after all.

Now, the miniaturised front section of the Rolls, the gnome's hutch, had a First Aid kit prominently attached to the inside of the driver's door, reducing the driver's space yet further of course, with a large red cross painted on its casing. This First Aid kit had been the subject of intense cogitation on the part of my uncle and the result of this cogitation was that the alleged 'medicines' that had formerly snuggled up in the green baize interior of the box had been replaced by bottles of spirituous liquor.

All went well at first, but as we neared Shepton Mallett (you know, where the road goes through that rather lovely soft country around the Longleat Estate) I noticed through the glass that Dick's ears had gone a sort of saccharine pink, invariable sign that he had been at the bottle. Or in this case, since the First Aid kit contained a large number of small bottles, at the bottles. He was pushing the immense car round the corners with a gusto unusual even for him. If there had been fewer tons of metal between my self and any possible contact with a third party I would have felt nervous.

We got to Bristol in one swerving enormous piece and pulled up on the quayside. The Great Britain was impressive for her age, rusty and unvisitable. A few minutes drinking in her lines quickly palled and it seemed time to Move On. Unsteadily Dick re-mounted and the rest of the party (Piers, my Cambridge friend

Johnny Brooks, others) climbed and slid into the back compartment. 'We're going to see Monty!' cried Dick, or it may have been 'Max' or 'Murgatroyd', and away we thundered towards the property of this enigmatic friend.

Some miles outside Bristol we turned into a drive that led to a very pleasing Georgian house set in an extensive park (am I starting to sound like Jane Austen?) where we were greeted like Victorian explorers who have Made It Through to the Lost City. Much clutching of old naval comrades occurred at the door and we were ushered into the house. The tour which followed included an upstairs bedroom where we were shown a Flying Fox, one of those high-wire contraptions that enable you to hang on underneath and go zooming down to wherever the Flying Fox goes to. This Fox started at the bedroom window and the wire curved gently downwards, following the lie of the land, to a large lake about a quarter of a mile away, rising slightly at the end as it reached a jumping-off point. All one had to do was to hold on like grim death and know when to let go. A bracing swim was the inevitable result of getting aboard this fearsome if attractive contraption.

Its principles were explained to Uncle Dick, who listened owlishly, blinking and hiccupping slightly. The owner of the Fox, Max or Marmaduke, began clearly to feel that only physical demonstration would make the point he was trying to impress on his guests and suddenly, with an eldritch screech, he seized the swing-bar and launched himself out of the window. For what seemed an age we watched as heaven held its breath and Max sailed away with increasing speed towards the chilly green water. Then the sounds came to us: first a tremendous yell and then, after an appreciable gap, an enormous splash, faintly but unmistakably audible on the still air. 'Bloody fellow!' exclaimed Uncle Dick.

We got back to Silton in time for the hoisting of the Gin Pennant, a symbolic moment opening the evening festivities. I must have been a mere nineteen years old and by seven o'clock I was entirely drunk. The next morning I quizzed Johnny Brooks about the parts of the evening I had missed. 'Well', he said, slowly and with much consideration, 'put it this way… I felt I was in the presence of masters.'

6. JACK

Uncle Jack and my Uncle Dick, brothers and only siblings, had come from the same stable, their father being a master at Charterhouse. Of this father I learnt only that he had taken a cold bath every morning and had shared the staff common-room with two History masters, Sellars and Yeatman by name, authors of *1066 And All That*, geniuses of a sort to whom the family always referred as 'surprisingly dull.' But if Jack came from the same stable as Dick he was a very different kind of horse.

'Horse', in fact, was one of the words that came to mind when one met him. He wore an air of the paddock and the racecourse, also wearing, less metaphorically, a brown bowler hat, a yellow waistcoat and a tie with a pin that I can't swear wasn't made in the shape of a horseshoe. This was in considerable contrast with his taller brother's elegance: Uncle Dick wore Edwardian suits in grey without turn-ups, with double-breasted waistcoats but never with a double–breasted jacket; these suited his long legs and his Bertie-Woosterish élan. Looking back on him I realise that even in the 1950s he was something of an anachronism though of course one made the mistake of taking as natural what was simply a cultural protest. Like Edward VII he spoke of 'gels' instead of 'gurls' (I think even 'Edwardian' came out with its second syllable pronounced to rhyme with 'card') and in 1970 thought that the idea of Britain joining 'Europe', then the Common Market, would be a good thing because we would 'run the show'. He had seen Johnny Foreigner in action and had on the whole been unimpressed.

His brother Jack, *pour revenir à mes moutons*, was louche in comparison, shorter and tubbier, another sort of late-Victorian or Edwardian figure but from the shadier side. He had about him something of Raffles, the minor character in *Middlemarch*, and of scores of other minor personages in the novels of the period and in the films that have since been made around them. Not quite Chevy Slime (really Dickens... the names!) but more something out of Sherlock Holmes – the plausible Bad Egg – or from Anthony Powell - not quite Uncle Giles, though Jack too had money troubles as we shall see, but not quite Dicky Umfraville either. In any event word had it in the family that 'Dick and Jack mustn't meet', an injunction that baffled me as a small boy but which turned out to be a fair assessment when I finally saw them together at a tricky supper in Knightsbridge where the air between the brothers was pure frost, and on another occasion when it was reported that at a family wedding they had 'come to blows in the bar.' Something pretty terrible must have lurked in Dick's unconscious for this to have happened; a kind gentlemanly figure, he would have wished to preserve dignity at all times, although it has to be conceded that he enjoyed the electric soup to a very considerable degree and could become wildly incensed when driving.

After one trip through London my ashen-faced aunt emerged from the Jaguar XK140 that they then drove (mostly keeping the Rolls for the country) saying that Dick had 'got cross' with the other drivers, had driven too fast and had indulged in swearing. When I raised my eyebrows at this to me incredible notion she added 'He has a fine flow of Quarter-deck language when he needs it' – another baffling idea that only time and research would elucidate.

Jack was thus a rare visitor – indeed the supper in Knightsbridge was almost my only exposure to the old chancer (in my mind he went along with those vague English expressions of another generation – he was a *chancer*, a *fellow*, a *cove*, possibly a *chiseller*, the sort of man often referred to, inaccurately enough, as *squire*.) But the denouement of the story so patently implicit in his very existence was narrated to me before he was finally gathered to the great Bookies' Tent in the sky. It has often made me think of the things people can get away with, and it went like this.

Jack lived somewhere in Cheshire - is it called The Wirral? It sounds as if it ought to be. This was because of the family connection with the Liverpool cotton trade which had brought Dick and Jack their fortunes when the legendary 'Uncle Arthur' of a previous generation and many cotton-mills, went down in the *Lusitania*, as described. Apparently there was an Exchange in Liverpool devoted entirely to the cotton which flowed through the port and helped to clothe Britain, even Europe, during the nineteenth century. The cotton-picking slavery behind the trade, which lasted until 1865, seemed marginally more acceptable to the traders, I suppose, because it benefited by the contrast with Liverpool's other trade of earlier years: the transport of the actual slaves across the Atlantic in the first place.

Uncle Dick had a hoary story from the old days known to us as the Liverpool Cotton Exchange Disaster story. His tales, few in number but intensely realised in his imagination and inflamed by the alcoholic stimulants necessarily imbibed in advance of the telling, were epic in proportion, wildly punctuated with strong emphasis and frequently muddled with one another. On reflection I don't think I ever really got the hang of this one but I do know that it involved some ancestor of his rushing into the Exchange with *his hat brushed awry* and, with this as supporting evidence, declaring some run on cotton or sinking of a cotton ship the result of which was that everyone started to buy, or to sell, cotton futures in a manner that permitted him, the ancestor, to make a packet. What the hat had to do with it I never fathomed although the point seemed to be that it gave the impression of disarray on the part of its wearer; more puzzling was the fact that you *could* brush a hat the wrong way. How much brushable stuff did hats used to have, I wondered. Weren't top hats supposed to be *shiny*?

By the 1930s, when Jack started in on his career, or rather 'career', in cotton, top hats and slavery were things of the past but money was still to be made in Liverpool although not, as it transpired, by Jack. Ah, those days before widespread domestic telephones, when a man could go to work and not be teased by troublesome questions from home! The times when he would go off into the wide blue masculine world and there lunch and go to his club and come back as and when he wished, happy to find supper on the table and the children in bed. How simple an epoch it was! So simple indeed that one could get away with almost anything and certainly could manage some playing truant without the little woman at home being any the wiser; so simple that Jack got away with *not going to work at all*. Every morning he went out, brown bowler brushed and shoes shining, leaving a wife and four children to get on with whatever wives and children do, allegedly to look after his investments on the Exchange and generally be a businessman. He always took a briefcase. But he never went to work.

Champion skiver, he went instead to pubs, cafes and clubs, drinking dens, places where other 'businessmen' talked about business in its various widely-differing forms. Above all, he went to the bookmakers, to such casinos and gaming-establishments as then existed and slowly, very slowly, he lost all his money.

One fine day, after *thirty years* of this, he returned to the bosom of his family and announced the terrible truth: they were broke, bust, without a penny; the house would have to be sold, the children taken out of school, the usual middle-class horror story. His wife went out to work as a cleaner. Think Mr and Mrs Bulstrode without the religious aspects. Imagine it: you get away with it for *thirty years*! And his wife hadn't a clue! It must be a record.

I last saw Jack at Uncle Dick's funeral at sea where he behaved moderately well; after the ceremony we got him ashore and shovelled him into a taxi. I never heard any more about him.

7. SULTAN

Uncle Dick worked for a few years, after he left the Navy, in the old Ottoman Bank which had its headquarters in the City and branches in some quite surprising places – I mean surprising for the 1960s. Turkey, obviously, but also East Africa and the Persian Gulf. It was quite amusing looking after other peoples' money in the Middle East in those days, the place being awash with Petrodollars and moolah of all sorts. The mullah's moolah I suppose. Uncle Dick used to go out on visits to make sure that all the staff housing was up to snuff; back in London he would busy himself ordering sofas from Heals and air-conditioning from Harrods. He claimed that his Arab colleagues out East admired him because he always wore a three-piece suit on the hottest days.

Be that as it may, Uncle Dick was also used by the Bank's bosses as a sort of respectable host and entertainer for the occasional visiting Prince or minister from the Emirates or Qatar or Zanzibar. Usually this involved wining and dining them in London; sometimes he took them to the Garrick Club where their flowing robes presented delicate questions of sartorial etiquette to the club staff, trained as they were to insist on collars and ties among the members. But one desperate weekend in August he was asked to look after a royal personage from Abu Dhabi from Friday to Monday. Quite why the bank's normal weekend hospitality hadn't kicked in I never learnt, and what the young Gulf prince had had to say about the prospect of a wet weekend alone in a cottage in north Dorset with an elderly retired Captain RN I couldn't even imagine, but so it was.

Now desperation spreads itself about like those little chips of styrofoam you can't get off your hands and uncle Dick caught the 'What-are-we-going-to-do-with-Sheikh-Sultan?' bug quite badly, badly enough for it still to be contagious when I drifted into the flat in Knightsbridge at an unfortunate moment. He fell on my neck as one does in dire times, actually almost literally falling as he made those feeble gestures towards a hug that Englishmen of a certain class and generation knew were going in the right direction but which they were unable to bring off completely. 'I say old man' he smirked, 'can you come down to Silton for the weekend? Old man?'

Now I love Silton, it being my birthplace as we've seen and a sort of centre for my imagination, and I went there when I wanted to, but hitherto Uncle Dick had not often proffered actual invitations to the place. He put up, in a dignified silence substantially reinforced by gin-and-water, with the various nephews, friends and hangers-on that were wished on him by my aunt when he was in the country. But he issued no pleas for our company. So when he bleated out his request I was both flattered and uncomfortably aware that there was a large rat in the room. What was this?

'I've got someone coming that I think you'll like. In fact old man you might be a bit of help to him.' To *him* notice, not to me. The old fellow was too canny for that. So I was to be the entertainment for a Sheikh of Araby because the Directors of the Ottoman Bank had allotted my uncle that role and he had now passed it neatly on to me. I was the bottom of the food chain. As people began to say when Margaret Thatcher proposed a 'trickle-down' society in which the wealth of the rich would be encouraged to percolate through to the less fortunate, and in reference to an American phrase of dubious origin, 'That stuff tricklin' down on you ain't money.'

I added up the pros and cons. On the one hand wonderful Silton, my nice uncle and unlimited quantities of gin, on the other an unknown quantity in the shape of a dark and possibly monolingual Arabian horse. Gratitude to my uncle prevailed – or at least a desire not to leave him in the lurch.

I can't remember how the three of us got to the house but it must have been separately because my first memory of Sultan has him standing in the hall shaking hands with me a little coyly. He was a large tubby young man of perhaps twenty-five, dressed in a shiny suit of the sort fashionable in Beirut in about 1936. His shoes were astonishing. And almost at once the odour of immense rat began to take concrete shape. The fact was that this blighter, who had something about him that spoke of mild oriental menace, proved, as feared, to be virtually innocent of the English language.

Now I believe, although without absolutely persuasive evidence, that I can sometimes charm people if I put myself to it; but this charm, if it exists, comes not, you may well believe, from any external pulchritude or psychic appeal but rather from the subtle modulations of my speech – well, in fact, it comes from the oleaginous things I say to cheer people up and make them like me. Give me a pair of ears that can take in the language I am speaking and I will show you those ears glowing with pleasure. 'Oh, you're an *accountant*! How *interesting*!' Or 'What *is* Croydon like? No *really*?' I can do all that. But give me a monolingual chubster from the Crucial Trucial and even with my six words of Arabic I quickly run out of the wherewithal to make his evening a pleasant one.

My first calculation when I saw that Sultan couldn't follow a simple English sentence (Me: 'Do you like England?' Him: 'What you are saying?') was to balance the horror of his (and my own) linguistic incapacities against the undoubted fact that Uncle Dick, especially once he was a few sheets to the wind, would launch into his extensive anecdotage without fear or favour and, oh joy, also without any real expectation of audience participation. On the one hand things looked bad for my ability to charm, on the other Uncle Dick might unknowingly bear the heat and burden of the day by filling all known conversational space.

And indeed Dick did talk – talked well and mostly in the narrative mode; his stories were as usual brilliantly-lit vignettes taken from his past, some of them involving louche ancestors, others the many occasions when the naval vessel he was commanding had sunk under him. In the family we had become so familiar with these tales of his life that we were able when he absent-mindedly supplied the punch-line from one story as the climax of another to laugh whole-heartedly. After all, it was generally a good punch-line to a good story which we knew well, even if it didn't quite fit, so what was to prevent us bursting out? He would look at us a little suspiciously though, when this happened, puzzled by his sudden but illogical popular success.

There was no real hope that Sheikh Sultan would follow more that a few words of the preamble to any of these stories, let alone the story itself, and Dick's silence-filling efforts could have been substituted by putting on Radio Ulan Bator, but they did the trick. At least they did during meals which were Dick's favourite court-holding times of the day. Come the long stretches of the later morning, however, or the interminable afternoons of rain which beset us, other amusements had to be found. The formula usually went: Uncle Dick, 'Do you think Sultan would like to see the farm/church/stream/local town/hedges?' Sultan, 'What he saying?' Self: 'He is speaking about the farm. You like to see farm?' Sultan (suspiciously): 'OK.'

And so it was that on a wet Saturday in August I was sent off with our lumbering son of the desert up the hill to Manor Farm where Geoff and Wendy Harris lived and worked as their forebears had done since at least the fifteenth century. These Harrises are very fine people but back then, in those antediluvian days almost before the Beatles' first LP and certainly before the Summer of Love, Dorsetshire farmers were not known for their sparkling liberal conformity to modern culture or indeed their wide knowledge of very much beyond cheese, cows and tractors. I had for instance been taken by my cousin Hugh, with Geoffrey Harris, when they were both about thirty and I was perhaps twenty, to a local cinema to see *The Killing of Sister George*, a film about Lesbians. Afterwards, on the way home to Silton, I chattered away in the car and Hugh invited Geoffrey in for a last whisky. Geoffrey had been entirely silent on the journey back and now sat in the drawing room nursing his glass. At last, unable as ever to bear social silence, I asked him 'Well Geoff, how did you like the film?' 'UR' said Geoff, and then: 'you know, Lance' (he pronounced the vowel like a longer version of the A in 'pants'), 'you know... Oi didn't know ladies did them things.' A few minutes later he put down his glass and stumbled out into the night a sadder and a wiser man.

So it was with some slight internal self-doubt on my part that I led my new friend up the two hundred yards of road past Silton Church to the old farm. It had been raining all day and now there was just a steady drizzle. Sultan had not brought any form of outer garment and had refused all offers of replacements. His astonishing shoes, white in parts when he bought them, were the only ones he had to loaf around in indoors and out. The road was filthy, though it was not as filthy as the Harris's farmyard, which was a pigsty and cow-

wallow rolled into one. I foresaw some slight trouble
ahead, at least in the footwear and getting-clothes-dry
areas. But it was worse than that.

As we approached the farm door who should
come out but, yes of course, the happy farmers, man and
wife, like an illustration in a children's book. I had
spotted them over the wall as we went round the corner,
and then it happened: as we came into full view of the
Harrises Sultan reached down and took my hand. He
swung our joint hands slightly as we splashed forward
through the cowflop. With my free hand I waved as
blithely as I knew how to our neighbours who continued
to stand in their doorway and to stare.

Quite unable to think of a decent way of
releasing myself from Sultan's firm grip I decided that
the way forward was bravado. 'Hello Geoff, Hello
Wendy' I shrieked, 'Can I introduce you to my new
friend?' This may not have been the most neutral
expression as I realised after I had said it, but it was
better than silence. Sheikh Sultan bowed and extended
his free right hand while still using his left to cling
intensely to my right. He made some noises. 'Oh' said
Wendy, 'Down for the weekend is he?' 'Yes yes' I said
as though no other explanation were necessary. 'The
Captain all right?' 'Oh yes' I squeaked 'Right as rain,
and down there as we speak. The Captain's here for the
WHOLE weekend too. With us. I mean he's Sheikh
Sultan's host' (what idiot would ever say that?) 'I
mean…'

Somehow, wet, muddy and blushing we returned
to the house. 'Ah, did he like the farm?' asked Uncle
Dick. 'Well Uncle Dick, up to a point.' 'Good, good.
Now perhaps he'd like a bath?' With great care I mimed
a man washing himself modestly and came out with

42

'*Hammam*?' Sultan looked at my writhings and said 'Like Gin and Tonic.'

The next day was the Garden Party given by the Lord Lieutenant, who at that time was a chap we knew as Colonel Jim, a neighbour of ours. Many years later my cousin told me that after Colonel Jim's death his house was sold to someone who became known locally as the Complete Shit. Great was the joy at Silton when this undesired specimen of Homo Suburbanus (*nouveau riche* among we *anciens pauvres*) suddenly, within a year, put the house back on the market and left the area. When the truth about this came out it was, as ever, quite unexpected: the Complete Shit had been unable to stand the hostile visits paid to him with military precision every evening by Colonel Jim's ghost.

The rain held off for the first part of the Garden Party so my uncle's Phantom III - its name referring presciently to our host's future existence - was able, instead of blocking the lane outside, to take up about three-quarters of the field allotted to car-parking. From it my uncle and I stepped in our suits (he perhaps in Morning Coat) followed by Sheikh Sultan in full fig, that is to say the complete Arab / Renaissance-Angel / Desert-Bandit white kit, looking menacing and for all the world pregnant. He seemed a little surprised to see dozens of women standing about in inadequate clothing, several military people in uniform and, best-dressed of all, the caterers in wing-collars, all bellowing over a brass band more to be admired for volume of sound than for delicacy of playing.

Not unnaturally Colonel Jim, himself in maximum sartorial splendour as Lord-Lieutenant, homed in on our exotic guest. It fell to me to act both parts of the non-conversation that ensued between them. Jim: 'Aha! Er, er, from, er, from, Out East eh? Very glad, very glad.' Self, mixing my two words of Arabic anachronistically with the style of Manuel from *Fawlty Towers*: 'He say you welcome to his tent.' Sultan: 'Like very much…*kef-el hal huwa*?' Self: 'the Sheikh is very pleased to be here and asks how you are.' Jim: 'Errm, splendid, splendid.' Self : '*Kullu quais*. Are you OK?' Sultan: '*Tamam, tamam*.' I'm not sure that Jim didn't end on 'Capital! Capital!' like Lord Emsworth but Sultan certainly ended with 'Drink?'

Uncle Dick had drifted over to a gaggle of cronies; Sultan and I walked the lawns in a sort of Arabian two-step; every time I thought I saw the approach of his hand to mine I skipped to his other side and introduced him to a countess or a cake, though usually without much result. Until, that is, we arrived at a familiar figure in monster clericals. 'My God' I thought, appropriately enough, 'It's the Archbishop of Canterbury!' Lesser clergy backed away and I skipped about some more, which left the field clear for a Meeting of East and West. 'This', I ventured from a vantage point near a small curate, 'Is Lord Fisher, he's…' but cleverer men than I have baulked at the prospect of explaining quite why the Protestant Church of England has an Archbishop at its head and why he dresses in mauve; 'He's a big priest… a mullah *kabir*, an imam…' Turning in the other direction I said 'This, my lord, is Sheikh Sultan of Abu Dhabi.' 'Aha!' cried his Episcopal Greatness, 'Aberdovey? I didn't know there was a Sheikh of Aberdovey' and with that he clutched Sultan by the forearm in a grip learnt over years of practice in the Athenaeum and said in the ringing tones of one addressing a deaf and possibly hostile foreigner, 'It's in Wales, isn't it? Do you like Wales?'

I discovered a little time later that Sheikh Sultan, although nominally over in Britain to attend some sort of course at the Police College at Hendon, was in fact being treated in a London clinic for impotence, with what result I'm afraid I don't know.

CHAPTER 2. PREP 1954 - 1958

1. INFORMATION

My grandmother, before she was married in 1909 to my grandfather had developed the opinion that on her wedding night my grandfather would cut off his penis and insert it into her navel. Presumably my grandmother was gently shown the error of her views, mercifully unfounded, as is demonstrated by the fact that they went on to have three children, one of them my mother.

The result of this intriguing piece of misinformation concerning the *omphalos* was that when my grandmother was bringing up her two daughters (I think their brother, my uncle Dudley, was allowed to find things out for himself) she preached a strong line about Informing Girls As Early As Possible. In spite of this my poor mother was perhaps not very happily married in this department, but thanks to my grandmother's efforts my mother was at least Informed, she had had The Information. And the result of that was that she had a strong urge to Pass The News On to her own offspring and pass it on early. We were boys of course, but her belief was strong and, plucking up her courage I suppose, she decided to Inform us one day in about 1953.

This Talk, this Information provided by my mother, happened only once, in Egypt where we were supporting our father, a professional soldier as we have seen, who was part of the British Presence there which was keeping the Suez Canal open and the Gippos in order. He would go off to see his troops drilled or oversee the testing of a new form of cross-desert vehicle while we remained in Kensington Village, wittily named in contrast to Chelsea Village, which was for

46

more junior officers, a few kilometres away in another part of the Canal Zone.

It wasn't a bad life, playing all morning, swimming all afternoon at the Families' Beach on the Great Bitter Lake, talking to the Egyptian cook in the evening, dodging mosquitoes at night. But one day my brother had to be sent off to school in England, and I was warned that I would soon be going to the army school a few hundred yards away from our house across the *meidan*. Because of this the time had come, my mother clearly felt, to do the Informing before we entered these hotbeds of sexual activity. The only thing being that we were, at the time of the Information, respectively, eight (my brother) and seven (myself).

We were playing in our room, which served the purposes of playroom and bedroom in our bungalow and was open on both sides to the hot Egyptian air. I had, inexplicably, stolen a bottle of my father's gin and hidden it in the bottom of a cupboard there. From time to time during the morning Piers and I would take a swig and giggle; it tasted horrible but it made us feel good. So, looking back, I suppose we were several furlongs south of sober, little boys pissed, when our mother strode sternly into the room. We looked up. 'Come over here' she said, without any of the usual endearments. We shuffled across to her, reeking of Gordons; but she was On A Mission and didn't notice. She sat on a cushion between us and spread out a blank sheet of paper on the floor. Then she started to talk and draw.

I can clearly remember the swirl of her pencil and my sense of bewilderment but, despite best efforts, cannot remember any of the gory detail. She spoke in apparent anger, presumably about such birds and bees as were then in fashion: 'The Man' does this and that, puts his something here and there; 'The Woman' does whatever she does. It all seemed very unlikely. We listened in silenced bewitchment; we had never seen Mutti like this before. It went on for some time, the drawing becoming more complex and intimidating. Then she finished, stood up and walked out as firmly as she had come in shutting the door decisively behind her. We paused in our motionlessness. Then, no word being spoken, Piers leant forward and, picking up a red pencil that had lain beside the drawing throughout, with great precision added a pink nipple to the left breast of the naked and partially disembowelled lady on the paper before us. Our silence went on until lunch.[2]

This Information was, I think, not stored in us in any meaningful way and the Facts of Life came as the same surprise to me as they would have done had I never been exposed to my mother's embarrassed explanations. But my parents' generation was not finished with me in this matter. When I eventually got to prep school, and got right through it, and came to be twelve years old, I was summoned, with all the other Leavers, by the headmaster, one Caspar Tremlett (only Dickens at his most stylistically brutal could have made up such a name) for The Talk in the Sixth-Form Room. This Talk, of which we had heard rumour, was to prepare us for going to public school which was at least, in contrast to my poor mother's efforts, at a time a little nearer to puberty.

---

[2] Like most of her generation my mother did not talk freely about sex. She once told me that during the war various Canadian Air-Force personnel up against whom she brushed had suggested to her that she 'fly with them to Brighton', an expression whose actual meaning only slowly penetrated my thick boyish skull. On another occasion she passed the opinion that she would as soon 'fly to the moon' as 'sleep with a black man'. And that was it. Somehow her ideas about sex had become mixed up with flying.

Caspar (known to us as Mr Tremlett, and to the staff as 'Charles' for reasons both obvious – I mean no sane adult is going to tolerate being called 'Caspar' by his subordinates - and obscure) Caspar, then, a man to inspire cliché in the beholder, beat around several substantial bushes before getting down to brass tacks; these again, with shades of my grandmother present, involved the Importance of the Wedding Night. Again, too, I find it hard to recall much gynaecological detail, but I do remember the Advice that followed: 'Under these circumstances, boys, you will be well advised not to expect too much on the first night and you must be prepared to cuddle your new wife – just cuddle her, hold her in your arms so that she can get used to you – and not to Try Anything Else for a few nights until she is Ready.'

This advice I took as a valuable piece of knowledge. It is one of the ways in which I know that the world changed utterly in the 1960s that when, finally, I did get married it was not to a virgin and the Information was well past its date. But then even in my earliest encounters with women, although I found that they indeed liked to be cuddled, as we all do, it was not quite for the reason that Mr Tremlett gave.

We were sent to Caspar's school in the Malvern Hills because my father had fallen out with the headmaster of our first prep school which was in Lancashire. This first head, one Mr Trevor whom my father always referred to as 'Trevor' in a subtly insulting way, had a wife obviously twice his age known to the boys as Goosey. We had gone to his Dotheboys Hall because my grandmother was vaguely acquainted with Goosey's mother or aunt or somebody. My parents never visited the school and we might not have been sent there if they had. Tales of infant misery

49

in early education are dull and uniform, like the
education itself, but luckily there was a falling-out over
The Bill (my father: 'Nobody has ever been as rude as
that to me in my life!') and we were whisked off to
Caspar's school at Malvern where at least we had
proper cereal for breakfast, Guernsey sweaters instead
of jackets and two afternoon activities, besides the usual
Sport, called Games in the Hills and Fighting in the
Gym. Neither of these had recognised international
codes, but they managed to explode the tension of
boarding school and get some of the screaming out of us
on the fun side rather than the horror side.

At the first and less good of these prep schools,
Mr Trevor's, I had my first and only fight. Fisticuffs are
rarer than you might think from watching American
films; that has certainly been my experience throughout
life anyway. I was in the dormitory one evening
preparing for bed when the boy from the bed opposite
came over and challenged me to fight on some recondite
pretext. I laughed at first but then saw that I had to
concur with this offer of belligerence, and do so before
Lights Out. Given this insight my dense self wasted no
time. I at once strode... no, not 'strode' for a shrimp of
a nine-year-old, I *scuttled* across the narrow corridor
between the beds and advanced on my challenger
without much thought or fear. The boy in question was
called Fairie, which might have had something to do
with my insouciance. Fairie was the son of a manager at
the Tate and Lyle sugar factory in Liverpool who had
just given his name to the Fairie Cube. Perhaps as a
consequence young Fairie was inordinately fat well
before Obesity became fashionable.

There he stood, smirking in his floppy flesh as I
advanced. He, although the challenger, seemed to be
unprepared for action, perhaps expecting a grovelling

submission or a little sparring before the main event. I however, unversed in any of the niceties of the ring, simply punched this tubby boy in his stomach. To this day I can remember the strangely yielding corpulence; my hand seemed to go on and on in. When I eventually pulled it out Fairie collapsed onto the floor and, with an arm raised above his head in the regulation manner, cried 'Don't hit me! Don't hit me!' I stood there for a space then turned and went back to my bed, put on my pyjamas, got in and went to sleep. That was that.

Such activities at the other prep school at Malvern were restricted to Fighting in the Gym, and to a lesser extent, to Games in the Hills; so perhaps those activities served their purpose after all. There was no sex at either school, anyway. The Information was premature.

Come the time that it might have been of real use to her sons, my mother's open attitude had changed. Still just as angry, she was now hostile to the operations her information had been designed, presumably, to facilitate. Perceiving, one melancholy afternoon during our puberty in some remote Married Quarter near Moenchen-Gladbach, that my brother had an erection baffling the front of his trousers, she seized it, fly and all, and shook it about with cries of 'What's this? What's this then?' It isn't clear to me that my brother survived this encounter psychoanalytically unscathed.

2. HOME

It is odd for the very young to be sent away from home; it puts the word into question. At seven or eight one thinks one knows very well that Home is where Mummy and Daddy are, but it is in reality an internal space always present inside one, heavy and dangerous

51

('heavy and dangerous' - Beckett's definition of *past time*, as I came to learn centuries later.) Home is a *meidan*, an empty quarter, the unfilled. It is there when the dormitory is cold, the uniform scratchy, the masters cross. It is there when you turn involuntarily towards your mother when you are told you have done something well in class and find she isn't behind you to smile. It is there when the bully approaches, when punishment is handed out, and she isn't there.

This internal space can change its contours a little, say when Mummy and Daddy move house or, in the case of my parents, move house-*and*-country, *again*. Home is the usual ornament on the different sideboard, the blankets from Heals that are always the same on the different bed, the copy of *Alice in Wonderland* your father gave you that lives in your bedroom wherever that bedroom is. I wonder what, in default of any such possessions, supported by nothing at all, Home would be. I mean, parents dead, houses gone, objects displaced to the great blue elsewhere. What then? What is the minimum definition or rather *support* for the word? Just memory of course, and that is what the young schoolboy boarder has, really all he has, as he confronts another twelve weeks (twelve weeks!) without touch of Home. I feel a retrospective pity for the enthusiasm we felt when we spoke of the Summer Hols. Christmas and Easter Hols, glorious enough, were only three or four weeks, but the summer was eight. Only much later, as an adult, did it occur to me that this was another of those pieces of self-delusion that help us get through life. 'Eight' in one context we believed to be deliciously long while in another 'twelve' is horribly infinite: 'Only eight more weeks of term now' doesn't sound very encouraging. *Three* weeks more of term was a long, aching age. But eight weeks of *holiday* was the Holy Grail.

By what extraordinary sleight of mind did we all accept it as normal that small boys (and sometimes small girls too) should be taken from their weeping mothers (she tried to conceal the tears but we saw), their weeping *unemployed* mothers (no officer's wife worked and what work, anyway, was available on a British Army of the Rhine base in Westphalia in 1955?) and sent hundreds of miles away (when we were in Egypt *thousands*) to strange cold unknown establishments and there be 'educated'? On my first day at my first prep school I noticed someone who seemed, astonishingly, to be worse off than me, a tiny bespectacled creature tightly packed into what was clearly someone even-smaller's school uniform, blubbing in the corner of the Day Room. I went across, faintly aware that the agony in front of me would take my mind for a second off my own. 'What's your name?' I asked. 'Peter' said the sobbing post-toddler. The dreadful tyranny of an undigested culture came over me quite unawares: 'You're not Peter *here*. What's your, you know, your NAME?' The dissolving creature produced a surname and added 'And they don't let you have a teddy-bear here either, do they? I've got one in my... my...' but he was unable to finish. 'No' I said, 'They don't.'

Great gods. Home is furry. Home is my first name. But I've had to entomb it here, inside.

Put onto a York, an aeroplane wittily re-named but in reality a converted Lancaster Bomber, we flew from Egypt to Malta where, at three in the morning, we were regaled with bacon-and-eggs which then fought the airsickness all the way through the second leg which went from Malta to Croydon (was it?) There our aunt met us and took us to her London flat. The next day we joined a train, with special reserved seats, at Paddington for the West Country; it was full of Boys, excitedly canvassing the prospects for the new term. I chattered too, but the sense of unreality, the memory of the warmth, when we had got out of the hellish din of the aircraft at Malta into a soft Mediterranean night, could not be excluded. I lived inside; I always would.

Coming to Derrida in later life I felt it: something in the attitude towards the real in poststructuralist thought spoke immediately to me. The impossible real. The unavailability of the essence, the absence of foundations, the relativity of all consciousness seemed to me what the French call '*une évidence*' – something so obvious as not to need explanation. Coming to Proust whose major key is the separation from the mother, I found it easy: '*Les vrais paradis sont les paradis qu'on a perdus.*' Coming to Beckett much the same.

Here is one of his last-published texts, a poem called 'Neither.'

Neither
to and fro in shadow from inner to outer shadow
from impenetrable self to impenetrable unself by way of
neither
as between two lit refuges whose doors once
gently close, once turned away from gently
part again
beckoned back and forth and turned away
heedless of the way, intent on the one gleam or
the other
unheard footfalls only sound
till at last halt for good, absent for good from self or
other
then no sound
then gently light unfading on that unheeded neither
unspeakable home

3. GHOST

I am ten years old or so and back from Prep-school for the holidays, the Easter holidays I think. My father has been posted to Oswestry in Shropshire for some unfathomable military purpose and we live in a bungalow outside the town, my father and mother, my brother, a year older than I am, and me. My father has a batman called Popple who comes every day to stoke the boiler and clean shoes. The bungalow has only one upstairs bedroom, which doubles as a playroom for us boys, and two bedrooms downstairs. My brother and I take it in turns to sleep upstairs, an odd arrangement since I hate sleeping up there so far away from my parents, who have one of the downstairs rooms, as I am terrified of ghosts.

This night, anyway, I am unfearful because it is my turn to be in the downstairs room and I can hear my father snoring in the room next to mine. I wonder about my brother, distant but impervious a few dozen feet up the staircase, and about his dashing indifference to the hauntings and weird creatures that populate my imagination.

I have to say that in spite of my fears I never saw a proper ghost then and I have never seen one since, but this once I saw something paranormal though not dead. I have never entirely lost my fear of the night and do not for instance spend nights alone in a house of any size or isolation even to this day, but, with the exception of what I saw that night, ghosts of all kinds have eluded me. Rather a pity, I now feel, for what happened that night was not at all frightening, rather the reverse, and for many reasons I did not then think of it as 'seeing a ghost' at all. It aroused a question in my mind that I have been trying to answer, off and on, during all the years since.

As I lay, slightly nervous in spite of being downstairs, listening in the quiet night to the regular sounds of sleep coming from my parents' bedroom, I became aware of a slow change taking place in the light at the foot of my bed. The hall lamp was on and my door ajar so I was not entirely in the dark but now my eyes were finding it difficult to focus; at the end of the bed, between the bed and the wall, in a space big enough for an adult to walk through but no more, the air seemed to be revolving and shifting about in various circular patterns covering a few square feet at about chest level. As I watched, the revolutions and glimmerings gradually solidified into the figure of a man who was looking at me. Accelerating his materialisation a bit, he came into full view rather suddenly, properly dressed and smiling a smile definitely directed at me. He had all the usual bits and pieces – head, hair, moustache, shirt and tie, trousers, legs, arms, hands. He was, as it happens, in the Gunners' Full Dress uniform.

I felt no fear and watched, as they say, in silent fascination. I had no compulsion to react until I suddenly realised, in a moment of enlightenment which included some surprise at the fact that I hadn't noticed this before, that the man was my father. At that point I said 'Pa?' which was the way I always addressed him. As I did so he began to move to the right and then to come up the space between the bed and the right-hand wall, towards the low bedside cupboard in fact. His smile increased; my fear however rather surprisingly did not, though I began to feel a little puzzled. My father looked rather younger than his then forty-three years, a touch handsomer perhaps, a little gayer and more light-hearted; I had rarely seen him looking so friendly and relaxed. He was definitely focussing on me and doing so with a good deal of rather unusual benevolence.

I may have said 'Pa?' again as he arrived at the level of my shoulders. He said nothing but kept on smiling and then, turning at the last second slightly away from me in order to look straight forward, he walked slowly and unconcernedly through the bedside cupboard and the wall. I remember clearly that at one point he was only half-way through, then that he had gone. There were no doors or windows in that part of the room.

I now realised that throughout this episode, which lasted for perhaps fifteen or twenty seconds, I had been unconsciously listening to my father snoring in the next room. His snores continued uninterruptedly as I sat up and looked at the wall through which he had vanished. I lay down again and all was as before.

The next morning I taxed my father mildly at breakfast with having sleep-walked, something he at once denied just as I expected him to; I had after all heard him sleeping next door throughout his visit to me. The subject was dropped, the holidays went on.

According to the experts, if such really exist in this field, I saw a Phantasm of the Living that night. Which tells us something about the nature of human existence. After all, people do report Out-of-Body Experiences (OBEs) in which they fly around above familiar scenes and can on occasion notice something veridical – that is, something which they didn't know before about the scene being looked at and which can be verified as real after the event. And if one were to notice such people flying around they would be living but also phantasmic.

Then, more often, people say that they see the ghosts of the dead. This could perhaps be 'explained' by the notion that somebody else, usually a medieval monk or beheaded milkmaid from the seventeenth century, is having an OBE and simultaneously an Out-of-Time Experience and paying us a visit in the 'here and now.' But, whatever it is that produces the ghost effect in such stories as are not obviously false, we need a concept such as the OBE to make sense of them. Overall they suggest the existence of another, usually unconscious dimension to which we seem sometimes to be connected. And so it is with a Phantasm of the Living. My father when he appeared at my bedside was, like a sub-atomic particle in Quantum Physics, in two places at once though he didn't know it.

If you add the Telepathy evidence and the Clairvoyance evidence to these points, not to mention the Healing that goes on in places like Brazil (and also in the Home Counties, Belgium, Russia and elsewhere), it really does begin to look as if there is another side to existence – a side where Dogs Know When Their Owners Are Coming Home, where one gets the Sense of Being Stared At[3] and all the other paranormal phenomena. Now the painstaking accounts of this sort of thing by Rupert Sheldrake, Dean Radin and many others are *either* all completely misguided, every single one of them, *or* just one of them is 'true' and then the materialist universe is broken open and new dimensions (more dimensions than four being, after all, demanded by science) may have to be called on to explain the new structure of things.

At all events I have had half an NDE (in 1967, in the Sahara), half a dozen experiences of Cosmic

---

[3] See the two books with these titles by Rupert Sheldrake.

Consciousness (one at school at Belmont Abbey in the
late 1950s, one when walking my dogs in King's Park,
Stirling, in the early 1980s, and three at the Catholic
church in Callendar in Perthshire during Mass in the
early 1990s) and I frequently get the Sense of Being
Stared At. On one occasion I was forced to move my
body involuntarily by a Norwegian shaman who was
standing several yards behind me, silent and well
outside my line of vision. He didn't say what he was
going to do and I was expecting nothing, but what he
did was extraordinary and rather painful as I writhed to
his unspoken commands.

All this is enough to make me feel fairly sure
that there is More Than Meets the Eye in the universe.
Enough to suggest to me the faint possibility of Life
After Death for instance. I have spent some time
collecting the best stories I could find, in publications or
from friends and acquaintances, stories tending to
present veridical-seeming evidence of something
ghostly, paranormal, 'spiritual' happening to people.
And I put all this alongside the New Age spirituality of
writers for whom the spiritual is real and our 'lives' a
species of identity-less delusion. The result is that I
think it likely that some people retain some
consciousness of themselves for at least some time after
death.

4. GOAT

At the second of our prep schools Piers and I gazed with
unstinted admiration, on those rare occasions when we
saw her, at the Headmaster's pulchritudinous wife. I
cannot at this distance recall her name but she was
tallish, blondish and endowed with a sort of Artistic
Charm and a nice smile, in sharp contrast to the bald

lunatic that was her husband for whom, as stated, one needed to exert one's sympathies in consideration of his having the considerable handicap in Life's Race of being called Caspar.

This lady painted. She lurked away from the smelly boys, though in our defence we had baths three times a week at St Richard's, another improvement on the once-a-week-whether-you-needed-it-or-not system at Mike Trevor's Bishop's Court. Caspar supervised bath-time and there we were, stark naked, getting in and out of the baths one after another in a large open attic and having our feet inspected for cleanliness by the Beak. He sat in a chair and we approached him in our innocence and placed our feet into his hands. I think it *was* innocent but today he would be in prison.

His wife, anyway, painted. All over the Main School and the Junior House (about a mile away along a main road, but we ten-year-olds walked it unsupervised after dark *sans gene*) there were some truly remarkable canvasses of Madonnas-and-Children (that doesn't sound quite right but you get the, ha, picture), nymphs and shepherds, warriors in incredible quantities of armour or equally incredible semi-nudity (I mean, who would go into battle with *naked legs*, really?) That sort of thing. Pictures of High Art you might say, but remarkably perfect, as if painted yesterday, which in fact they had been, by the headmaster's wife.

I stared at these Mrs Tremletts during boring lessons or when I was sick because in the Sick-Room there were a couple of fetching 'Renaissance' scenes of exquisite colouring, one involving what I now think must have been 'Susannah and the Elders'. It involves voyeurism in ancient Israel, and gives the viewer a chance to scope what the Elders got an eyeful of, viz. Susannah as Porn-Star.

These pictures lived with me and had me wondering about Mrs Tremlett's extraordinary talent until I began to look at Art more seriously. Then, when I had glimpsed a few real Renaissance paintings in books and magazines, I thought it miraculous that these famous works not only hung in my school but that they had been painted by my Headmaster's wife, and that they still looked so fresh. Astonishing. Only gradually did it dawn on me that she had, of course, *copied* Michelangelo and Raphael. The 'Susannah' wasn't actually the Rembrandt or the Guido Reni but just another Mrs T. *Quelle déception.* I saw her now as a mere dauber, an imagination-deprived parasite, a painter-by-numbers. Actually she was really rather a good imitator and when, years later, I took on board poststructuralist ideas about representation I was able to forgive her and see her as frightfully *avant-garde.*

Art, incidentally, in the sense of Painting, was completely omitted from our education except for some weird sessions at Belmont Abbey with Brother James, a tubby tonsured lay-brother and raging queen. Father Illtyd once said that 'De La Grange' (the headboy in my first year and a noted beauty) had been 'the love of Brother James' life.' Poor old Bro James, brilliant but unfit for most purposes, taught Drawing, after a fashion. But there was no Art at all at prep school beyond the fake Old Masters.

But it transpired that Mrs Tremlett fulfilled herself in other things too outside the Realms of Art. Goats, for instance, she found particularly fascinating.

Now goats have had a bit of a poor press and, even when you have made all allowances, one might expect the prejudice against them to have prevented a female aesthete in the 1950s from wishing to take them to her bosom. Yet take them she did and, what is even more remarkable, she took Piers there with them. Or rather with *her*.

To my immense surprise, but surprisingly to no one else's, La Belle Tremlett and my brother went off, in a slightly furtive manner, the schoolboy and the reproducer of Rembrandts, in a car, to Goat Shows and other cabrine events around the Malvern Hills, penetrating as far as Birmingham once I think. Piers even stayed on at school at the beginning of one holidays in order to accompany her on one of these expeditions. I think I was a touch jealous, but then… goats? At home, in whatever Married Quarter we then occupied, Piers would corner me and make me look through *Goats Monthly* while he explained the finer points of the beasts as photographed. None of them were as nice looking as Mrs Tremlett. Mark you, when Pauline and I were in London in about 2008 we went to see the Edward Albee play *The Goat*, a parable in which an ordinary American falls in love, quite unexpectedly, with a very fetching nanny. It made me feel that Piers, given that his first experience of the divine passion involved goats and the Tremlett in tandem, may have dodged one of Cupid's more unusual bullets.

Retrospect does make things look odd. I mean, the modern parent, learning that their ewe lamb (sorry – I do it unconsciously) is being taken from school without a by-your-leave and promenaded round the Midland counties of England by a tasty middle-aged woman in pursuit of *goats* might possibly ask for an explanation. In my own parents' generation however Pa's reaction was the normal one: 'Oh yes?' And that was all.

Piers has… (oh, my spell-checker doesn't like that, offering instead 'Piers have' or 'The pier has', I'd never thought of that.) So, try again: Piers has always been an enthusiast, enjoying passionate relationships with a variety of pastimes and causes, some of them arcane. In his early days these enthusiasms were directed towards the female of the species and at sixteen he left home in order to cohabit with the daughter of a renegade Anglican vicar – at sixteen, note. But once Love had proved too much for him, as it tends so easily to do, and he had preferred the quieter shores of matrimony, parenthood and a proper job, thus selecting the other Freudian possibility in life (they are Love and Work) he didn't allow his *coups de coeur* to languish but diverted his extra energy into a wide variety of other channels. One year it was Save the Seals, another Brew-Your-Own (beer), then real tennis, then the recorder (I mean the musical instrument, of which one can only say that one was thankful that it wasn't the violin), then the Compositor's Art (printing, but via the computer), then sailing yachts and so on. But prime among these benevolent manias were horses. Piers learnt to ride virtually in middle age and then went in for it in all possible forms: Hunting (dangerous and expensive), Point-to-Pointing (cheaper but exhausting, and a sport for which he had to lose two stone and put up with being called 'Grandpa' by the other jockeys), Polo (very expensive and impossible to do well) and Dressage (suddenly a bit cheaper although it also leads into Classical Riding which takes one to places one never knew existed.)

Given the opportunity, he would smile winningly and introduce into the conversation by some subtle means such as 'Look at this saddle!' or 'Have you ever wanted to make your own wine?' his latest infatuation. Hours of happy fun followed during which he explained in minute detail, using wherever possible the recondite jargon of the field he had fallen for, the history, present status, rules, good and bad points and detailed costings of the topic. You would doze off for a bit and then come to as he reached what was clearly the climax of some narrative or explanation: 'Wallis is going in for a bumper!' he would cry and look at you with the smile. One groped a bit: this was probably a horse being talked of, OK, but then? He had no horse called Wallis, and what was a bumper? As the afternoon (or weekend) wore on it became clear that his currently favourite nag, officially called Dorset Eagle the Third, had a stable name ('As all horses do. Surely you knew that?' he would add scornfully) which 'we' used. 'Ah' I said. And junior races, races for beginner horses, are called 'bumpers.' 'Ah' I said again. So Wallis went in for bumpers. See?

Goats are also animals - I mean, as well as horses - so perhaps they were the forerunners of all these equine enthusiasms. Beyond that I don't have much of an opinion in the matter of those-who-are-not-sheep although, since the photographs of them were always in black-and-white in the magazines Piers brought home, I notice that I never think of them as being coloured. A faint element of un-politically-correct wordplay becomes unavoidable in this paragraph. For I was confronted by multitudes of rather fetching brown goats in the Caribbean when I was there in the year 2000 and, flying home on Air Jamaica, understood their purpose when I noticed that while the white passengers were offered 'Lamb Korma' by the nice stewardesses the black passengers were offered the same dish, for I assume this wasn't some strange form of culinary racism, under the more honest if more brutal soubriquet of 'Curried Goat.'

5. CLASS

My grandmother D and her two daughters, to mention a topic once of some importance, were as I have said consciously *ladies* in every sense that that term then meant. My father and Uncle Dick were equally self-conscious gentlemen, as indeed was my other uncle, Dudley, the older brother of my mother and aunt. He joined the Indian Army too and remained in it during the war but in 1947 he saw the end of the road, the end, that is, of both the Raj and the normal future for his profession and type. The sign at the end of the road said 'Australia' and he went there. Some of his English class-consciousness seemed to rub off in the land of the okker bloke, but he only came back to Britain once so I have a single memory of a tall Australianised English gent talking to me in the unconcerned way that such people then had, as though I were a brief acquaintance of marginal interest recently met on a train (rather than what I actually was - his nephew) and, accurately enough, never to be met again. Dudley lived and died in Australia where he and his Scottish wife produced four cousins for me: Bill, Peter, Patsy and Gillie. At the time of writing (2016) these four are all alive, pretty well and living Down Under.

One of the oddities of this social categorisation stuff ('ladies', 'gentlemen') for people of my age and generation is that what was absolutely normal during our early lives (such things as servants, accent, schooling, dress, behaviour, interests, *politesse*, deference, education, *class*) became, in the twinkling of an eye, absolutely *ab*normal and often derided, criticised or simply abandoned as the tidal wave of the 1960s did its work. We were left somewhat stranded in between. I remember the broadcaster and comedian

Alan Coren, perhaps ten years my senior but *dans le même bateau,* lamenting that as a child in the 1950s he had been dragged to endless and expensive dancing lessons, elocution lessons and other such things, in order to raise him from his lower-middle-class background to something more gentlemanly, just in time to discover, as he emerged into adulthood, that the dancing he had learnt was entirely useless because now we were jiving, twisting, rocking, rolling and generally jerking around instead. Such people sometimes had to *re-learn* their own original accents to get back down to the plebeian speech that became fashionable in and after the 1960s.

    Piers and I were taught, naturally, to speak the Queen's English ('proper' English, RP, BBC, what you will); we were taught to call grown-up men 'Sir', to waltz, to wear ties, never to wear a belt or brown shoes with a suit, to shop at Harrods. Then, in 1963 say, we entered a world that was suddenly full of successful people, in the media, in parliament and elsewhere, who spoke badly (some like the disc-jockey John Peel deliberately choosing to lose their Public School accents), dressed like unmade beds, listened to pop music (the Beatles' first LP: 1963), shopped at the new supermarkets (first one in Britain: 1964) and showed no deference at all. After a while women joined in the chorus of protest and ribald mockery and the Prime Minister (Harold Wilson) had HP sauce on his dining-table in Downing Street. But this change has been documented a thousand times, by Bernard Levin among others and most recently in the highly intriguing account given by Richard Davenport-Hines in his book on the Profumo Scandal of the early 1960s, *An English Affair* (2012.)

    I was very glad to get to Cambridge under these circumstances. Here, although I found a number of young men (no girls at my college then, not many at the university) who had espoused the left-wing views that were then fashionable, the majority of my contemporaries were from private schools and spoke properly. It was said that 75% of Cambridge freshmen in my year were Public School educated. Certainly in the Pembroke College Boat Club where I spent a lot of my time even the Rhodesians talked RP.

I remember once, in about the year 2000, trying to telephone Pauline, the Scots girl who would become my second wife, at her council-house family home near Glasgow, I heard her sister, who had answered the phone, calling out to her '*It's for you. It's that man off the radio.*' The BBC goes ever on.

CHAPTER 3. BELMONT 1958 – 1963

1. BEERBOHM

The school play, so important to the children and so painful for the parents as they participate in the jealousies of casting and in the horrors of performance, often comes from the fevered brain of the English master or mistress, though the latter was never, alas, my case. By way of female care and attention at Belmont Abbey we had only Matron, a brick-built lady of many summers who would countenance no narrative of illness ('I think my arm's broken Matron!') without first making the patient drink a glass of undiluted TCP, a disinfectant suspiciously advertised as being equally efficacious whether administered internally or externally. As if this were not bad enough she would hand you the glass with the standard encouragement 'This'll get some of that spunk out of you.' Years later, reading late-Victorian fiction, I realised that this expression wasn't quite as near the knuckle as we assumed at the time.

School plays are chosen for a variety of reasons, but the one I am talking about, performed in about 1959 and an unquestionable lemon, was unfortunately to be put down to our English master's notion of Quality. I remember objecting that it was, though I now shudder at the word, 'boring.' 'No' said Mr Jenkins, 'It is a play of Quality.' 'But sir, the parents won't get it or, or like it, or...' 'That doesn't matter... that'll be their fault in not being able to see the Quality.' I sighed and accepted a part as a Guelph, or possibly a Ghibelline.

Those among you who have been exposed to the nameless horrors of school dramatics may recognise from my Guelphs-and-Ghibellines business that this was the only (please God the only) play in English that focusses 'humorously' on events in the life of Savonarola and the political situation in Renaissance Florence. The Guelphs (or the Ghibellines) had to run about in the background of the 'action' making the noises of ancient and modern protestors ('Down with the Inquisition!' 'Vote Liberal!' or some such) and I, unwisely but hoping to get good marks in English, was one of them. The play was I think by that Great Unknown, certainly that Great Unread, of Eng Lit who enjoys the unlikely name of Max Beerbohm, he of *Zuleika Dobson*, once regarded as a funny novel.

Other boys were in Mr Jenkins' good books too of course, or wanted to be, and they too had been roped in to impersonate the compatriots of Dante complete with stuffed breeches and lines that would have been improbable even if the play had been set in the Edwardian England of its writing and not in the Italy of the Quattrocento.

One of these boys was Coppage. A nice enough chap, and the School Pianist and Organist, he was equally essential to our single-sex productions of Gilbert and Sullivan and to High Mass on those Sundays when Brother Wilfred, a former Gurkha officer and the official Abbey Organist, was Having a Crisis. In this present production Coppage, no actor, had the part of Messenger. The cue for his entrance was the obviously Italian-Renaissance line 'I'll take her maidenhood to Maidenhead!' delivered by some Borgia or other and to me pretty much as near the knuckle as Matron's description of her universal panacea.

69

The weather that June was terrific. Such parents as lived near, together with the Great and Good of what would now be called The Community including local bishops, mayors, Lords lieutenant and who not else, were selectively invited to an outdoor performance on the Abbey lawns where Mr Beerbohm's incomprehensible farrago would be laid before them without benefit of microphone (Mr Jenkins: 'So unnatural. No, no – the human voice for me') or scenery or music, in the open air. Inaudibility was to compound the inherent difficulty of following the plot.

The metaphorical curtain rose and we ran about. People delivered their lines. Coppage, some considerable number of minutes into the production, was to be seen, well *was* seen by me as I skulked behind a rhododendron, himself skulking behind a large mildly-topiarised yew, provided originally by Nature but in this case Nature aided by a century of monkish clipping. Peeping out I could also see the Mayor of Hereford, complete with shining chain, sound asleep in the front row of chairs, snoring gently and getting burnt by the sun. Looking back at Coppage in his yew-bower I saw him stiffen at the gnomic words about maidenhoods. I watched as, summoning his Messenger persona from some deep within him, he plunged out of the yew-shrubbery towards the action, itself at some distance from where he was.

Once he had crossed the mossy sward and drawn up about level with the other actors he delivered his message in tones obviously inaudible to the sleeping Mayor and to most of the other three-hundred people snoozing or bewildered in the sunshine. I knew that, delivery complete, he was to stand his ground until such time as the female Borgia or Mafiosa or whoever it was that hadn't wanted to hear this bit of news had struck him to ground and followed this aggression with the clunking line 'But I am not such a woman as not to know how to reward the messenger of bad news' which, if you come to think of it and take into account the political situation in Renaissance Florence, could only mean 'I am now going to kill you.' This was to be followed by the murder of Coppage by stabbing.

Of course, ours being a boys-only school, our female Borgias and Mafiosi, like our Gilbert-and-Sullivan heroines, were masculine. The 'woman' who had to kill Coppage was thus in fact one Duncan Grant brother of Patrick Grant, twin fifth-formers with tremendous stammers who never quite seemed to know whether, as people used to say in those days, it was Christmas or the Marble Arch. Grant Minor thus, in full transvestite fig not omitting blonde wig and heavy make-up, having knocked the messenger to the ground, started off on what was to prove a long and dramatic speech, much more dramatic in fact than anything envisaged by Beerbohm for whom the theatrically-convincing was clearly something unrecognisable at five paces. 'B-b-b-b-but' he began, 'I-I-I- a-a-a-am n-n-n-not s-s-s-such a w-w-woman a-a-a-as…' The long afternoon wore on while this Duncan manfully attacked consonant and vowel. Coppage lay on the short grass, his messenger uniform riding up to reveal elements of school uniform.

After some considerable time Grant Mi arrived at the end of his immensely-extended soliloquy and, seizing from its sheath a knife whose blade flashed in the sun like the scimitars of the orient in a G.A Henty novel, plunged it into the recumbent form of our school organist. I was watching in a desultory manner (the Guelphs or Ghibellines not being due on again for few minutes) but even so I wondered what was really happening as the blade went in. 'Ah!' I remember thinking, 'It's one of those retractable blades, probably rubber.' A pause ensued in the performance during which some Cardinal or Pope had obviously dried.

"Oh do get on with it!' I thought. But then I saw Coppage's lips moving, and I knew that he didn't have a line there – unsurprisingly as he was supposed to be dead. What was this? 'Get me off the stage!' he rasped in tones a good deal more audible that those used by the majority of his fellow-actors. 'Get me off!'

At that moment Grant Mi staggered backwards dropping the knife as he went. It Fell From His Nerveless Grasp in an action considerably more convincing than anything he had yet achieved in the play, even in the rehearsal where he was drunk. He stammered out some gasps: 'G-g-g-golly!' and sat down showing the audience a pair of (masculine) Chelsea boots, forbidden under school regulations and rarely worn by Florentine women in the time of Savonarola. 'Get me off!' moaned Coppage. 'Gosh, this is terrific!' I thought. 'Mr Jenkins was right after all!' 'G-g-g-g' went Duncan Grant. Coppage twitched feebly discreetly imploring help.

You will have guessed that the Guelphs and Ghibellines were sidelined as the ambulance charged into the Abbey grounds a few minutes later. We took the opportunity to have a smoke behind the yews. The Mayor of Hereford had woken up and was giving advice to the ambulance men and everyone else was running around in a sort of controlled frenzy, many parents clutching their children as if they were on the Titanic.

What, we asked each other, had happened? Calmly but palely Mr Jenkins called us together. 'Coppage has been stabbed in the liver. He may not live. We must pray for him. Duncan Grant is being

interviewed by the police. We must pray for him too.'
Even at a Catholic abbey school this counted as rare and
refreshing fruit. Golly! This was exciting.

The facts of course appeared, when they
emerged, as folly rather than as malevolence. Duncan
Grant, detailed off to obtain some species of knife, had
remembered that his friend Sampimon, one of two silent
Malay brothers in his form, had come back from Malaya
last holidays with a *kris*, a stunningly dangerous ten-
inch knife with a wavy blade of the most fearsome.
Borrowing this to add verisimilitude to his Renaissance
character's ensemble he, Duncan, had wielded it too
forcefully and, his aim impaired by his voluminous
clothing and his agonies of stuttering, had thrust it
enthusiastically into the entrails of the recumbent
Coppage.

We never finished the play that day, or indeed
ever. The excitement over what we called 'Grant
Minor's Arrest' died away when it was obvious that a
murder trial was unlikely. And as if that were not
disappointment enough we also came rather to dislike
poor Coppage because the Abbot, overriding the
headmaster, decreed that until our schoolmate was out
of danger we would have to go into the Abbey church
(again!) every evening and say a whole rosary for his
preservation. 'If only he'd just DIE' was the commonest
expression of our resentment. He did, however, for a
while at least, insist on living.

2. HENDERSON

Although we were a Catholic school there was a certain
realpolitik among the monks and lay masters when it
came to entertaining the troops. In particular we were
allowed to celebrate Guy Fawkes' Night on November

73

5th just as if poor old Guido F hadn't been the last man to try seriously to reinstate Catholicism as Britain's national religion (oh, except for James II in 1685 I suppose, and perhaps his son and grandson in 1715 and 1745 respectively). Antonia Fraser has rather a good book about it called *Gunpowder Plot* which I find sad to read in the way that I tend to with narratives about the hopeless (and pointless) causes for which people died horrible deaths in the past.

So naturally we had no Guy. That would have been a jollity too far considering the fate of the poor old Roman Candle himself. Fawkes. But we had a bonfire out on the edge of the rugger pitches, and we had fireworks. Somehow these were always many in number and of considerable violence, the sort that appeal to boys, as they say, of all ages.

This year, I must have been 15 or so, I participated in 'Fireworks on the Pitch' in the usual way after dinner, running about in the dark and being something of a nuisance. It was windy and the fire went well, but it was a cold evening so the anti-papist shenanigans weren't extended much beyond the usual bedtime. The next morning however, Fatty Henderson sidled up to me in break and made a suggestion that seemed altogether good. He, Henderson, had been told by his father, unwisely perhaps, that most fireworks don't explode fully and that there is in the bottom of an unexploded firework a small residual quantity of gunpowder that can be recuperated by the dedicated arsonist. Would I like to go out to the rugger pitch with him after lunch and see what we could find? I would.

All over the area where the bonfire had been there lay the cases and cartridges of the supposedly finished fireworks. But, looking more closely, you saw that inside the little cardboard tubes there was, in every

case, a pinch, sometimes rather more than a pinch, of
dark grey powder. Henderson tore open the cases one by
one as I supplied them to him. My circles of collection
round the pitches got wider and wider but I went at it
with a will, bringing more and more. Henderson's
handkerchief became fuller and fuller. Then we found a
jam-jar, which increased our scope and, when it was full
(full!) we put the remaining powder in our pockets. By
the time we had to wander back to the classrooms
Henderson was a sort of walking Hiroshima but, in the
way of boys inured to disappointment (the one outcome
that never fails to disappoint) neither he nor I really
thought that we would be able to get so much as a
whimper out of our damp collection of smelly powder.
So he took little care as he walked.

　　After Geography (Father Hildred the Sub-Prior:
'I know I'm writing on the blackboard, but I can see you
in the reflection of my glasses Bennington Major.
You're TALKING. Nothing escapes me. What IS an
Armchair Valley?') our class had to go to something
optional – before Tea, which would be optional for no
known schoolboy of my generation, indeed too often the
only edible meal - and all the other boys slid vaguely
away while the Geography master went into the
Chemistry Lab nearby to discuss a problem boy with the
Stinks fellow, or possibly to smoke a quiet one among
the fumes. Thus Henderson and I were left alone. Fatty
wanted to get the powder out there and then and use it to
burn down this particular classroom block. Almost for
the first time in my life I realised that I was being called
upon by the fates to Be Responsible. 'No, not in here' I
cried, 'Outside!' 'Well. On the steps then' said
Henderson. And out we went.

　　The steps were of stone; so far so good; the
powder was tipped out of jar and pocket and placed in a

neat Mount Fuji on the lowest step, perfectly formed but not small; so far so better. What could go wrong? Henderson took out his matches. Still, in truth, neither of us believed that this was going to be that much fun, or even work at all. Then Fatty made his mistake. He removed his spectacles (all fat boys have spectacles).

Now, I don't know whether your chemistry is up to that of Mr Stinks and I can't offhand remember the formula for the relationship between distance and explosion, I mean in terms of How Near You Can Safely Get to How Big A Bang, but Henderson, intent only on doing a good job in what were probably hopeless circumstances and by nature extremely short-sighted, peered forward, burning Vesta in hand, looking for the best spot to apply flame. Choosing one he thrust his arm forward into the centre of the not inconsiderable heap of innocuous-looking dark-gray powder.

At once there was a huge WHOOOOOSH! that knocked me backwards and a searing flame that sprang into the air and blinded me for a moment. Recovering a little I took stock, though at first I had to accept that I could neither see nor hear. No master was thundering towards us like an avenging Fury; indeed no sound was to be heard at all. I did not see that the Chemistry Lab door had come flying open. Where, indeed, was Henderson? What of his inevitable cries? Was he already residing among the morning stars with Guy Fawkes in a sort of Idiot-Martyrs annex of the Catholic heaven?

As the temporary blindness passed I was able slowly to make out Fatty sitting about ten feet from where he had last been. His face was totally black and, it would transpire, he was without eyebrows or eyelashes; his hair was burnt to a crisp and the only thing that enabled you to know which way he was facing was his mouth which was opening and closing rhythmically to reveal, alarmingly, pink gums and black teeth.

My first thought was 'What a pity he took off his glasses.' My second was 'WHY? Why would he take off his glasses when they would have helped him see what he was doing and have provided some minimum protection? Was Fatty now blind? These questions resolved themselves into the fatuous single enquiry 'Did you break your glasses?'

Henderson was only a couple of days in the Sanatorium. Nobody asked him how he had become so burnt, and most of it of course washed off. And in the event we got away with a school crime that would normally have been taken with dismal seriousness Scot-free. The masters seemed unable to believe that we had been so stupid as actually to do what we had done. But worse was to come.

Fatty was Scottish in that sort of Anglicised way that involves neither accent nor habitation and relies on genealogical connections of a remote kind. My own mother once said, in that way that so baffles thick children of the sort I was, 'We are entitled to nine different tartans you know.' I didn't really *feel* very Scottish, but then Henderson perhaps didn't either. So when we had a Mock General Election in the school, encouraged by a master with more imagination than sense, Fatty stood for the Scottish Nationalists, then in reality a non-existent force in Caledonian politics. He pleaded with me to act as his Agent. Nobody could stand for the mock-seat of Belmont Abbey Central without an agent, so in my usual thoughtless way I agreed. Some of the debating that occurred in the Sixth Form Debate and elsewhere left me mildly humiliated by my lack of knowledge of both Scotland and the political process, but I hung in. There may have been an extra tea with the appropriate master to lure Agents and Candidates to stand. Or perhaps I felt sorry for my semi-pal. In any event things went along, with posters being made and displayed and arguments being had, in quite a surprisingly satisfactory manner until the day of the hustings which took place in the gym. The entire school was crowded into this Deep-Heat-scented place and candidates were paraded in front of them on a species of stage. The Head Boy gave a reasoned speech about voting Liberal (I think it was) and a rather posher-than-average chap went in for the Tories; I don't think there were any serious contenders for Labour so then it was the turn of the fringe parties, first among them Fatty's bloc which consisted, largely, of myself and the two Malayans who had no clue whatever as to what was happening and one of whom, at the end of the day, refused to tell me how he had voted (it wasn't Scot Nat, I know, as we only got one vote: mine) 'in case he was arrested and deported.'

Now Fatty Henderson had been taken ill the day before, possibly with hunger pains (at his size school food was conspicuously inadequate) or with repletion if he had managed to sneak into Hereford for a blow-out, or perhaps nerves. So he was in the sanatorium (again) sweating and burping as I took the floor in his place. Unabashed by ignorance and irrelevance I set about the task of convincing a large mixed body of English Catholic teenagers to pretend to vote for an all-Scottish party.

At first all seemed to go well. The catcalls and boos subsided, to my surprise, and looks of attention began to appear on the faces of my schoolmates. This effect spread quite rapidly in fact and by the second minute of my useless rambling there was what is known

78

as a deathly hush. 'This is going well' I thought, visions of a career at Westminster already forming at the back of my brain, 'They like me!' For another thirty seconds I ploughed on while glassy stares, accompanied by slight but noticeable smiles began to spread among my wrapt audience. All eyes were upon me. I got as far as a quotation from one of those horrible French thinkers who gave a *raison de massacre* to all left-wing tyrants from Robespierre to Lenin and Pol Pot, one St Just by name (a name that manages, if you consider St Just's ideas, to be a double oxymoron) about how 'Nobody can rule guiltlessly' when it happened.

While I was speaking I became aware, with that animal sense for danger that we all possess, that a threat was looming and that it was looming from behind me; but the show has to go on, no? So on I spoke as the silence became absolute and my chimpanzee brain yelled 'Watch out behind you!' at increasing volume. The attack was perfectly timed. As I opened my mouth to let them have a bit more St Just at high pitch, an unknown hand reached round from my left ear and stuffed a large slice of fruitcake into my mouth. Several things then occurred at once. In order as I perceived them: a huge roar of laughter swelled up; I began to choke; a fight broke out among the various factions in the hall and a visiting rugger team came charging into the gym to see the fun.

Extricating some of the cake from my mouth I ran across the stage in pursuit of my assailant who was fleeing down the steps into the auditorium and caught him by his coat tails. He took a tumble into an assembled body of fourth-formers and I heard above the din 'Let's have another game!' at which members of our own First Fifteen set about forming a scrum and charging the visiting team whom they had just beaten under stricter regulations on the pitch. I pushed some partially-masticated cake into my attacker's face and looked round to see our star Centre running into the gym with his well-known Mach 2 speed, eager for the fray. Unfortunately he ran straight into one of the fourth-formers and knocked him over. All the other small boys at once screamed 'He's got weak bones!' for this was the famous Twistelton or Ashby or whatever-his-name-was who had come to the school with the warning 'His bones break easily.' Twistelton, or Ashby, lay on the floor writhing in agony and then passed out; the impromptu rugger match passed over him like a tsunami and at that point the headmaster looked in to see how the election was going. 'You won't believe it Father!' I shouted at him. 'No, I can see that Butler Minor' was all I caught of his reply.

The boy with broken bones joined the malingering Henderson in the sanatorium. The school calmed down. The democratic experiment was abandoned and never repeated.

3. PORT

My penultimate crime before being expelled from Belmont started promisingly enough. The English master had to find a room for me to sit my Oxford Scholarship exam (remember those?) and after some negotiating with fellow-masters in the school, where there was apparently No Room At All, and the monks in the monastery, where Boys Were Never Allowed, the compromise was reached that I would be allowed to sneak across the shortest possible monastic corridor and sit my four-hour exam in the Abbot's private study. The Abbot was away ('Sunning himself in Rio' as Father Illtyd rather darkly said from time to time at this period) and the room quiet. But I was to understand how privileged I was. Very.

The Oxford Scholarship in those days was an exam taken in December to allow the Cambridge version to be taken in January; successful candidates were then invited to the college of their choice for interview. It was these two exams that enabled me to make so near a mess-up of my Oxbridge applications, but in the event I never went back to Lincoln Oxford after my interview there (crusty don: 'Tell me about the aesthetic in the modern novel'; me: 'Ah.' Don: 'You know, Joyce and Lawrence?' me: 'Ah. Er, Yes! Joyce and Lawrence.')

The exam was a sort of freestyle essay (you know the sort of thing: 'Write an Essay About Compromise', 'What is Decadence?' or 'Write an Essay about Writing Essays') that just suited my unconcentrateable talents. I wrote for a while and, at about half-time, losing the will to go on being profound and witty, started looking round the room. I was expecting signs of monastic poverty (Poverty being the vow they take in the Benedictines along with Chastity and Obedience) and not a drinks cabinet, yet there it was. There wasn't much in it but there was something I had never heard of before: White Port, about half a bottle.

Now half the enjoyment of the scandalous, the funny and the extreme is sharing the event with a like-minded pal. In this instance I at once thought of my then-best buddy Caradoc King (where do parents *get* these names?) who, I knew, would be hanging about in the Sixth-Form Common Room at lunchtime and I determined to end my witterings about 'The Aesthetic in Literature' forthwith and, concealing the port about my person, surprise him with it there. But think if you will

of the relative sizes of a schoolboy's uniform and a
bottle of port. The best I could manage was to put the
bottle down my trouser leg and, putting my hand into
my pocket, grasp its neck.

What I had failed to count on was the presence
in the monastic corridor of... a monk. From the gloomy
distance he hailed me, 'What are you doing up here
boy? Who are you? Come here.' It was Father Martin,
the foolish old once-Austrian housemaster of a house,
not mine, where discipline was little known. But not so
foolish as to take in his stride a boy in the monastery
(horror!) with one hand in his pocket (forbidden, even to
sixth-formers, when talking to a monk or a master.) 'Ah,
Butler! Take your hand out of your pocket Butler.' 'I
can't' I said. 'Take it out' he said. I saw we had reached
an impasse. I had a moment's interesting fantasy of
doing a runner, bolting down the dark corridors and
going quickly to bed, pretending to be ill and denying
everything. But instead I started laughing and tried to
pull out the bottle of white port. If you think about it
though, my hand was in my pocket holding the neck of
the bottle but the bottle was actually in my trouser-leg. I
had therefore to unbutton my fly and reach into my
trousers with my other hand. This operation caused
some raising of Fr Martin's substantial Teutonic
eyebrows but I thought I detected a glimmer of what I
can only describe as hope in his suddenly-enlivened
blue eyes. Once I had retrieved the port and rearranged
my clothing Martin took it (the port of course) and
looked carefully at the label. 'But this is port!' he said
intelligently. 'Yes Father.' 'But you're not allowed
Port! Where did you get it?' Sheep, lambs and hanging
came to my aid; 'From the Abbot's study Father.'

The Headmaster, to whom I was sent, was
extremely cross. He claimed later to have said 'If this

sort of thing happens again....' But I don't remember it. When it *did* happen again however he referred back to this threat, possibly mendaciously, and used it as a pretext to expel me. A couple of pals and I had gone out to one of the few remaining cider-pubs in the Herefordshire countryside, where, having ingested several quarts of disgusting apple-flavoured vinegar of great alcoholic strength, we started to challenge one another to Dares. Mine involved, as we lurched back to the Abbey in the small hours, stealing some significant object with which to decorate the Sixth-Form Common Room. I spotted a large Goodyear Tyres flag at the top of a flagpole outside a closed petrol station and managed, by what means I cannot now remember, to get it down and wrap it around my person under my waistcoat. (What *is* it about young men that urges them so inexorably towards the stealing of traffic-cones, flags, fire extinguishers and the like? I once even stole a *punt pole*. I mean, why?) On arrival back at Belmont I was waylaid by a lurking monk who, in his turn, issued a challenge, 'What have you got under your clothes?' His acumen needn't have been very great since I was about twice as fat as I should have been. I remember unwinding the huge flag from my person with what I took to be a great dignity, a dignity surely confined only to my ability not to fall over. The Head had had enough and next day I was on a train home.

'Home', as we know a tricky entity for me as for many, was at this time in Wilmslow near Manchester where my father now took it upon himself to organise a little education for his wayward son ready to go up to Cambridge with the minimal barrier of one further A-level (I had passed A-level English at the end of the Lower Sixth; with the Scholarship Exam successfully negotiated Cambridge was not really interested in my

A-levels but had to nod to government *minima*) and some Latin. Any grades would do. So Pa found a crammer in central Manchester and I commuted there a couple of days a week. It was a curious establishment where some first-class teachers lurked and plied their shameful trade of bringing the children of the better-off up to scratch. I did some History and some French (surely I could get a bare A-level pass in *one* of those?) and also a fair amount of Latin with an excellent chap who taught three of us the dead language of Rome with considerable invention. One of my fellow-pupils was Ezra, an extravagantly Jewish-looking male midget of great charm as well as actual Jewishness with whom I lunched. The other was a woman in her late thirties (I now suppose) of intense pulchritude and great warmth with whom, in the emotional vagrancy of adolescence (I was only sixteen), I at once fell hopelessly in love. Think Rousseau and Mme de Warrens.

At this stage I fear can't remember her name, but I found myself thinking about her all the time and talking to her throughout all available pauses, in class and out. I remember a day when I sat on the train with her and, because of her, felt that the ugliness of the dreary Mancunian suburbs through which we were travelling *didn't matter*; her existence on the planet and within my ken was enough to redeem the whole sorry spectacle. And they say that women have no power.

She had the most beautiful curves, at least when fully clothed which is how I always saw her, of any woman I had even seen until then, and the warmest smile. You have to remember that I knew only one other woman at the time – my mother – and had never touched or even really spoken to anything more female than certain dogs and horses and even then it was often hard to tell. Looking back I think this Lady of the Latin

Class must have resembled my mother but in a more cuddly edition. One day, finding the Subjunctive a bit stressful, or the Manchester afternoon too warm (this was May or June), she took off her shoes. I carried them for her as she padded to the coffee-bar. I would have carried them in a golden casket over broken glass barefoot to Vladivostok without a murmur. I remember her skirt, her hair. On the train back to Wilmslow I decided I would announce my passion to her after our next Latin class, but I never did. She thus joined the long list of might-have-beens that are strewn along the life-path of any man of feeling. The worst thing is that I can still feel the feeling, the love, fleetingly and faintly, when I think of her unexpectedly. I was much consoled, many years later, to come across Hardy's poem 'I look into my glass' with its last stanza:

> But Time, to make me grieve,
> Part steals, lets part abide;
> And shakes this fragile frame at eve
> With throbbings of noontide.

Though I suppose that 'throbbings of mid-morning' would be more suitable than 'noontide' for a sixteen-year-old.[4]

Of course my Cambridge College would be all-male too. I can't believe I didn't turn out gay.

---

[4] I have a friend who went through this precocious process younger than me. He had been sent home to prep-school from Thailand aged 5 (*sic*) and by the time he was 12 had fallen in love with the New-Zealand Under-matron, a young lady of 19. She offered him tea, sympathy and cuddles but their affair, such as it was, was brought to an abrupt end when, in distress over something or other, he visited her room one evening to find her under the Latin master.

4. SURMAN

When I was about fourteen I had had enough of the discipline at Belmont Abbey and, threatened with a caning by Fr Aelred my fairly sadistic housemaster, decided to run away before he could get his hands on me.

Looking back, this was the moment at which I had the option to become a hero or to discover my own special level of incompetence. Of these two possibilities I embraced the second with quite stunning single-mindedness by running away, for instance, *in the wrong direction*, by being entirely unprepared for the contingencies of such an adventure and by having to rely on others at every turn.

I managed to get out of the Abbey grounds during the afternoon, to cross some fields and dodge down some lanes until I got to a main road. There I set out for what I thought of as The Nearest Town. Unfortunately this proved to be Hay-on-Wye, some ten miles from the school and well west of it, when I thought I was going to London many miles to the east. I just seemed to walk and walk through the increasing darkness.

Once in Hay I felt the need of bed and board and rang the bell of a small hotel (this was about 11 pm) of which the front door opened in the full Hollywood Sinister Castle manner and I found myself in a species of private parlour answering the questions of a definite though not unkind hag. I said I had been left behind by a bus driver who was taking a school party to London. They had simply forgotten me. I needed food and a bed.

Before the hag would take me in she telephoned the police who sent a constable. This bluebottle, astonishingly, swallowed my story without question and

86

said he would return in the morning. I was given something to eat and retired, but not for long. Spotting that my painfully thin cover would be blown at dawn, I slept for a few hours and then at 3am got up again and crept out into the chilly streets of the town. There, going round a corner, I ran into a policeman. Another policeman. This is getting to sound like a Flan O'Brien novel, or a Beckett.

This second policeman was every bit as astute as the first one had been. He peered at me in my school mac, tie and damp shoes. Which I was wearing at 3am. In Hay-on-Wye. But what was even more astonishing was the question he asked me. 'Ah' he said, 'Tell me… Are you Richard Surman?' I goggled at him for a bit and said, quite truthfully, 'No, no. No I'm not.' Now the reason for my surprise was that one of my friends at Belmont was, precisely, this Richard Surman. I was hard put to it to imagine what was going on. Were there actually two Richard Surmans ('Surmen'?) I wondered, in Herefordshire, one at Belmont Abbey and the other wanted by the police? But why would this constable whatever-he-was think that I was one of them? Why didn't he ask me my name? It was unfathomable. In due course the enigmatic peeler dismissed me and sent me on my way without further enquiry in the same way that his colleague had left me unquestioned in the hotel. I staggered on into the night, getting ever further from my destination and puzzling over Life.

Of course this running-away was not really intended to separate me forever from my school; it was quite obviously, I now see, a cry for help. The horrors of the housemaster's study were only the tip of an iceberg of fear, confusion and sadness and I needed to make a very loud noise and get an audience, some notice, parental help, a good laugh, anything to help me break out of these feelings. It was megaphone diplomacy. As ever, this unconscious tactic to attract attention, to protest, to ask for help was altogether unavailing among the non-analytical relatives and schoolmasters by whom I was surrounded.

So it didn't work. When eventually I managed to find a telephone box and call my aunt (my parents being in Germany) and told her what I had done she made little comment, offered no sympathy and merely asked where I was, in great detail. When I told her my whereabouts she said I should go back to the hotel and wait there, which eventually I did. In the morning the hotel-hag told me that 'Father Martin' was coming from Belmont to collect me; and in due course the ancient black Monastery Car pulled up outside the hotel and the even more antique Father Martin, the Austrian monk of the Port saga, took me into custody and back to school.

On the way he said that I had set a trend and that another boy had run away during the evening. 'Ah' I said, 'Was it Surman Father?' 'Yes, yes it was' puffed the old God-botherer, 'How did you know?'

My housemaster treated me with kid gloves for the rest of that term at least. But I was left with some questions. First, how could I have been so grossly incompetent as to go in the wrong direction? And yet how come I was so amazingly competent at telling improbable stories to strangers? Second, as my aunt never mentioned the matter again and I think that my parents were never actually informed about it, the escapade vanished into a sort of *oubliette*. Why?

Today, when I think of how I followed my own daughters through every detail of their education and how seriously I would have looked into either of them *running away*, I am astonished at the lack of seriousness with which my protest was greeted. If Alice or Miranda

had run away from school I would have been on the
very next plane from Timbuctu or Anchorage to sort
matters out. If they just had a *cold* I was all for keeping
them at home (they didn't ever really board, thank God)
and their slightest anxiety would fill my head. Perhaps I
went a little too far as a father, but if I did it was surely
a fault in the right direction. Unlike the road from
Belmont Abbey to London via Hay-on-Wye. But in my
parents' generation one merely accepted things and
carried on.

When, a couple of years later, I took an overdose
of sleeping-pills in Cheshire (another cry for help I
suppose) my father came down from a holiday in
Scotland to scoop me up. But even then his
investigation into my plight, such as it was, consisted of
making me promise 'Never to do that again.' After
which we discussed the weather.

5. TERRIBLE

Father Aelred must, I suppose, have been genetically
human but we were inclined to see him rather as a sort
of vicious greasy machine. At Belmont he was
Housemaster of Kemble House, to which Piers and I
belonged, and a notorious wielder of the cane. In one's
early teens one regards such phenomena as
schoolmasters as fixed stars in the constellation of
adults that surrounds one: Aelred seemed to have been
born in his Benedictine habit and appeared to have a
shining blue chin of exactly the same degree of growth
(zero, but *very* blue) at all hours of the day and night
although no one ever saw him shave. We never learnt,
indeed, where he slept. Perhaps he didn't sleep but crept
about the monastery at night, slithering up and down the
outer walls like Dracula.

89

At seven every morning this Aelred would burst into the Kemble Junior Dormitory ringing a large bell of extraordinary penetration. 'Come along! Up! Up!' he would intone in his 'I-am-really-Welsh-but-the-Abbot-sent-me-to-Oxford' voice. The choir-monks at Belmont, destined to be unpaid schoolmasters, were often sent off to Oxford after Ordination; there they lived at Bene't House (there was one at Cambridge too), a small college for Benedictines. Aelred had read History and had lots of expensive and intriguing books in his study, among them Koestler's *Darkness at Noon* which I stole but later returned. Read it sometime gentle Communist.

He would return to the dormitory at three-minute intervals to roust the sluggards from their beds. By 7.30 we were washed, dressed and hearing Mass in the Abbey church. I found this short, astonishing ceremony to be a cold but beautiful moment; it left me subsequently reluctant entirely to ignore the whiff of pontifical incense in my psyche.

Within minutes of his final harrying operations around our sleeping quarters Aelred would appear in a side-chapel of the church in full vestments, saying his own Mass (no Concelebration in those pre-Vatican II days) complete with angelic altar-boys from the junior forms. Then, almost immediately it seemed, we would see him back in his habit enjoying his breakfast bacon on High Table while we stared at our grey gloopy porridge below him. After a brief post-breakfast pause it would be Double Maths, taken, ye gods, by Father Aelred! Later in the day he might appear as Coach for the Colts Rugby team, organiser of that year's Duke of Edinburgh's Award expedition or, in his most wonderful transformation, on Thursdays, in full army uniform as Captain Cousins, Commanding officer of the

Belmont Abbey School CCF. He was, in short, ubiquitous. Perhaps he was God.

He was also self-appointed sex-tutor to our house, perhaps more widely in the school, and had earned himself the nickname of 'Kinsey' after the famous Reports of 1948 (men) and 1953 (women) which had explained the birds and the bees to a new generation of Americans. Luckily I never experienced any Information at his hands. Unless you count his astonishing decision to ask a sixth-former to cycle down to Hereford to buy *Lady Chatterley's Lover* on the day it was published after the famous trial in 1958. Aelred allowed the book to be passed around among the senior boys in the house. I remember that very soon the paperback copy fell open spontaneously at page 144. I didn't read the whole book until I was about thirty by which time it had a lost a lot of its sting.

There was a *canard* in the school that this character's priest-name, strange as it was, meant 'Terrible' in Anglo-Saxon. In fact St Aelred, a monk of the twelfth century and patron saint of bladder-stone sufferers, was a historian, an abbot and a suspected homosexual; he has been adopted by certain gay-friendly organisations in the USA as their patron too. Fortunately we did not have this information. And 'Aelred' actually means 'noble' or, confusingly, 'counsel', seeming unable to choose between being an adjective and an abstract noun. But someone with a smattering of Old English must have picked up 'Aedreclic', which does mean Terrible, or perhaps 'Aelreord' which means 'of strange speech, barbarous.' Unsurprisingly the Anglo-Saxons had dozens of words meaning bad things like 'terrible' and Kinsey deserved some of them.

In any event this frightful fellow did, as hinted, have his moments of quasi-humanity and one of these occurred on a November 5th, a date when things were likely to go off-piste a bit, as in the Henderson episode above. Hardy has a good comment in *The Return of the Native*, which opens in November and proceeds with a bonfire: 'At the winter's ingress…. the fettered gods of the earth say 'let there be light.'' So it was, even at Catholic Belmont where presumably we should have been lamenting Saint Guido Fawkes' failure to incinerate the Royal Family and the entire political class of London in 1605. Instead of which we celebrated like all other Englishmen but, as we have seen, without a guy.

Perhaps to make up for this lack of point, Fr Aelred tried sometimes to lay on an extravagant bonfire for the house behind the Fifth-form classrooms in a random field which seemed unused for any purpose, even by Brother Peter who kept the pigs.

One November 5th when I was myself in the Fifth form he went beyond his usual arrangements. For some reason a simply monstrous pile of wood and rubbish had been collected in advance for the bonfire and this must have excited his less-monastic side because, with a certain amount of greasy giggling, he led a few of us to a storehouse where some previous housemaster had collected a large number of broken chairs. These he gestured towards with the words 'Take them all!' rather like the Bishop of Foix outside the walls of Beziers during the Albigensian Crusade who, when asked what should happen when the town was taken considering that besides the renegade Cathar heretics there were some Catholics in there too, replied 'Kill them all! God will know His own.'

We rushed the chairs to the pyre with shrieks of delight, heaping them up and casting about us for other fuel, finding old clothes, less-old clothes, books, jotters, small trees, new-boys. There was (need I say?) a tradition that the older boys could take a little beer on this occasion and we had interpreted this informal licence liberally. A boy called Aitken had sold his gold cufflinks to buy vodka for instance; I myself had first learnt what a 'pin' of beer was (a barrel, but not as small a one as it sounds) and then ordered one from the grocer's in Hereford where I had an account. The Head of House had pinched some Glenlivet from his father's drinks cupboard during the summer holidays and now brought it out. The combination of this supply of mixed alcoholic substances with fire and destruction was extremely productive. Wild confidences were exchanged, wilder songs sung and competitions proposed as the long evening wore on. Among these last was one that I subsequently thought of as Aelred's Disgrace.

The chairs we had liberated from the hidden store had included several metal ones which even I could see would not burn. These were seized on at about 10pm by a red-faced Aelred who, I realized, had been celebrating in the same way as the rest of us and was now a fiery greasy whirl of hysterical beer-fuelled energy. 'Racing!' he cried. 'Time for racing!' and in what seemed only a few seconds he had set up a sort of hurdle track round the bonfire with the metal chairs and was urging the boys to try it out in a finely competitive spirit. As we hesitated for a moment or two, perhaps because of a certain mistrust brought on by this unusual behaviour of our housemaster's, he decided, with the rapidity of early-stage drunkenness, to Show Us How.

93

'I'll show you how!' he shrieked and, tucking up his skirts, set off at a good lick.

All went well for a dozen yards as he got into the correct orbit round the monster fire, accelerating as he went. Then his trajectory closed in on the chairs and he took the first of them with mixed success, trailing a leg so that although he received what must have been a painful crack on the shin he was able to continue at almost unreduced speed. The second chair went worse: he placed a foot on the raised back part and vaulted over at high speed; in the air he performed a kind of *entrechat* with his legs, waved wildly with what seemed to be several arms and then came down astonishingly still upright and still moving. We yelled encouragement interlarded with carefully-modulated obscenities. The third chair was Aelred's last. Taking it too early he smacked into it squarely and carried it forward a few yards before coming to rest with a final gurgle in the darkness beyond the fire.

We carried him back to the Abbey, though even that night we somehow failed to find out where his sleeping-lair was. He slipped from our grasp into the cloisters (Out of Bounds to us) with a groan and was not seen again for about twenty-four hours. Next time we had him for rugger practice he was wearing long trousers to conceal what had happened to his shins. This was in the days before track-suits of course.

The last I heard of Aelred was in the 1990s when I visited Belmont again, to see Mr (by now Father) Jenkins. It turned out that the Terrible One was now in Africa, Uganda I think, where he was still a priest and still teaching. He was alleged to have changed Catholic horses and now belonged to some white-robed order of missionaries. I found it hard to imagine.

6. GNOSTIC

Standing next to Mr Jenkins the History master one dull afternoon in the bike sheds outside the main refectory, I mentioned that I was scheduled later that day to discuss something (Oxbridge entrance?) with Father Jerome. 'Ah' said Jenks, 'well, good luck. I always think he's a bit agnostic.'

Watching Jenx smoke and wondering if I knew him well enough to ask for a drag, I considered this. Could it really be true that that most monastic of monks Father Jerome was in fact an *unbeliever*? Or did it mean just that he had once expressed Doubts? And how would Jenks know that, and why would he tell me? As ever with my interactions with this super-master, himself later to join the monastery, take orders and become headmaster, there was a secret agenda. With extraordinary subtlety I sounded Jenks out: 'What do you mean?' I asked.

'Nothing to do with religion' he replied. 'It's something I have developed with Father Robert. You know those people who are *with you*? Who understand, who *follow*? Robert and I call them Gnostics because they really recognise that there is another person in front of them, they *know* that the world is not entirely orientated in their direction, that they aren't the Centre of All Things. It's perhaps easier to think of the *ag*nostics to get the point. You know, those chaps who interrupt your story or explanation or plea with something of their own before you have finished talking. Who aren't concerned when you clearly want to be serious, who can't manage to crank up some amusement when you are light-hearted. People who can't follow St Paul's advice to be 'all things to all men' but plough on doggedly along their own furrow.'

I did. I do. Watch. It's easy to imitate and you'll recognise it at once:

You: 'How are you old man?'
Them: 'Pretty terrible actually; I've been feeling bad all morning.'
You: 'I'm so sorry - a bad day then?'
Them: (puzzled) 'No'
You: 'But you're feeling ill?'
Them: (dubiously) 'Well, my day's been OK. I mean.... I'm not *ill.*'
You: 'Oh but I thought perhaps...'
Them: 'I'm never ill. I just get these bugs from time to time.'
You: 'Oh yes. I've had one recently. It...'
Them: 'No no; that's different.'
You: 'So... you don't think you've got a bug?'
Them : 'What makes you say that?'
You (internally): 'Jesus Christ! I don't really care that much about this chap or his bloody lurgy. I was only being nice, making conversation. All I wanted was to play the game he started – and for his sake!

Quite a lot of the people I have met in life have been agnostics. I was going to write 'to one degree or another' but in fact I fear that there are no degrees in this matter – one either is Gnostic or one isn't. Politeness can be instilled, so agnostics can fool some of the people some of the time, but the truth will out. I remember turning to an apparently very nice Cambridge friend of mine with whom I had shared a lot, apparently on equal terms, when my first wife left me and I was distraught. I phoned him and he listened to me for a while before coming back with 'Well old man, it's your problem', and that was that. Looking back I realised that all our interactions had in fact taken place around him, not me, and on his terms; also that he had never

96

cooperated in anything at all of mine, never visiting or
inquiring or calling or proposing anything. He was not
at all a *bad* person and his level of selfishness was not
noticeably higher than my own – he seemed a bit lazy
but he had some charm to make up for it. We had
laughed together, but only at *funny* things I now saw.
Perhaps he cared for me deeply, but as he wasn't *with*
me he didn't in the end appear to care at all. He wasn't
gnostically connected to my existence as I had always
assumed he had been.

In short Gnosticism is love and he just didn't
have that in his make up. Did he love others? On close
inspection I realised that I couldn't say that he really did
love anyone. Love is also an absolute: you have it or
you don't. This insight has paradoxically made me less
tolerant as life has gone on, less able to bother with
agnostic people. Which makes me a kind of horrible
purist I suppose, and surely someone who has set the
bar too high. But I mention it all here because it has
been a great surprise to me to see how the world goes in
this connection and I still can't quite understand it.[5]

Other people are a strange lot. They are so
important, so immense a part of the life of our very
social species, yet so difficult to stay enamoured of in
the longer run. Friends are easy to make, I find, easy
even to keep, but there comes after a while a moment
where one realises that they are very *full* of themselves.
Now of course that's the most obvious thing in the
world and altogether natural, but the trick of social life,
a fortiori of gentlemanly behaviour, is to conceal this as

---

[5] One of the uses of fiction may be to provide readers with a world
in which gnostic behaviour is common. Narrators and heroes, the
'good' people in traditional novels and stories at least, understand
and care for each other in a gnostic way. But why, then, does the
great agnostic majority enjoy fiction so much?

much as possible and not let its whiskers show above the parapet. Some people can manage that; some of my pals manage it a lot better than me, but many have fallen at the eighteenth hurdle – I mean at that point where it becomes apparent that between your interests and any of their interests the contest is hopelessly uneven.

But here is one person I knew who, without pretension or protestation, cut the mustard and earned my unchanging admiration and affection. She must have been sixty-five and I a mere twenty when we met, Irene Swainson, and she died fifteen years later aged eighty. She was the same age as the Queen Mother and thus as the century itself, so I must have known her from 1965 to 1980. Why she took to a puppy like me must remain a mystery.

Irene had been, by her own account at least, the first British girl ever to be given her own car, during the First World War. She then spent her life propping up the Empire in such insalubrious places as Ghana and Nigeria where she coped with extraordinary resilience. There was much to cope with, and her stories were legion, but I will restrict myself to two details. One is that she drank like a fish but not as much as everyone in the colony thought because she had her houseboys serve cocktails, much consumed in the Tropics in those days, at her parties, which had been doctored. Where everyone else had gin in their Pink Gins or Tom Collinses she had hers served with water only. She would throw them down at great speed and thus force many of the men present to keep up, often with revealing results. The other detail is that she survived Blackwater Fever, a disease universally fatal to white people, not once but twice.

Irene made no fuss about being very nice to me indeed and spoke as if we were equals and always with understanding and warmth. I felt the rarity of this at the time. When she was buried in 1980 there was a Requiem mass for her said in the Catholic church in Gillingham near Silton. Contrary to the specific behests of the Second Vatican Council the priest had the humanity to say it in the language that Irene had always spoken to God in - Latin. I have no doubt He was feeling a little nervous about Irene's arrival and must have welcomed this.

CHAPTER 4. CAMBRIDGE 1963 - 1966

1. ENGLISH

'English', then often known as 'Eng Lit', was the starry
arts subject for my generation. Since its acceptance into
the Tripos at Cambridge in 1917 it had slowly taken
over the mantle of Classics and was expected to do
something of the same job that Latin and Greek did,
whatever that was. Eng Lit was big in America, where
Classics had died slightly more quickly and where
'English', disguised for instance as 'Freshman
Composition', was a matter of learning about the
language as well as the literature. In Cambridge there
were heady days both before and after the Second
World War, the days of New Criticism which starred
I.A.Richards, T.S.Eliot, F.R.Leavis[6], *Scrutiny* and the
whole post-Arnoldian work of Practical Criticism and
moral intensity. All of this was still alive and well when
I went up in 1963.

Things changed, as they do, but in general
'English' was a rising force through most of the second
half of the twentieth century and I seemed to rise with it
as I progressed from naive Freshman to hoary Professor.
It seems hard to imagine now, but the new and
relatively small University of Stirling, opened in 1967,
had an English department that by 1974 numbered
twenty-five full-time staff. In those early years our Head
of Department was appointing two, three or even four

---

[6] The comedian Eric Idle, made famous by *Monty Python*, was up
at Pembroke with me. I heard him give a spoof lecture in which he
impersonated Leavis doing a New Critical analysis of the
Cambridge Telephone Directory. The climax of this piece of
nonsense was his account of finding his own name in the book,
phoning the number and discovering that he couldn't get an answer.

100

lecturers per year; I arrived with three other young men in 1972 for instance. Of course, a couple of years later the doors slammed shut and the department gradually diminished. Other flavours of the decade emerged: Film and Media Studies, Politics, Religious Studies, Computing, Japanese. By 1987, after I had been at Stirling for fifteen years, the doors hadn't re-opened an inch: I was still the youngest member of the department.

This was the time of the expansion of British universities in the 1960s (seven new universities including Stirling) when the great majority of applicants to higher education had no Latin or Greek at all. And it brought about a heyday for 'English' that lasted, with ups and downs, until the next great expansion in higher education that took place in the late 1980s when the number of UK universities simply doubled. After that Information Technology in all its forms, together with an increasing ignorance of the cultural bases of English literature, meant a relative decline.[7]

But there was something else as well. After about 1980 'English', which had seemed so static and comforting to those of us educated before 1970, turned out to be both the birthplace and the victim of some new ways of thinking that none of us had expected. Indeed, at a certain point after 1980 statements such as 'there is no such subject as English' or Terry Eagleton's 'there is no crisis in English - English IS crisis' would become commonplace. Once we had been got at by Structuralism we put on seminars and conferences

---

[7] When in 1995 I was appointed External Examiner at one of these new-new universities, a former Anglican teacher-training college, I discovered that 'English' now mostly consisted of dull girls studying Children's Literature and producing portfolios of 'creative writing' not dissimilar to the work my own daughters did in the later stages of their prep-school education though with added sex.

called things like 'The University in Ruins'. This was
the Structuralist and, very quickly, Poststructuralist
revolution that came across the Channel from Paris and
carried all before it. It even got into *The Times* where I
saw a Calman cartoon in which, over the breakfast
table, Mrs Average is asking Mr Average 'Have they
caught the Cambridge Structuralist yet?' This was in the
wake of the Colin McCabe affair – he was sacked, from
Trinity I think, for being too theoretically advanced in
the direction of Paris. Oh, and of course in the wake
also of the arrest of the Cambridge Rapist, famous in his
day, a tiny man who assaulted young ladies while
wearing a mask with 'Rapist' on it in childish letters, to
give the poor girls a clue as to what to expect I suppose.
He turned out to be the drayman at the Cambridge
branch of Dolamores, a wine shop run by a red-nosed
friend of mine who was terribly surprised to discover
that he had been nursing a viper to this extent.

So being in 'English' was a two-sided affair for
my generation. Before 1980 all was sweetness and light,
literally if you consider the impact of Arnold's *Culture
and Anarchy* of 1868 where he pleads in those very
terms for something more liberal than the then-current
British class system. 'English', in default of a credible
national religion or the long haul of learning Classics,
was the obvious answer to the lacks in British
intellectual and spiritual life, and we 'English' people
thrived. It was a political position of course, though we
didn't know it, and it was a moral one. As one
Structuralist sniping at this *ancien régime* put it, we
were engaged in a process whereby young men were
encouraged to love George Eliot and then to love the
tutors who had been the means of introducing them to
her.

It was all most pleasant. As a student at Cambridge I was engaged in reading 'the best that has been thought and felt' (Arnold again) and explaining to an undemanding don how good it was, or perhaps how the metaphorical structure of the text worked, or something about 'Milton's language.' One would get essays back with 'Quite interesting' written on them – and usually no grade since there was no such thing as 'continuous assessment' in those days. This was how I was taught and this is how I myself started teaching in the 1970s – an agreeable occupation, presumably humanizing and good in itself for the student on the receiving end and, at the very least, not doing anyone any obvious harm.

Then that unexpected slow-release bomb was sent in among us, from Paris with love. The alarmingly dry and *difficult* work of the Structuralists was bad enough and it made us think beyond the boundaries within which we had been so comfortable. Suddenly we had to think about people like the anthropologist Claude Levi-Strauss, then a name so big that at Stirling we awarded him an Honorary Degree even though he was too important, blasé and gonged-up to bother to come to the university to collect it. Psychology, philosophy, politics all reared their Gallic heads and shouted at us. But then, very quickly it seemed, the Poststructuralists came over the horizon too: 'English' became about Roland Barthes, Michel Foucault, Jacques Lacan and Jacques Derrida even before we had properly absorbed Genette and Todorov, Structuralists who were at least literary in orientation. Departments were split between those who thought that all this Gallic obscurity had nothing to do with reading Jane Austen and those who thought that it was a paradigm-shift in intellectual life equivalent to the work of Copernicus.

Arguments ensued in articles, conferences and common-rooms; people fell out; some rejoiced that this was confirmation of the left-wing agenda that they had been proposing since the 1960s and went about observing that if their traditionalist opponents weren't careful they'd be 'back with liberalism', something that many of us thought might be rather a good thing if a bit optimistic, but which was meant as a synonym for 'Satanism.' Some departments went the full fissiparous hog and split into two parts, one called 'English' and the other 'Literary Theory' or 'Critical Theory.' But, de facto, the intellectual force of the new thinking was such that it proved irresistible even to those opposed to it.

As for me, after a brief flirtation with the Rejectionist position ('It's all French tosh. Go away and read some proper books for heaven's sake') I too saw that there can be no such thing as neutral reading, that interpretation is infinite in the sense that there can be no *a priori* exclusion of possible future meanings and, yes, bowing *contre coeur* to the political interpretation, that cultural circumstances and political arrangements do to a great extent determine our reactions to works of art.

Eventually one realised that this was amazing stuff but amongst it one trod warily. Voices outside the academy were quick to sneer, to laugh and to shrug their shoulders. 'Silly Relativism' was the cry, and people published books called things like *Fraud* and *Not Saussure*. But inside English departments it became obligatory to learn the new language of criticism. It was called 'Literary Theory' by most and 'Critical Theory' or just 'Theory' by the intellectual imperialists who thought that the deconstructions that we were getting used to in English were going to spread across the whole range of subjects. But a very substantial baby was thrown out with the bathwater of the older way of doing my subject.

Seconded to the University of Pau in 1986 for two years I found myself at least feeling that I would now, here in France, be at the fountainhead of the new wisdom. Expressing this opinion to a new friend in the *Département d'anglais* I wished I hadn't. He looked at me with a degree of contempt and said 'Oh, Derrida and all that. No no. His stuff is all Old Hat here my dear. We've moved on.' I was torn between irritation at this usual failure of the gods of Time to get things in order for me and admiration of my colleague's excellent English.

2. CLIMBING

It was sometimes said in the family that my uncle Bunny Fuchs, Arnie's second husband after the demise of Uncle Dick and an Antarctic explorer of some renown, had been a climber in his Cambridge days, and in a special sense of the word. He was thought to have been a member of the group of young men at who, under the collective pseudonym of 'Whipplesnaith', had written *The Night Climbers of Cambridge*, published in 1934. It is a college-by-college description of the best climbs complete with murky black-and-white photographs of young men setting about self-harm with extraordinary determination in the dead of night.

Besides descriptions of the hairiest ways of getting about the roofs of the colleges some assessment is made of the nature of each sort of inhabitant that might be found dwelling under the roofs in question. When it came to my own college the description included some uncompromising summary judgements. On going through a window into a chap's room

105

'Whipplesnaith' comments: 'The traditional Pembroke greeting of a punch on the jaw was noticeable by its absence'. And on our students in general: 'Pembroke men are the sort that suck pipes in far Malayan jungles, but do not pass exams.' (Note the redundant comma for dramatic effect.) Of course when, at about my time and certainly in the years that followed my graduation, intelligence became the only criterion for entry into Cambridge such characterisations became anachronistic. I recall the amusement caused among us older stagers when the comparative Tables came in (how many Firsts did *your* college get?) and Pembroke one heady year was an astonishing Top. Quite incredible to us. In the Pembroke Boat Club, my year, our dismal performance was only surpassed by our neighbours on the river, Downing, who managed five total failures in the Tripos out of the nine men in their first eight. By the time we came Top we had got cleverer obviously, but it was because by then we had Girls.

The tradition of climbing about the buildings of the university is quite old, presumably at least contemporary with the Alpine maniacs who in the Nineteenth Century assaulted the Eiger and the Matterhorn with nothing but a stick, a Norfolk jacket and stout length of rope. Or, in the case of Gertrude Bell, with two strong Swiss guides and clean underwear because on the tougher stretches she was often required to divest herself of her outer raiment so that they could push her up chimneys and whatnot. The guides apparently looked away as much as possible while pushing. By the 1930s Climbing was evidently still fashionable and was, surely, preferable to the alternative tradition of Stalinism-and-sodomy in vogue among the Burgesses, Macleans, Philbys and Blunts of the period.

106

In Cambridge such notorious pitches as King's Chapel Roof, Trinity Hall Backs and the Senate House Leap were talked of still in my day, and we used to try out our own college when the evenings became a little short of excitement and the nights darker. When a man called Lomax left a bottle of Laphroaig whisky in my rooms in Red Buildings the hair-curling smoky Water of Life, of which I think I consumed half in ten minutes, had the almost immediate effect of quadrupling my courage and doubling my foolhardiness. I sprang from my fifth-floor window onto the parapet outside and whizzed round the Victorian architectural decorations thirty feet above a stone-paved court with a sense of invulnerability that has never been matched in my dreams of the event in the years since.

It was I think with the same Lomax that I set out one night to climb round the Hall, not too difficult a climb except for one stretch above the Screens. These 'Screens' were an arched passageway between Hall and the Kitchens. Where the arch debouched each end into the courts there were only upper bedroom windows above and no ledge below to put one's feet on. One had to hang, in other words, by one's fingers from the gutters above the bedroom windows to get across a dozen feet of effectively empty air. 'You go first' said Lomax. And, like the tramps in *Godot* discussing which of them should hang himself first, I thought I saw the logic and went first.

Half way across the yawning chasm, with my face pressed against the glass of a window and my feet dangling, a Thought came to me. The window was lit but curtained and there must surely be some chap in there studying or making toast whom it would be a joy to surprise. I felt the certainty of the comedian who approaches a really good punch-line. This chap would be *so* very surprised to see a face at his window at such a distance from the ground. He might shriek or faint. I couldn't resist the temptation and, insanely letting go of the gutter with my left hand (my legs turn to water as I remember this), tapped on the window. There was a pause during which Lomax whispered in an acid tone that mixed agony with fear and impatience, 'What's *wrong?*' 'Just watch!' I whispered back. And behold! The curtain slid back.

Now perhaps I had miscalculated where we were or perhaps some other force was in play, but far from the sight greeting our eyes being one of undergraduate pyjamas and chaste toast or possibly even light Anglican prayer in a well-ordered set, what was before me was (a) the enlarged face of one of our Oriental Studies dons, an obese Arabist called Mattock, and (b) a small lavatory. The former was sitting on the necessary furniture of the latter and was clearly in the process of relieving himself of the High Table meal he had eaten only hours before. His trousers were round his ankles. His wide flabby face, so close to my own, was flushed with effort and port, his eyes popping. I looked at him through the glass for a space; he looked at me. I could see the dandruff on the horn rims of his horn-rimmed spectacles. Simultaneously I had the following thoughts: (a) if he opens the window it will knock my arms from their hold and I will plunge to my death, (b) I shall shortly be Sent Down and what will my father say? (c) this fellow (ha!) seems amazingly calm. To his eternal credit the seated scholar of Eastern Lore neither opened the window nor, to anticipate, reported us to the College Authorities. He simply raised the arm not involved in holding back the curtain and, without changing his expression, gave me a big fat V-sign and shut me out. We traversed on into the darkness without a word.

108

Cambridge, of course, is associated with climbing in other more metaphorical ways. My contemporaries did not, on the whole, go on to be prep-school masters or local government officers; they were inclined to go on to do Research and become Academics, join the Foreign Office, to go into the City, to be elected to Parliament, to become head of MI6, to infest the Bar, to appear as famous comedians on television, to be surgeons, to do well as public-school masters, to join family firms, to open high-end advertising agencies, to work in the more recondite reaches of the civil service.

Pembroke was known as a college for comedians. We had had Ted Hughes on the serious side but also Bill Oddie, Tim Brooke-Taylor, and in my time Eric Idle, Clive James and others. I once saw these last two in the Pembroke Smoker (Smoking Concert, that is, the annual college Revue) alongside Germaine Greer and Johnny Lynn; I have never laughed so much. You can look at Clive James' fragment of autobiography *May Week Was in June* of 1994 for an account of the Pembroke and the Cambridge of those years. Clive and I shared a supervisor in Ian Jack, a specialist in eighteenth-century Eng Lit and Romanticism, and *May Week* includes a description of a supervision with the nice but dreary old Scotsman complete with his twitch and snap-of-the-teeth that interrupted every second sentence he spoke. I think it is the only part of Clive's marvellous memoirs on which I could improve.

Jack, at any rate, had a few things to compensate for besides his twitch. Prime among these for my generation of undergraduates was the fact that he was currently writing a book on 'Browning and the Visual Arts', a fairly recondite topic concerned with a fairly unreadable poet. But the matter that seemed to explain the twitching was his frank admission, after a sherry or two, that he was colour blind. We were too kind to react adversely to this piece of information.

3. BOATS

Every afternoon of my Cambridge career except Sundays I went from lunch in Hall across the town, over the river and to the Pembroke Boathouse where the day's Outing took place at 2pm.

As a day-old Freshman, on my first evening in my new rooms in Red Buildings, after Hall, there had been a tap on the door and a large man with dark hair came in. 'Butler?' he barked with a minimal smile. 'Er, yes...?' 'What are you doing tomorrow at two?' 'Er, nothing...' 'Down at the Boathouse, two pm then. All right?' 'Er. OK...' A short pause followed. 'You *are* a cox aren't you?' he asked. 'Well, I coxed at school, first eight.' 'Good, we need a cox for *our* first eight. See you tomorrow.' And he was gone with the wind. I hadn't even asked where the Boathouse was.

For the next three years I walked or cycled daily to the Victorian building on the Cam where we kept our boats and oars and where Fred the Boatman presided. On the wall of the best changing room (the 'May Room', never used for any purpose whatever) were small brown wooden plaques with the names and weights of all the May Boats since time immemorial. My name is on two of those plaques, listed against eternity in a forlorn gesture, weighing in at 8 stone 6 pounds.

The oarsmen put on shorts and sweaters, I put on longs and sweaters and steered them down the river and then back up again, shouting a bit, passing on orders from Stroke and generally encouraging the boat. It was the greatest fun. I only have to close my eyes to remember the feel of the rudder strings and the kick of the boat in the small of my back when the eight got into their rhythm, a kick every stroke. But alas it wasn't exercise. That would have to wait until I was in my twenties.

On the other hand Pembroke, the years I was up, had the fastest boat on the river, at least as far as the First Eight was concerned and that was what mattered. We had good support from the dons and rather a lot of success. We never became Head of the River, missing bumping First and Third Trinity by a few feet on an astonishing number of consecutive nights. But in my first term we won the Fairbairn Cup, the major trophy competed for by the colleges in December, and in my second term we made our four bumps (the maximum) and set the college up to go Head of the Lents the following year. Then in the summer we won the Ladies' Plate at Henley, beating the Oxford second boat (Isis) in the heats and the RMC Sandhurst in the Final. A fair haul. I got a Trial Cap in my second year but never coxed the Blue Boat, to my everlasting regret. Nonetheless the rowing ethos did a great deal for me and made me some good friends. It was a part of the Cambridge experience barely available even in pale imitation elsewhere. I may add that coxing a fast crew in a bumping race is one of the more exciting things you can do.[8]

---

[8] For those who may not know, a bumping race actually involves bumping the boat ahead of you. Eighteen crews set off in each division in line-ahead a length-and-a-half apart. If you are neither bumped nor bump you 'row over'. If you manage to bump the boat in front of you you both pull into the bank to allow the following crews past, but the next day, when racing commences again, you each start in the other's place. Thus over the four days of the Lent or May races you can move up four places (in which case you 'get

At Henley, in the nice Long Vac of 1964, we were in a species of very English paradise. The crew stayed at a pub outside the town, the White Hart at Nettlebed, where a genial female monster by the name of Clemmie sat at a bar-cum-till in the centre of the old building directing the operations of her splendidly motley crew of Italians, Spaniards, alcoholics and gay Englishmen who provided a first-class service including excellent breakfasts and enormous dinners. On the one hand the oarsmen weren't allowed alcohol, on the other hand it was frowned on for the cox to eat too much. A trade off. Fred-the-Boatman was accommodated, I can only presume, in some squalid den of his own from which he emerged to look after the boats and the oars and give words of opaque advice.

Every day of the regatta – warm-up period, heats and so on - I was ordered by the Captain of Boats to walk down into the town - four miles I think – to keep my weight to the minimum, but I usually managed to sneak into a car. There were moments of quiet evening discussion, gentle strolls and other nice things. Then on all four afternoons of the regatta we beat our opponents over the mile-and-a-quarter. The Final pitted us against Sandhurst, the college for training army officers, and I shall never forget the yelling (mostly for Sandhurst) as we approached the Stewards' Enclosure and thus the finish. Crossing the line was a riot. I was thrown into the Thames. We then drank a lot, stroked the silverware we had won and felt on top of the world.

In the Stewards' Enclosure later that day there was a Special Announcement. The Harvard crew of

---

your oars' a literal process of being awarded an old oar with the names and weights of your crew painted neatly onto the blade.) The Ladies Plate at Henley is a trophy that was given to the regatta by lady supporters; it is not a competition for women.

112

1914, who had won the grand Challenge Cup in that year, were back on the river fifty years later and would row past the assembled members. We watched as they paddled gently by and we thought, surely to a man, 'These guys went back to the States with their silverware *before the First World War*. They all managed, although of exactly the age and the class to become officers in the US Army, to survive that and then to go on surviving till now. Wow.' It was as if a herd of mammoths or a flock of Dodos had been driven past for our entertainment.[9]

The sporting authorities in Spain, in that same summer of 1964, wanted to inaugurate their new rowing course on Lake Banyolas outside Barcelona. They turned to the Boat Race or, as they called it, 'Oxford and Cambridge' as the most famous rowing event in history and decided that they would repeat it over their nice 2,000-metres of water. Now Oxford was ready and willing to participate, but Cambridge (*our* Blue Boat) were all away on their hols or preparing to run the country or some such, so the captain of the CUBC asked if Pembroke would like to pretend to be Cantab for a week or so. We agreed and were flown out to Catalonia with some ceremony. We took our own oars but were provided with boats 'of Spanish construntion', as the letter of invitation said, that were a bit primitive. It was the same for Oxford of course and they very sportingly agreed a deal: they would row alongside us for about

---

[9] When in 2014 we had the opportunity to do the same thing to celebrate the fiftieth anniversary of our own victory (we were allowed a 'row-over' on Henley Saturday, euphemism for a gentle paddle past the crowd) I wondered how old or Dodo-ish it made me. It certainly gave me what the French call a '*coup de vieux*'. See 'Henley' below.

1500 metres and then pull away. We had beaten Isis, their second boat, at Henley earlier in the summer, but these were the big boys. This way the Spans would get a bit of a race and there would be some excitement for the considerable crowd that pitched up that hot afternoon.

Alas, come the launch, we found that the other six lanes of the course, provided according to Olympic regulations, were not going to be empty. *Au contraire*, the cream of Spanish oarsmanship would be on display for us to make mincemeat of, if we could. We looked in particular at the large Basque bruisers from the San Sebastian club Ur Kirolak (immediately pronounced 'Erki-rowlack' by the merry Englishmen they were competing against) and felt a bit nervous, not least because we had let ourselves get out of training over a month of sybaritic living since Henley.

We had attempted a bit of rowing on the lake in the days before the great occasion but this had mostly ended up, in the heat of July in Catalonia, with members of the crew falling out of the boat into the cool water with affected cries of anguish. I myself spent more time swimming about pretending to fix the rudder strings than I did steering and shouting. And now we were going to be humiliated by the Basques. We suddenly remembered their prowess at sea-rowing, a heavy and hairy sport only for the strongest. The Oxford captain came up to us and suggested that they had better just row as normal without waiting for us; at least that way some English honour would be saved.

And so it was. The starter, who, we had been told, would start us according to the international conventions of those days in French - '*Attention! Etes-vous prêts? Partez!*' - sprang onto his podium slightly before we were expecting him, raised a flag and shouted at the top of his voice '*Preparados? Va!*'

114

The Spanish crews had anticipated even this brief start by a second or two and were digging in for all they were worth. Oxford got the point and took off into the hazy afternoon at a good lick; they were soon well ahead of the field and then they stretched out to a nice rhythm, ready to accelerate if any danger threatened; but we panted along in their wake absolutely neck-and-neck with Erki.

My crew sweated and heaved, and so did the Basques who were alongside us. This was going to be harder than we thought. The lads began to get stuck in. And then it came to me: inexperienced oarsmen, aware that nearly all crews leading at 1500 metres go on to win races, tend to give up if they are not ahead at that mark. I attempted to convey this to my crew but they were too far gone; their chests were heaving and their eyes were rolling as I called for an extra-hard Ten and they responded, up to a point, as we approached the kilometre-and-a-half mark. When we reached it the whole Spanish crew looked across at us. Realising their position, slightly behind our steaming boat, they chose, to a man, to pack up and go home. Their boat virtually stopped dead and we shot on to come second in the Grand Inaugural Regatta.

So we came an honourable second at Lake Banyolas and the order of the universe was restored for a time.

4. FRED

As mentioned, the boatman at Pembroke was Fred, a bachelor as far as we knew and a person whose life was entirely dedicated to the rowing men of the college. Fred had never learnt to drive a car and instead got about in a three-wheeler, inaptly named a Reliant Robin, whose main characteristic, apart from the fact that you only needed a motorcycle licence to drive it and Fred had one of those, was its unsurprising tendency to fall over on account of its only having one wheel at the front end. Mercifully its top speed was so low that the occasions of its toppling mostly failed to result in death or major injury producing instead merely mild embarrassment among the traffic. In spite of which, sad to relate, Fred did in the end shuffle off his mortal coil in his car, wiped off the road by a monster Euro-camion quite unable to believe its eyes.

When I knew him Fred was in his fifties I suppose and was one of the last relics (there were many others at Cambridge then but their days were also numbered) of the old British class system of Deference. He called the young gentlemen 'Sir' and they called him Fred; it made everybody happy. His role, besides messing about with boats and blades and riggers and things, was to coach the First Boat at the beginning of each year and then gradually slide down the scale of boats from the First to about the Fourth as old Pembroke men came up from the City or from their country vicarages and took over the coaching from him. This he resented. 'Well, how would you like it Sir?' he asked me once, 'if just when the boat's beginning to fly it's taken from you? I mean I do all the 'ard work putting the crew together and teaching them 'ow to row and then the gentlemen coaches come here and just cycle along the towpath saying "Come forward a little more number seven" and easy things like that. I mean, it's me what does it really.' 'I'm sorry you feel that way Fred' I answered, 'perhaps you could ask to take the First Boat for an extra week this term?' 'Oh no Sir, I couldn't do that.' Not a thoroughgoing revolutionary our Fred.

Fred was very clear about how a boat should be handled. ''It it broad Sir!' he would shout, ''It it broad.' When we pulled into the bank for a breather and a little coaching he would expand on his method. 'Sit up compact Sir and work it off accordin'' he would confide to us, artful Dickensian boatman that he was.

But he didn't like to be contradicted while working a boat. I had the blithe folly to question one of his proposals on a grey Tuesday afternoon in the Lent term of my first year. He called us in to the bank ('Easy cox, Easy!') and, dismounting, threw his bicycle into the grass between towpath and river. He pushed his thick spectacles up his nose, in a manner that I would soon recognise as betokening respectful anger, and criticised my steering. 'But Fred', I remonstrated, 'that's how I felt it was best to go round Grassy Corner.' Fred looked at me and there was silence in heaven for a space. Nine of us waited on the water, Fred considered. Then, having found the gem he needed, he delivered it: 'Look at it my way Sir. You're wrong.' An exceptionally useful method of arguing.

In a democratic spirit Fred was invited to some of the Boat Club dinners where he stood out in a suit that had been through the Blitz and a long tie among the oarsmen in their Ice-Cream Kit (Boat Club evening wear) complete with bow ties. He was unmoved by the most drunken behaviour and the worst stories. One night I was chatting to some friends after a Bump Supper when Fred came up to us; we made space for him and put him abreast of the conversation. 'Butler here is a Catholic, Fred' said someone in explanation of something. Fred considered this and then got it: 'I don't 'old with foreign religions' he said. 'Neither do we!' chorused the inebriated mostly-Anglican boaties, to my curiosity. I didn't know they cared.

117

It may have been at that same dinner (in memory they tend to run into each other somewhat, though not perhaps to the degree of the cocktail parties given and frequented by a highly-sociable Golf Blue of my acquaintance, a man called Midgeley, who woke groaning one January morning with the exclamation 'Good heavens, the Christmasses are starting to merge together') that I performed one of my worst degrades[10]. Desperate to go to the loo, I had held on to a full bladder through a very long dinner but, the toast to the Queen seeming still a long way off, was unable to hold out any longer. In front of me was a large piece of College Silver, masquerading as a species of Greek urn, complete with lid. This I took from the table, unnoticed by the carousers around me and, affecting deep interest in the hallmarks, lowered it to crutch level. There, under the table, great relief came to me. When I put the silver urn back on the table, lid on, it slowly developed condensation to about half way up its height. "Good heavens!' said the man next to me, 'The silver's sweating.' Luckily the toast to the Queen was then announced and he forgot the ominous phenomenon.

In a fit of public-spirit I attempted to leave the dinner with the silverware under my arm imagining I could empty it in the bogs on 'A' staircase and return it; Herbert, a college servant of preternatural antiquity, took it off me at the door: 'I'll 'ave that sir.' 'Ah yes

---

[10] Pembroke slang. A 'degrade' was a disgraceful episode reflecting poorly on the perpetrator. Similarly 'genial' meant 'good' in almost any of its senses and 'pragger' stood in for that piece of social interaction that English so strangely lacks, the equivalent of *'de rien'* in French, *'de nada'* in Spanish or, uncoincidentally, *'prego'* in Italian; the thing you say to people who thank you. 'Pragger' was short for 'pray don't mention it'. I draw a veil over the ghastly Americanism 'You're welcome' and an even thicker veil over the more recent 'Not a problem.'

Herbert' I said smiling cunningly, 'much better that you do.' At lunch the next day Herbert was serving. When close enough to me to recognise who I was, and that had to be pretty close in the case of Herbert, he said ''Ere sir, that thing you give me last night' 'Yes Herbert?' 'It was full of You Know, wasn't it?' 'Yes Herbert' I said, 'It was.' And after that, well, what could he do that wouldn't be almost as bad for him as for me? We got on famously thereafter, though with a guarded demeanour.

You might wonder about the likes of Fred. Was Carlyle right when he said that people were happier when they knew where they were? Who they were. What they had to do. Their place in the order of things.

There is no order of things, of course, which is why we have invented politics, and philosophy I suppose, to order them for us, out of our heads, without foundation, randomly, though somehow not quite randomly. But Fred. He was what he knew himself to be; he was concerned with things utterly trivial in a universe in which, however, it may be that all things are equally trivial, equally (un)important. He seemed not to question. If you had offered him, say, promotion, he wouldn't have accepted it. I know that. He was asked if he would apply for the vacant job of boatman to the CUBC, the big one, the university club, the Blue Boat, 'Oxford and Cambridge' and all that. Fred looked shiftily indignant, 'Nah' he said, ''Oo'd want to do that? Think they own the river they do.' And that was that. The pay would have been better, the prestige higher. But Fred was the Pembroke boatman, he knew that and he liked it. It was him.

Why not be anti-Catholic? Fred's Protestantism had no foundation in practice or precept. He wouldn't have been able to quote even one of the Thirty-nine Articles and probably couldn't manage the Ten

119

Commandments all the way through. But he knew he was an Anglican and that Catholics ('RCs'; 'Romans') were a dubious foreign lot. Was it true? Does that matter? Isn't one fiction as good as another? Better than none? Especially when 'none' is not an option.

There are limits. Had he set about murdering Catholics that wouldn't have been good. But he didn't. Because he knew well enough who he was not to have to resort to febrile assertions of identity of that sort. He knew so well who he was that he actually needed Catholics in order not to be one and in order for his mild Chauvinism to have a little trot out. 'Pembroke' is nothing, an entirely arbitrary identity. And being French? Christian? Modern? A Scientist? All equally made up of course. And often much more dangerous than just 'being a Pembroke man' and liking it.

What we do, we others, is to move house all the time, to aim high, to have ambition, to want, always to want more than we have, of course to want what we don't have. With the result that we never do have it. Is that happiness? What would Schopenhauer have said? What Beckett? And Pascal: 'We are always preparing to be happy; it is therefore inevitable that we never are so.' Better to be Herbert. Or Fred. Unless it is really better to be Socrates dissatisfied than a pig satisfied as Mill thought.

5. PUKER

Johnny 'Johannes' or 'Puker' Brooks, a man with whom I shared college rooms for two years, was a minor legend at the university. In our very earliest days at Pembroke, during our Matriculation Dinner in Hall, he had become overwhelmed by the unstinted wines and, briefed fiercely that he shouldn't leave Hall before the

Master had said the final Grace and had himself left, found it impossible to maintain the iron grip on his peristaltic system that public behaviour normally requires. Looking wildly around for a local depostorium for at least a substantial part of his main course he lighted upon his own sleeve and, with a horrible eructating noise of last resort, filled, via the sleeve, one side of his evening clothes with an amalgam of vegetable matters, mostly peas for which he had an inordinate fondness and which he had consumed in unwise quantity.

Leaving Hall with his left arm held above his head he attracted attention and in the court outside it became clear to a small but eager band of college drunks that here was a phenomenon to be inspected. They were quite amused up to the point where the full horror of Johannes' shirt was exposed to them. So that night they looked elsewhere for further entertainments. But next day Johannes B had become 'Puker', the soubriquet which stuck with him, like many substances, for three years.

A local Cambridge man, Johnny made friends at the college with a variety of young East Anglians and, as he explained to me while licking his wounds and huddling over our gas fire one night, was unwise enough to accept an invitation, near the end of our last year, to the low-quality wedding of one of them in King's Lynn or, worse, *near* King's Lynn. I say 'unwise' because Puker was almost bound to live up to his nickname at times of emotional stress, high boredom and free drink. These three elements would have been more perfectly united, as the French say, had the drink at this ghastly shindig been actually free. Instead of which the invitations had included the dread words

'Cash Bar.'[11] But two of the three components were actively present and the third could, surely, be compensated for by drinking a lot of other people's leftover drinks, scrounging some directly and even, when desperation struck, paying.

Still, unwisdom on Johnny's part seemed like something that might be kept at bay as we bade the poor lad goodbye at Pembroke and wished him well until evening. He took a train north from Cambridge into the Fens. His return would, we foresaw, be furtive and involve climbing in and/or considerable apologising to his bedder.

And indeed, arriving at the Register Office in King's Lynn (or *nearby*) Johannes was unable to behave other than well. But arriving at the hostelry where the reception was to take place he began what was to prove a thoroughly successful hunt for free drink. Astonishingly a meal was provided *with wine* and he sat for a while amongst the other guests like a rare animal in a Primary School. One course followed another and all seemed well, but with Puker Calm seemed to lead with great regularity to Storm. While pudding was being served he decided to make a dash for the bog (no waiting for Grace here.) Standing up, he felt the old familiar head-spin of those whose Bacchic devotions have been too assiduous. Reaching out with his left hand, the very one he had so liberally deluged with high-fibre green matter three years before, he clutched at what he took to be a table.

Now it was indeed a table at which he clutched, but, alas, on that table was a tray of drinks, some fifty glasses full of the unspeakable (but free) wine provided

---

[11] Weddings are bad enough in themselves but if, in addition to the usual horrors, you have to buy your own drink they become altogether farcical.

122

for the assembled revellers to drink the toasts to the Happy Couple during the speeches. The waitress who had put this tray-in-waiting on the table had left a small but significant corner of it sticking out over the edge of the mahogany and it was this corner that Johannes firmly seized and on which he exerted much downward pressure as he steadied himself against giddiness. His arm plunged down canting the tray up in a swift and perfectly Newtonian action-and-reaction. Down went Puker, up into the air flew fifty glasses full of warm Blue Nun. There was a moment of astonished silence as wine and goblets flew through the air, falling to earth in every possible place, on the table, all over the carpet, into the laps of the wedding guests. Most affected by this vinous tsunami was Puker himself. By the time the glasses and wine landed he was on the floor, positively rolling and, very soon, soaked, bruised and cut.

'Never mind!' he cried, levering himself up into the view of the stricken party. Drink had given him eloquence and determination. 'Never mind! I shall buy everyone another drink!' He was offered a napkin, which he took. Then he said 'I think I'd better go and clean up a bit first.' Wiping, tidying and clucking were going on all around him by now in a light *scherzo* of broken glass as he slid out of the door narrowly avoiding collision with an entering waiter. He had remembered where the bog was! It was up *those* stairs. He lurched forward (what do they *put* in those cocktails I stole?) and went up the thick sticky old stair-carpet on his hands and knees. At the top he locked himself into the lavatory and inspected the damage. Not too bad, all things considered, but what was this? The return of the nausea! Ye gods.

Johnny knelt before the great white telephone and opened its lid. Then he did what he did best, the thing that had earned him his nickname, creating volume in both senses. But what did *he* care? It wasn't *his* wedding! He chundered on blithely, sometimes hitting the spot and sometimes vomiting into his trousers. Standing up he caught sight of himself in the mirror again. Good heavens! I *do* need to clean up a bit, he thought. He removed his trousers and tried to set about them. Was this one ruined suit? Well, perhaps not although the trousers were in a terrible terrible... But joy! Here was a handbasin ready for action, complete with tap and nailbrush! In nothing but his underwear he washed and scrubbed like a good-un.

What he had not realised, alas, was that when he had knelt to deliver a good piece of his mind to the Great White T he had clung to the water-inlet pipe at the side of the lavatory's low-level cistern. In his paroxysms of puking he had contrived to wrench this pipe away from the basin and water had been flowing steadily over the bilious carpet all through his subsequent clothes-removal and ablutions. He had scrubbed on unconscious.

When finally the hotel staff broke down the door to the lavatory they were greeted by a wall of water (its flow down the main staircase being what had alerted them) and the sight of Johannes asleep in several inches of mixed liquids, semi-naked and clutching a nailbrush. He was physically expelled from the party, from the hotel and from the village.

Late that night he recounted the last stage of this odyssey, this degrade, this *epic* of poor form. He had finally made it to King's Lynn Station for an evening train back to Cambridge in which he had fallen asleep. When he woke up he found himself fifty miles beyond Cambridge at London Liverpool Street where he crossed the platform and, after a suitable delay, got on the next train back north up to Cambridge. In this train also he fell asleep, again overshot his destination and woke up, oh horrors, in King's Lynn. Only on the third attempt did he get out at Cambridge station, whence he walked back to college, climbed in and prepared to tell the story.

Of course some of Puker's degrades I experienced at first hand. There was, for instance, the occasion when we spent the night together in my family's flat in Knightsbridge after a considerable evening entertainment of some sort. To understand this episode you have to know that the room where we slept had been curtained by Uncle Dick in full maritime fashion with thick navy-blue curtains trimmed with gold braid just like the uniforms which he had worn in the service.[12] These excluded all but the very dimmest light from the room. Johnny, then, waking sweating and naked in the small hours with his usual imperious need for the bathroom, proved unable to fathom where he was. Deciding on general principles that he was most likely in his flat in Chatham, he sprang from his pit, waking me in my bed a few feet away as he did so, and, clamping a hand firmly over his mouth because his chronic reaction to excess food and drink had come upon him with unusual suddenness, *ran* towards what he took to be his bathroom door. Alas, this portal to relief was a phantom of his drink-crazed brain or, rather, not so much a phantom-door as a very real large chest of drawers with, amazingly for a Georgian antique, all its keys in place sticking out of the keyholes. Colliding

---

[12] In fact *exactly* like the uniform which he had had made during the war which looked regulation issue but was in fact dark blue velvet. He was able to catnap in his bunk in this elegant *tenue* and be out on the bridge in time not to go down with his ship on several occasions.

with this substantial object, and bruised by several of the keys, he squeaked as much as he could considering the alternative uses to which his reverse-peristalsis was inciting his mouth and, despairing of direction, turned randomly left and tried again. This time he managed only two paces before he hit the back of a sofa and toppled over onto the cushions with further muffled cries and, as later investigation was to reveal, the loss of some of his supper onto the chintz. I watched his shadowy form with absolute fascination as, wild with confusion and the need to vomit but still with a hand over his mouth, he rose from the sofa and, spying at last the faint line of light that showed where the curtains came together, sprinted the few steps to the window and threw back the naval hangings. There before him Hans Place shone in the lamplight and down on it, from the third floor, he gazed with hope. Unfortunately my aunt kept plants, Busy Lizzies I think they are called, in pots on her window-ledges, along with ceramic objects of doubtful purpose, and the windows, furthermore, opened inwards. Exercising initiative, Johnny, with his one free hand, swept the *impedimenta* from their places in a series of hieratic gestures and scrabbled for the window handle. Pots and curios crashed onto the carpeting and after what seemed to his audience of one, as no doubt to himself, an age he worked out how to open the window and opened it. Only then, removing his hand from his mouth and bending his naked torso over the sill, could he permit the fluids and solids that so urgently wished to say farewell to him to shoot forth. His tremendous chunder was followed, as my ears attested, by a brief silence which ended when the load, falling past pavement level and into the basement area, met the housekeeper's geraniums.

126

I switched on the light. There he stood, modern man at his apogee, swaying and hiccuping and feebly trying to wipe the vomit from the velvet. 'Ah' he said, 'I couldn't find the bathroom.' Then, smirking, he added 'But I did shoot the most enormous tiger!'

Puker had a modestly successful career in a suitably louche profession - journalism. Starting on what we came to call the Chatham Evening Chunder and graduating to a larger paper whose soubriquet I shall not mention (its real name was the Kent Messenger) he ended up as a sub-editor on the Daily Express where he became known as 'Bertie' and 'The King of the Time Off'. Retiring early (he was ever what Beckett called his Murphy: 'a chronic emeritus') he married a Holiday Rep on Ibiza where, although well cared for by her in rather a nice little villa, he died of MS when he was about 60.

When I went to visit him on the island he could no longer move or speak. This pathetic sight touched my heart as may be imagined and I talked long and earnestly to his wife about the poor chap. She, a person of great kindness and realism, comforted me in an unusual way. Without inventing anything she was able to say 'Well, Johnny always wanted to get into a position where he had nothing to do and could be waited on hand and foot and I think he's found it.'

6. TUSSAUD

In this memoir there are stories about school, university, travels during the *Wanderjahre* that we all have in our twenties, as well as snippets of later life, and they will have to stand in for a lot of tedious padding about school-friends, academic failure and success, My First Job and so on. But, come to think of it, I can't help

127

slipping in here the fact that my first paid employment was during one Long Vac from Cambridge when I was taken on for the summer by Madame Tussaud's Waxworks in Marylebone as an attendant. I was paid eleven guineas a week and was, or should have been, appointed at the same time as a Thai student of my own age who was stuck in Britain for the summer because he couldn't afford to go back to Thailand. I say 'should have' because Dong, charming and discreet as he seemed, was instantaneously sacked by the Mr Tussaud of the moment as soon as he saw him. Tussaud was the sort of heir known as 'Young Mr T' in the family firm, a hefty bruiser who, spotting the oriental features of the poor Thai, growled loudly, turned to his lieutenant and said 'We aren't having any of *those* in this place! Out! Out!' Poor Dong was out of his uniform and, indeed, of the staff door within three minutes. I think I was told later that Tussaud had had a thin time of it in a Japanese prisoner-of-war camp. So it goes.

The only other incident of note that ghastly summer in the appalling fraud that is Tussaud's was when a very substantial Frenchman fainted in the Chamber of Horrors while I was on duty there. The crowds of disappointed visitors (in the case of Tussaud's you could just say 'visitors') parted like the Red Sea leaving me at one end of a darkened plastic imitation torture-chamber and the obese unconscious Frog at the other. Everyone was watching to see the fun as I ran down the alley between the exhibits and picked the poor fool up in my arms; I ran back between the racks and guillotines and then up twenty-or-so steps and out into the semi-fresh air of the Euston Road. I was around 8 stone in weight at the time, and not strong with it, the Frog-body twice my size. You can imagine how I marvelled at the power of the mind: sometimes it can make the impossible really quite easy.

7. TORTION

In those days, before things began to change in the 1970s, students at Cambridge still had to Keep Term. This involved sleeping in college for fifty-eight nights each term, that is three times a year, a rule that could only be circumvented in one of two ways. Either one obtained an *Exeat*, a slip of paper from the Dean permitting one to stay out for some purpose, or one stayed out but climbed back in before the Bedder found one's bed unoccupied in the morning. The gates of the colleges were locked from 11pm to 7am when the flood of Bedders came in chattering and brandishing cleaning materials ('Come on Mr Butler, time you was up!') These ladies had, allegedly by statute, to be *'Senex et horridae'* to reduce the temptation young gentlemen of the college, full of naïve self-confidence, might feel to invite them to join them in bed with the cry 'No no, Ethel. I'm up already. Time you was in here with me!'

So when I became ill in London, after a visit of now obscure purpose to the flat in Hans Place and found myself doubled-up and groaning with pain on Platform 5 of Liverpool Street Station I was obliged, as we will see, to miss three of the sacred nights and thus ultimately explain myself to a sceptical Dean.

It is strange how one lives in denial. I had felt a bit odd as I bought my ticket back to Cambridge at the station and odder as I sat waiting for the train. When it came in I was surprised to see that I was walking along its length bent over more or less into the horizontal; I noticed my crooked form reflected in the carriage window and only found it slightly unusual. Reaching the carriage-door, however, I had a definitely queer turn and suddenly sat down on the platform. This brought a degree of reality to my perceptions and I realised I had to take some sort of special action. As so often in my time in London, action meant a cab and I staggered out of Liverpool Street and found one.

Back in Hans Place I found my condition worsening and that the pain was focussing on my groin. Within an hour I was rolling about on the floor tearing at my trousering and emitting hollow whimpers; within two hours I was entirely naked and groaning fit to die while still rolling around on the close carpeting. At some point I must have had the presence of mind to telephone the doctor because the flat doorbell rang and I crawled out into the hallway and, reaching a desperate hand to handle level with a gasp, opened it. Stepping over me, in came a man I vaguely recognised wearing a three-piece tweed suit and a deaf aid. Holding out his hand in the general direction of my naked and prostrate form he said 'McCluskey.' Such is the force of breeding and habit that I took one hand from my agonising groin and waved it towards him. 'Lance Butler' I said. He shook my sweaty palm with some hesitancy; I immediately clamped it back in my crutch. 'Not feeling so good?' he asked. 'No', I said. 'No.'

A little more of this sort of discussion led Dr McCluskey to the conclusion that I had a Tortion of the Testicles and he sprang into action as I wondered whether to faint or not. He called an ambulance and gave me a shot of morphine with the words 'Some people find a tortion rather uncomfortable.' Dear God, I thought, Life with Litotes.

But then the morphine started to kick in. I rose to my feet and, pulling a sheet or towel around my lower reaches, attempted the part of host. I asked the doctor how far he had come and whether I had disturbed his day. I'm not sure that I didn't offer him a gin-and-tonic. Myself I had no need of one because I was now feeling as chipper as a well-iced glass of Gordons. 'Make yourself at home!' I cried and fell into an armchair with a brilliant grin. He watched me as if building up to a wild surmise. It was a sort of standoff. Luckily some time later, say ten seconds or an hour-and-a-half, the doorbell sounded again and this led after a space to the panting ingress of two large men in a species of fire-fighting kit carrying a stretcher. 'How nice to see you!' I carolled at them. 'DO come in!' Gins and tonics were in the air again.

With some asperity I was ordered to lie down on the stretcher when I knew, of course, that it would have been childishly simple, and surely easier for everyone, if I simply floated down the stairs to the front door on my own and without their aid, possibly without the aid of my legs either. 'Get on!' said the gruffer of the two thugs. 'Oh, OK' I giggled. They made heavy weather of carrying me down and I remember for my part making a special effort not to say 'I told you I'd be better on my own.' They shoved me into the back of the ambulance and both of them got into the driver's cab. We started off into the London traffic, siren blazing. 'Wow!' I thought, and possibly 'Whoopee!' as we sped and swerved. I knew the direction we would take and managed to spot Big Ben before the accident happened. It was just after the Houses of Parliament, on Westminster Bridge, that we crashed. Attempting a manoeuvre to overtake some slower user of the road, the ambulance-jockey had driven straight into an oncoming vehicle. I felt the shock of the crash with unfeigned delight. There was much shouting and swearing that entertained me vastly; I think people even screamed. I sat up.

The impact of the crash had burst the back doors of the ambulance open and I had rather a good view of the floodlit Palace of Westminster as well as of a gathering crowd of interested persons and blocked cars. Blue and golden lights flashed, sirens sounded, people yelled. I saw what my role was in this melee and rose. I was wearing, remember, a white blanket and a white towel and resembled a species of Indian guru or just possibly the Risen Christ. I stood and, drawing myself to such height as I have and the ambulance would allow, spread my naked arms in a hieratic or prophetic gesture. 'Everything is perfectly all right people!' I bellowed, 'Do not distress yourselves about so trivial a matter! All will be well and all manner of things will be well!' The crowd of onlookers took this in surprisingly good part. 'You all right then?' they chorused. 'You OK?' 'Naturally good people I am untouched.' I yelled in reply, 'I am The Untouchable!'

But at this point a couple of bruised and muttering paramedics came round the end of the ambulance and got to grips with me. 'Come on you', they said, 'enough of that.' Somehow we got to St Thomas's.

I was taken into a reception ward where a young doctor explained my condition to me and told me that they were going to have to operate immediately otherwise infertility might ensue. 'Carry on!' I cried, being still brilliantly lit inside from the morphine, 'Do your worst!' 'But we have to ask you some questions first' he said. 'Ah' I said, 'Ask away old doctor, ask away.' He quizzed me about any recent, er, *use* to which my contorted parts had been put. 'Ah!' I said again, more loudly, 'Well, last night....' And I proceeded to regale the entire room in ringing tones with a description of my evening with a young lady of my acquaintance, sparing no details. At some point in this desperate monologue I heard the doctor say 'For Heaven's sake, I think I've heard enough' and soon I was under the ether. When I woke up I felt rather sore and puzzled. I remember the removal of the stitches with unaffectionate precision though it is true that when the trainee nurse who came to remove them, shaking slightly under Matron's beady eye, offered me a respite half way through I replied, quite unconsciously, 'No no. Just keep your eye on the ball.' Matron shied and snorted.

Eventually I got back to Cambridge where I found a written summons from the Dean. I went straight to his rooms and found him *in situ*. 'Well Butler?' he began, 'you've missed three nights of term, and this isn't the first time you've been in trouble. What is your excuse on this occasion?'

He was not always very fierce but he had a fierce streak. Enough to provoke some rugger hearties one night, after a particularly good dinner, into chasing him round the Dean's Garden, where he worked in the cool of the evening during the summer term looking after his exotic plants. He was watering his floral pets when the hearties grabbed the can from him and pursued him with the cry 'Grow you horrible little bugger! Grow!'

On the other hand it was he, the Dean, who told this story against himself, including the 'bugger' at the end, so he must have been all right really. In any event I now confronted him across the decanal carpet, pale but invulnerable with my medical certificate from Tommy's. 'I've been in hospital in London sir.' 'Really?' I could see that he absolutely did not believe me. I produced the medical certificate and handed it to him; he looked at it and blinked. I had one of those moments of intuition where one is altogether certain of what is passing in another person's mind. His disbelief was patent. 'Hmmm' he said, 'but you have missed three nights of term.' 'Well sir, I literally couldn't move. I had to have an operation.' 'Where?' he barked, unable to read the surgeon's scrawl on the paper in his hand. 'My, er, on my... well, down *here* sir.' He glanced at my crutch. 'It seems all right to me' he said.

Now it is true that undergrads in those days did sometimes get Medical School chums to cover for them with false sick-notes and the like, and the Dean, who had me down as a left-and-right-hand chancer of the first water by this time in my Cambridge career, just *knew* I was lying. I could see it in his face, in his shoulders, in his dog collar. But I wasn't. Yet if he wouldn't believe the surgeon's line what could I do? Only one fully-convincing course seemed open to me. 'Well sir' I said as I reached towards my fly-buttons, 'I can show you.'

For a moment I thought he was going to take me up on the offer. He looked at my crutch again. An age passed. The he said 'No, that's all right Butler. It won't be necessary.'[13]

As I left the august presence I felt his gaze on my back. It was clear that he still didn't believe me but felt he had been outwitted. Even in those days it wasn't exactly a career plus for an Anglican clergyman to be known to inspect the pudenda of young men in his care and I knew that he felt I had pulled a neat trick on him

---

[13] This Dean, one Meredith Dewey, features in Clive James' memoirs of his time at Pembroke, *May Week Was in June*, mentioned elsewhere in these reminiscences. He was one of the last old-world Cantabrigian dons.

when, in fact, I had just had my balls carved up and
yearned to spend the rest of the day in bed.

8. MORGAN

In E.M. Forster's autobiographical *The Hill of Devi* of
1953 there is a curious episode where he is on the staff
of the Rajah of a Princely State called Dewas Senior
somewhere in the depths of India in the 1910s and early
1920s. The photographs show him dressed in local gear
and (as Edward Morgan Foster certainly was)
diminutive in a way more characteristic of Indians than
of the average Englishman of those days.

Half-way through the book a visit is expected at
the Rajah's palace, a visit from the local British Raj big-
wig, some heavyweight member of the Indian Army or
Indian Civil Service. The Rajah, along with his court
and numerous semi-official hangers on, waits in a long
line outside the palace on the *meidan* with Himself at
the centre and the vague hierarchies of Indian life
stretching away in a downward curve of importance to
the less significant minions at either end. Forster, in
native garb and some distance down the pecking order
but not hopelessly inferior, waits with the others until
the British team arrives. The British-Raj-people line up
opposite the Dewasis in a similar order, with Maj-Gen
Sir Somebody Something in the middle opposite the
Rajah, his aides and regimental commanders flanking
him, their aides and the lesser officers flanking them,
and so on down and out.

Now the formal method of greeting in that part
of India at that time was to offer '*pan*' - bread and
water, possibly salt and water - to your guests; the
senior figure on the host side would offer these things
first to the head honcho on the other and then work

down the line. Perhaps two seniors were needed, one to travel slowly in each direction. Thus, in this case, a senior member of the Dewas staff offered *pan* to Major-General Sir Whatsit Whatsit and then worked his way down the left-hand line while another identical senior servant offered these tokens of welcome to the ranking officer standing beside the General and worked his way down the right-hand line. This process was then reversed with the guests in their turn offering *pan* first to the Rajah and then to his flankers down the line. The rub came when these official greeters had gone along each line as far as they thought decorous; they had to draw the line somewhere, and would draw it for instance, in all cases, well before the Untouchables.

EMF stood in the Rajah's line, quite a sight in his turban and strong spectacles, not to say in his height of five-foot-five in his stockings' holes. He watched as Colonel Thing, the offerer of *pan* from the British side, approached and he (EMF) was on the point of making some coy remark in suburban English when the said officer, looking down the line and seeing what seemed only an insignificant low-caste native next, decided to call it a day. The day in question had been long and hot for all concerned. He reached the person just above EMF, administered the *pan* and then simply turned and went back whence he came, to the bemusement of everyone present and the mortal wounding of the pint-sized novelist. Some of his more liberal and anti-military opinions may have dated from this incident.

Now the British officer detailed-off to perform this ritual of the *pan*, and generally keep things in orthodox order, was my grandfather, Colonel Sir Hugh Vincent Biscoe IA, as mentioned. And he it was, putting two and two into the same cliché, who refused to give EMF his official greeting. I felt a tiny secret thrill when

136

reading this episode in *Hill of Devi* to think that I alone knew the identity of the apparently-rude Englishman in question. Not even EMF knew it or, I believe, had ever known it.

Many years after this incident in Dewas Senior, and many years after the death of my grandfather and indeed the end of the Raj, I was at Cambridge and one day I rode a bike into the courtyard of the Eagle on Ben'et Street, parked it against a wall and went in to have a few beers with my friend Johnny Puker-da-Luker Brooks, as described. The pub became crowded while we talked and I had a fair degree of difficulty in extracting my velocipede when we emerged. Johnny walked me out towards the street where I vaulted into the saddle, as the expression goes, a few feet inside the archway exit. By the time I had gone through the archway and was crossing the pavement I was doing a few miles per hour and suddenly I ran slap into a small mackintoshed bundle of humanity and knocked it to the tarmac. Johnny stepped forward and picked up the frail elder whom I had thus so cavalierly abused. Between us we patted him and pushed him back into shape and got his hat back on to his head and apologised about a thousand times. 'It's all right', he said rather testily, 'I'm not hurt.'

He pushed on along the street in the direction of King's with a furtive and scurrying gait for all the world like a large rodent with a serious complaint against his lot. 'Ho!' said Johnny, smiling and looking after the retreating figure. 'D'you know who that was?' 'No' I said. 'It was E.M. Forster' said Johnny.

Good heavens! I thought. That's twice my family has done the poor man wrong. But we should take heart that he has survived all we can throw at him – I mean, he has managed rather successfully to get to be *old*! My Penguin copy *of A Passage to India* was already very

137

dog-eared when I ran Forster over. It is now fifty years older.

9. HENLEY

In 2014 I had the most Proustian moment of my later life when I again coxed a Pembroke eight at Henley. We had won the Ladies' Plate in 1964 when I was just eighteen and very extraordinary it had been. Now, fifty years later, we re-enacted a pale shadow of that triumph. The shaker and mover of this event was Hugh Burkitt, who had rowed Bow in our winning eight and who had brought us together at intervals since (twenty-five years; forty years) and other than on these occasions I had not seen much of the crew except for Hugh himself, who became a true friend in later life, and Zan Fell who happened to marry a woman near where I lived in Scotland in the 1980s and 1990s. But the fiftieth anniversary was special and Hugh went to town on it.

In 1964, as we have seen, we were waiting to be given our cup and our medals by the rowing enthusiast Sir Robert Menzies, then recently Prime Minister of Australia, and ceremonies had been interrupted by a row-past that we turned to watch. It was the Harvard crew who had won the Grand Challenge Cup, the only trophy senior to ours, in 1914. We stared as they paddled gently by, prehistoric in their antiquity. 1914! It was an almost unbelievable sight in these heady modern times, the Sixties, these years that we already saw were changing everything – or, as I would slowly learn, everything except Henley Royal Regatta. What weird old birds. And they could still row a bit!

Now in 2014 the whirligig of time had brought in its revenges and there we were, getting ready for our own fiftieth-anniversary outing on the river. How on earth could we be as old as those Americans had been? How had the half-century that had flashed by be the exact numerical equivalent of the previous half-century which had gone from Edwardian parlour-maids to the Beatles, from planes made of canvas almost to Concorde, from almost no cars on the road to the jams on the M1? From Suffragettes, Empire and top hats to Private Eye, ITV and supermarkets? And they say that the period, so much more familiar to us and thus less obviously one of radical change, from 1964 to 2014, has in fact been a time of even greater change than our parents' generation experienced. (My father was born just a year before Harvard won the Grand.)

But it didn't feel like it on the river that day, July 5th 2014. It felt as though we had been rowing in Cambridge just the week before, that almost nothing had happened since the last Bump Supper in the Old Library at Pembroke, that at any minute Fred the boatman would rise from the ground before us, that Jacko the Arabist would throw off his cerements and stroll up with a quip, that we would talk of that afternoon's opponents.

But there were no opponents. The greatest oarsman of all time, winner of gold medals at five successive Olympics, Sir Steven Redgrave, rowing Number Three in a light four, preceded us ceremoniously up the course in honour or memory of something, and another light four manned by some meaningless people called the Porcellian Boat Club also lurched up the course ahead of us commemorating the mere fortieth anniversary of their own triumph at Henley. Then it was the turn of the Pembroke Eight. We got going, took on a little speed, managed the last half-mile of the course and surged up towards the grandstands and the finish. The crew went pretty well all things considered; Pauline's film of it, taken on an ageing I-phone, makes us look

139

rather like the business. I was caught on it waving unprofessionally but jovially at the extraordinary enthusiasm of the assembled oarsmen, girls and drunkards in the Steward's Enclosure. But inside me something else was happening.

As we got into a rhythm (remember we had only rowed the last half-mile of the course) and came to the Enclosure lawns where a surprising number of Pembroke men and other more random supporters were cheering us rather loudly, I heard myself saying the last words with which I had urged the crew on to the victory of 1964. 'You remember' I bellowed... no, this time I had a microphone and amplifier and needed only to speak in a normal voice to be heard: 'You remember... what I said at this point fifty years ago?' And I quoted myself: '*Go for the silverware!*' And at that moment I was back in the old days. Just as Proust says, I was like a giant plunged in the years, touching at one and the same time points remotely distant from one another. I felt the feeling I had felt then, purely and clearly. There surged up in me a sweet version of that old drama, tempered now with the certainty of success, the ease of the whole thing. I was at once and simultaneously in 1964 and 2014. We were winning the Ladies' Plate again in a calmer manner. I was ecstatic afterwards for about a week and I think I have never since entirely recovered from the beneficent effect of Involuntary Memory at work that afternoon.

If I had to explain this I would say that at that moment I felt a powerful sense of identity. I have, all these years, been a Pembroke man without fully realising it – more accurately a member of the Pembroke College Boat Club, the PCBC as we called it. Silently it has sat inside me, this identity, largely unbeknownst to me, biding its time. Now it had a field day and raised my spirits to a pitch that I cannot forget. The crew members, most of whom as I say I hadn't seen except at rare reunions at College or for our twenty-fifth and fortieth anniversaries, seemed so deeply familiar, natural, normal to me that we hardly had to exchange any pleasantries or gossip – we just were what we were, without fuss or politesse.

We picnicked in Butler's Field (sic) and there the son of our captain, young Tom Stallard who had rowed in the silver-medal-winning British Olympic crew in 2008, told Pauline and me that for him and his family Henley was like Christmas: it came round once a year and never changed; it was something they looked forward to all year; it regulated their lives. He then went off to the river and Pauline and I were left alone by the table laden with Pimms and salmon and she pointed at the sky and said: 'Look!' Above us a pair of Second-World-War Spitfires flew low, saluting Henley from the past, calmly, just like that. The assembled buffers and boaties, young and old, nodded at them, quite at home.

Christmas and Spitfires do not change; the regatta finish-line and the grandstands and all the paraphernalia around them had not changed at all in fifty years. The Henley sky, always subtly different from any other, was putting in its usual shift; the crowd in the Enclosure was exactly that of 1964 wearing not merely similar clothes but in the case of some of the buffers the actual clothes of yore. Everything had changed and nothing had changed. Reasonably enough, it seemed, the very different person that was me now was exactly the same person as me then. Time does not defeat us as we think. What has been there is there still, is always there, available in another dimension, ready to tell us some truth about who we are. I felt, no, I *feel*, happier for that. All manner of things shall be well.

CHAPTER 5. BAGHDAD 1966 – 1967

1. ORIENT

A couple of months after leaving Cambridge, on an
evening in September 1966, I boarded the Orient
Express at Victoria Station, bound for Istanbul. I had a
couple of friends with me, a few Lloyd's Bank
travellers' cheques and a small amount of guarded
optimism about my return to the Mystic East (I had been
in Egypt as a child, remember?) I was going as a United
Nations Volunteer to teach English in a school and one
of my friends was coming with me on the same mission;
there was also another pal who was just coming for the
trip.

The train was on time at Munich the next
morning (9.18 am I remember) and thereafter became
progressively later and later, arriving finally in Istanbul
five hours behind schedule. And they say we shouldn't
resort to cultural stereotypes. But then, once we were
established in the city, the curse of lateness became
more marked: an Englishman called Hartley who, with
his family, was driving across Europe to pick us up to
go on to Baghdad was *five days* late. In a novel this
would be all very well, even an opportunity in some
way, but in the workaday world where bills have to be
paid and we are not all able to survive without any
obvious income, running out of money in a city where
the hotel bill is racking up and one has actually to eat
from time to time is less and less fun. Luckily a great
friend from Cambridge, the Arabist David Jackson, was
in town researching into the Arabic-Greek translation
literature (think Ancient Greek science and maths
translated in Baghdad and Cordoba in the 10th century
and collected in the Sultan's library in Istanbul when he

became Caliph for about four hundred years.) He (Jackson, not Suleiman the Magnificent) spent his days at the palace at Topkapi poring over manuscripts and his evenings showing us around the great city and drinking Raki. But even so I felt a little nervous when my last Lloyd's Bank five-pound traveller's cheque was cashed.

Finally our means of transport to Baghdad, the two motor cars belonging to this Hartley, headmaster of the school where we were going to teach, appeared at the hotel. 'Sorry I'm a bit late' he said and that was that. Saying goodbye to David Jackson…. but let me pause here to recognize that flawed genius. 'Jacko' was fifteen stone of high-octane conversationalist along the lines of Wilde; he had studied Classics at school but had then been sent to MECAS in Beirut to learn some Arabic before coming up to Cambridge to take a degree, like James Bond, in Oriental Studies. Jacko got a First and stayed on at Pembroke as a Research Fellow to start a doctorate. A couple of years later he was appointed Lecturer in Arabic at St Andrews where he stayed until his early death.

At Cambridge Jacko rowed for the college, played the clarinet and got a half-blue in Judo as well as getting his First. He also spent an extraordinary amount of time in the public houses of the town out-drinking most of us, a skill that led him to become an automatic selection for the annual Oxford-and-Cambridge wine-tasting match where he never failed to disgrace himself because, although fairly conversant with the ways and styles of wine, he proved unable to restrain himself from swallowing, thus becoming an early casualty of the evening. He was a man both physically and mentally larger that life.

At the other end of the time that I knew him, in Scotland in the 1980s, he was married twice – once to a lady who also liked to drink but who four days into their marriage developed a pancreatitis so severe that she was forbidden ever to drink a drop of alcohol again. Thus are some relationships abbreviated. *En secondes noces* Jacko, aged about fifty, married his 89-year-old neighbour on the Fife coast, pointing out to me on the telephone when he called to break the news that she had 'terrific tits.' Thus can some relationships sail forward, though in this case rather briefly as death intervened on both sides.

But I must make the regulation bow to the moral of the story. Jacko was probably always going to be neurotic and unhappy for reasons buried in his past along with his mother, his schooling and so on, but I have the feeling that had he been less successful he might have had a better life. The alcohol was a substitute for something and it may have been for the peace of mind that he sought. He was lacking something, anyway, and his great talents, even though they were recognized and rewarded, didn't automatically provide him with the something in question.

Meanwhile, on to Baggers. We drove, very slowly, for *a week* across Turkey, a bit of Syria (the bit that would be part of an independent Kurdistan if everyone had their rights), down to Mosul and then on to Baghdad. It was dusty and boring and Hartley had brought along not only his wife, a slightly mixed blessing, but also their ten-year-old daughter who tormented me for a thousand slow miles by making me play the sort of word-games usual, I imagine, in girls' prep-schools. Let me draw a quick veil over this with the shudderous revelation that one of these games was called 'Sausages'.

They say that old Baghdad, the magic city of Haroun Al-Rashid and the *Thousand and One Nights*, not only has left us no ruins to look at but has altogether vanished; like Ozymandias' kingdom it has just sunk into the sand and no one can even work out where it is supposed to have been. It is even hard to find much evidence of Turkish Baghdad, and you have to remember that Johnny Turk was only booted out of Iraq in 1917 after four centuries of cruelty, sodomy and mismanagement. So it goes. But these things might not have mattered to me in 1966 had I stayed well and happy in my work. Alas, I contracted jaundice and, after three miserable weeks during which my eyeballs and stomach were yellow while my pee was approximately Old Mahogany, I also realised that the 'Volunteer' tag had been a bit of a sharp piece of practice on the part of Hartley. My friend Mick and I were hoping, I suppose, to Do Some Good, but we ended up as unpaid teachers at the most expensive private prep-school in the country. This was galling enough, but when I also discovered that I was thoroughly incapable not merely of teaching small boys but even of controlling a classful of them, I saw that I was doing absolutely no good at all and quit.

The British Council Rep, seconded by the Ambassador, badgered us a bit: 'But you are the first western volunteers this country has allowed in, *ever*! They'll never let us have another one!' We asked to stay on in an Iraqi state school but that proved tricky. Then I wanted to stay on doing private teaching, but that wasn't allowed either. In the event we travelled back overland in February 1967 to Amman and Palestine, visiting Arab East Jerusalem just months before the Israelis invaded and took it over. Then by plane to Beirut, Cyprus, Athens (where there was snow on the runway) and, flying in what must have been one of the last BOAC Comets, back to London. Oh, and besides the well-known high fatality rate among Comet passengers I had a meningial infection on Cyprus that at one point seemed likely to finish me off; there were those who thought I would never make it back to England.

Back home I was whisked down to Silton for some recovery and on my first evening there Uncle Dick took the opportunity to hand me an open book before dinner telling me to read the page before me. It was a piece of Christian flummery by St Anselm or some other lice-ridden Desert Father about sticking to the task and ploughing to the end of the furrow; Dick clearly thought, without of course asking me anything about what had happened or how I was, that I had betrayed my calling in Baghdad and that I needed a bit of moralizing at. Being a weasel, I smiled and thanked him for his wisdom and that of St Whoever and poured myself a sherry. The topic was never mentioned again. I fear that Uncle Dick belonged to that generation that had neither the brutal self-confidence of Victorian parents nor the post-Freudian care and concern of the modern parent. So he thrust some useless and inappropriate medieval text at me and left that to do the work he vaguely thought needed to be done but had never got round to doing himself. It was like my running away from school or attempting suicide all over again: nobody gave a damn about why I had done the thing I had done, but they had an opinion or two, took their own line, shouted at me briefly and then shut up forever.

Shortly after my arrival in Baghdad, while I was lying in the YMCA in the full yellowness of the

146

jaundice, Hartley had come into my room and announced that my father was dead. He handed me a telegram, said he was sorry and left. (Once more no attempt at any kind of human interaction.) My father had been killed falling off the garage roof at my stepmother's house in Crowborough, Sussex. So it goes. Poor chap, only fifty-three and not a very happy man. Fifty-three. Seems rather young to me now. Piers made sure that there was a Union Flag on his coffin at the funeral.

2. HABBANIYAH

I have only been consciously spied on twice, and both times were in Baghdad in 1966. The first occasion was unexciting; it merely involved some amateur tailing by a fat young government agent who may well have simply been practicing. But on the second occasion I was approached by a thirty year-old chap in glasses, also rather tubby, and invited to go into the desert with him. He had a car, O wonder. I was with a couple of British friends and, oh yes, they could come too. We invited our sudden host to have some tea with us in one of the dusty little cafes of our quarter of town and planned a trip. Eventually I asked him 'But don't you work? How can you get the time off... and we've only just met you!' 'Never mind' he said, rolling the R in the most Arab manner possible, 'Never mind. I am doing my work while I am with you.' 'Oh' I said, 'how can that be?' 'Well' he said, 'I am a spy and I have to spy on you.'

The day of the expedition dawned, as they say, and there he was, the spy, honking his horn outside our house and smiling nervously. We drove off westwards. Soon the city gave way to desert and we settled in for a hot haul of a couple of hours. The good news was that we were going to Habbaniyah, on Lake Habbaniyah no less. Now, we were not altogether deprived of the sight of water in our curious Iraqi existence – we sometimes had supper beside the Tigris near the centre of town where huge cats prosecuted a Darwinian struggle for survival among the litter of fish and other comestibles that patrons of the temporary river-bed cafes threw onto the sand. Apparently when the Tigris was in spate the cafes were removed for a while, but while we were there we were in effect eating near a smallish river in a huge river-bed, on the sand. One of the cats, the alpha cat, the dominant male, was the largest feline I have ever seen of his species, bigger than a spaniel. But we needed more water to look at all the same.

So the thought of a lake was appealing. On the way there, which seemed to be an age of hot driving, one of my friends remembered that Habbaniyah had been the site of a large Royal Air Force base in the days when the British ran things in Iraq and Jordan. We wondered about that but when we asked our guide he merely grunted something like 'Yes, it's an Iraqi airforce base now. Much better.' Yet we saw no planes and no viable landing strips. Only, beyond the abandoned airfield, stretched the blue of real, extensive water. We licked our lips.

There was what seemed to be a concrete latrine block of the 1940s British-Forces-Abroad kind standing near the water, and not much else. Our guide, friend and investigator took us towards this building and said 'Changing Room.' There we put on shorts and rushed out to plunge into the water. The spy merely spied on us from the bank, smirking and smoking. But as we came out of the water severally he went into action. The first of us to emerge was a rather nice-looking blonde

148

student (male, as we all were) from some provincial English university who was with us and I noticed the spy putting his arm round the young man's shoulders as he led him back into the red-hot and rather odoriferous Changing Room. Quite soon the young Englishman came running out and fell back into the tepid water. He didn't say much. Then Mick went through the same process with the same result. Then someone else. A few minutes later, needing a hat or a towel or a drink, I got out of the lake and went towards the building. Ahmed or whatever the spy's name was sloped alongside me and did the arm business. We went inside together. As soon as we were out of sight he confronted me and said 'Come into this room and we will... Take Our Freedom.' Those rolled Rs again. 'Gosh' I said, embarrassed, 'that's not really my sort of thing' and then, with an inspiration born of pusillanimity and visions of trying to get back the hundred miles to Baghdad in the heat on foot, I said 'Perhaps you could try one of the others?' He looked annoyed, 'But they all said the same thing! Does not one of you wish to Take His Freedom?' He was genuinely surprised.

Somehow we got back to the city and the spy's Volkswagen vanished into the traffic. We went back to the café where we had started. 'Well', I said to the others, 'how was that for you?' They all had the same story to tell. The beautiful student was the quietest but after a while he said 'That always happens to me! I mean, what's wrong with me?' and he told stories of fighting off panting grizzled inamorati, whose loose robes bore clear proof of their ardour, all across the Middle East. From Libya to Iran he had had encounter after encounter and he was still puzzled. I said 'There is a long tradition of homosexuality in the Muslim world. You know about T.E. Lawrence, about the Turks?

149

About the poem which begins 'There's a boy across the river with a bottom like a peach, But alas I cannot swim?' All this was however new to him. 'Really?' he said. 'Really' I said. And I resisted the temptation to say 'Just look in a mirror my friend.'

Two things stuck in my mind from this experience. The first was what is known as the polymorphous sexuality of the male of the species. It is not quite true that, given the chance and in the absence of anything better, young men will consider having sex with vacuum cleaners, but I got a strong impression that our spy was not necessarily gay; the possibilities and traditions of his culture permitted him to proposition us, but then we were available, or seemed to be, and there was nothing much else on his sexual horizon I suppose. Notably he didn't appear to mind much which of us he took his freedom with, he just wanted sex, any sex, with anyone.

The second lesson was one of self-knowledge. The beautiful student seemed to be utterly unaware of the effect he had on people, but how was that, when his stories were all about the effect he had on people? Ever since then I have taken absolutely nothing for granted in this department.

3. PLAYS

Before a rioting mob, protesting I think about the First Gulf War in the 1990s, burnt it to the ground, the British Council Centre in Baghdad was rather successful. There was a library there, full of British books (I remember looking in vain for a Hemingway I wanted to read – 'Sorry Meester Butler, I don't think he was British, was he?'), classrooms where people like me taught English to adults in the evenings, an exhibition space and a

150

theatre. Not bad for the capital of a minor Middle-Eastern power but then we (the British) had had a special interest in Iraq ever since Gertrude Bell and T. E. Lawrence and the others had invented the place and turned it into a country after the First World War. And of course it had Oil.

This British Council effort, successful while I was there, turned out eventually to be a complete waste of time. The investment in Barbara Hepworth sculptures and the complete oeuvre of Anthony Powell didn't cut much ice with the Iraqi people, though of course 'Iraqi' is a concept invented over a glass of port by Sykes and Picot (they of the Sykes-Picot Agreement) and that rather interesting man Arthur Balfour in about 1917, not to mention Lawrence and Bell. Still, whoever the Iraqis were, one wondered if this was the way forward; and one was proved right in one's wondering when, after a series of bloodier and bloodier dictators (so much for Western liberalism spread by mild art and a little light TEFL) they scooped the pool with the appalling Saddam Hussein (referred to by my daughter Alice throughout the First Gulf War as 'Madam Hussein', a charming variant) who wouldn't have said Hello to a Hepworth under any circumstances and had a view of the world and of social behaviour rather at odds with those of the author of *A Dance to the Music of Time*. The British Council buildings lasted I suppose twenty years, Saddam an amazing twenty-five during which he destroyed his country and murdered most of his countrymen. So much for the hope one has of civilising the world.

De toute façon, there I was in Baghdad on starry cooling nights chatting to youngish adult aspirants for a better life, persuading them to distinguish between *sheep* and *ship* and *cheap* and *chip* ('Sir! Today I have

151

some ship for lunch' - which has only three mistakes,
two of them in the same word) so that they could speak
a language that might be useful when they eventually
fled Iraq; thus I helped the civilizing efforts of the
Council staff, good people to a man and occasional
woman but often barking mad. One of the maddest was
a chap called Raymond Tong whom I offended by
telling him that I had met his namesake in a bar in
Istanbul. 'Oh?' said Tong, brightening, 'Who was he?' I
replied, in all truth, 'A gigolo from the Ivory Coast who
was on his way home from Berlin where he made his
money by, erm, servicing well-to-do German Hausfraus
at a deutschmark a.... with his....' Mr Tong stopped me
before I got too near to his surname. 'How revolting!'
he said. 'I always thought we were a respectable
family.' And he marched off into a gathering dust-storm
muttering to himself.

    Back at the Centre excitements included an
extreme version of that well-known sport anti-semitism.
This was played by young Arabs by finding out when
the few remaining young Jews of Baghdad (they were
definitely the last of what had been a huge colony in
Iraq before the creation of the so-called State of Israel in
1949) were taking their exams (these Jews were trying
to get out not just by learning English but also by
getting British O and A-Levels.) Once the Arabs had
learnt the date of the exam they would stage an anti-
Israel demonstration outside the Council as the police
looked on smiling; then they would make a rush for the
entrance where the odd enfeebled Brit, replete with
thoughts about the latest in Concrete Poetry or planning
a concert of music by Benjamin Britten, would confront
them with the sort of 'You can't come in here like that'
approach that hadn't worked, really, since India in 1947.
Yells would interrupt a paper in A-level Economics

152

(Oxford and Cambridge Joint Board) and knives would be brandished. The young Jews would take to the fire exits before being helped over the back wall of the compound by my friend Stephen Nash who had been combining Invigilation with a little light Ethics in which he too, astonishingly, was simultaneously taking an exam - an A-Level (London Board.) 'Jews?' he would say, returning breathless to the classroom now empty of candidates and full of gold-toothed, flashing-eyed young murderers, 'We don't ask about our candidates' religion.' This flummoxed the desperados who went away to plot the assassination of the American ambassador instead.

Amongst this sort of thing we reacted in the only obvious way and put on Drama – British classic plays for the delectation of a select Iraqi audience. While I was there we did *Twelfth Night* (Feste the Jester for yours truly) and *Waiting for Godot* (Vladimir.) This latter play was not strictly British of course, but there. Beckett, when asked on one occasion if he was British replied '*au contraire*', which I think was rather neat. Anyway Beckett came in under the Queen's Shilling those nights in sunny Baggers.

With hindsight no better plays could possibly have been selected. The Girls' University was studying *Twelfth Night* and of course anyone in the whole world can relate to *Godot*.

Strangely we put on the Shakespeare during an incredibly cold patch of weather and had to wear extra clothes in rehearsal. In the Green Room (a sort of grown-up back passage at the back of the building, near the wall used by Jews to shin over at need) we had a paraffin stove. This gave a decent heat, itself becoming incandescent in the process. Unfortunately one of the actresses, the English teacher playing Olivia I think, put

153

a basin of water on top of this dragon and managed, during the dress rehearsal, once the water had almost reached boiling point, to knock into the stove pouring the water all over her legs. Much screaming ensued.

You can imagine the scene in the Green Room. But worse than this was the scene when they play opened the following night. In agony and with her legs visibly bandaged Olivia hobbled about the stage chatting to Viola about her (Olivia's) irresistible beauty with less and less conviction. The lines 'I shall give out divers schedules of my beauty as, item…' followed by the list of her features served only to draw the audience's attention to her lower limbs. Worse again, the play having been cut, insanely, on the grounds that it may have been rather long for Iraqi taste, Olivia and all of the rest of us were constantly interrupted as we reached the cut lines, by a noisy flurry in the audience who, to a female student, were reading the play as they watched it and were suddenly and frequently baffled by the omissions. Turning to one another they all asked at once in a sharp Arabic murmur 'What's going on? Where are those lines? Is your book the same as mine? Can one do this to Shakespeare?'

Later in the piece it became apparent that Viola was short of a sword and the confusion, already great in the students' minds, became total as her twin brother, dressed identically of course as he always is in productions of *Twelfth Night*, had to come onstage long before his cue and the great Recognition Scene, to hand it to her. There was a loud gasp from the hall and much more shuffling of texts.' 'Really?' the girls were all asking each other. 'Here? … Him?'

The play closes with a song by Feste which I sang solo, after a fashion, directly to the by-now largely-bamboozled audience. The entire cast, on the

154

last night, had conspired to join me without telling me they were going to and they crept onto the stage while I sang the first verse and then joined loudly in the chorus. I spun round in surprise and managed to get back to normal only just in time for the second verse. Being congratulated after the show by the British Ambassador over a glass of whisky I was silenced not by his genial remark that I had managed to 'do a good job in tricky circumstances' but by his further observation that it was a tribute to my acting skills that I had 'feigned surprise quite brilliantly' at the end. I remained silent but managed to look modest.

Godot was its own species of disaster. Although quite promising in its opening moments its capacity to run off the rails, always strong in a play whose dialogue is repetitive and inconsequential, suddenly emerged on the last night of the short run (which may only have been three performances though I can't quite remember.) I had been unnerved in the Green Room by Stephen Nash ('My surname means 'funeral pyre' or 'resurrection' in Arabic' he said; 'OK' I said) who had come to wish us luck and stopped briefly to paint his nose bright blue with the makeup we hadn't used. All I wanted to do when on stage was to see how this was going down with his diplomatic and British Council colleagues, which may perhaps be the reason that, as we ploughed through about page 15 of the script, I suddenly and totally dried. No word of any kind seemed available to my panicking brain.

I was playing Vladimir to the Estragon of one Nick Brimble, a chap who, surprisingly, went on to a successful acting career in film and television, mostly playing villains of the blackest stripe in historical dramas but also Little John in one of the many *Robin Hoods*. He was, you will have understood, about 6 foot

155

5 inches tall, nearly a foot taller than myself, and we made a very pretty couple if you happen to be an Absurdist playwright. We had prepared for our final performance, after comments had been made that our second-hand clothes weren't *trampy* or destitute enough, by dragging each other round the *meidan* outside the Council Centre to collect more authentic dirt. Now, though, Nick sat on his low mound in his filth gazing at me as I realised in the eternal instant of the dry that I would never, ever, find my line. After about three-quarters of an hour, or say ten seconds, he spoke up: 'Didn't you have a pain yesterday?' (not a line in the orthodox text of the play.) 'No!' I said, 'No, I had no pain yesterday' (an equally invented line.) As I said this some deep instinct kicked in and I looked desperately into the wings where a random Pole, in Iraq for obscure reasons of his own and currently courting our stage manager, a blonde of a certain age and big glasses, was supposedly acting as Prompt. Imagine my surprise, not to say horror, when I saw him dozing gently on a laundry basket, the text of the play slipping slowly from his nerveless grasp. 'NO!' I shouted again in his direction and watched as he very slowly opened his eyes, grasped both the play script and the situation and began hunting for our place in the text.

'' Do you think you will have a pain tomorrow?' asked Nick/Estragon. 'No!' I yelped, 'No. I do not think I will have a pain tomorrow.' 'Have you ever had a pain?' he pursued. 'No! No. I have never had a pain.' I was now quite enjoying this; I saw that it could go on and on; something like a play by Beckett really. But then, possibly exasperated by my uselessness, Nick changed tack. 'WHY have you never had a pain?' he cried, adding for good measure, 'In this painful world, this...' he remembered a good word from Sam himself,

from one of the novels I think, 'this… SHITHEAP?'
The audience, for a reason hard to fathom, began to
laugh. Some of our nervous tension had transmitted
itself and they began to giggle, snort and hoot. The
answer came to me, as they do: 'Because…. Because
(*inspiration!*) because I am in truth DEAD.' Even Nick
looked a bit aghast at that. 'You're *dead?*' he queried in
a voice much more normal than he intended. The
audience guffawed. 'Oh yes' I said, 'altogether dead.'

At this point our Pole found his place and from
the wings came a violent hissing as he tried to attract
our attention and give me the right line in a voice that
must have been audible in Damascus: 'Have you ever
known a moment's happiness?' he bellowed. I felt I
could answer that one but let it pass and instead turned
to Nick and repeated the line in horribly normal-
sounding tones: 'Have you ever known a moment's
happiness?' This was the signal for another paroxysm
on the part of the assembled glitterati of Mesopotamia.
Only when they quietened down could Nick say
'Never.'

Godot was once billed in Florida as 'the laugh
hit of two continents' by some impresario anxious about
his box-office. The American holidaymakers bought
their tickets all right and poured in on the opening night.
It was not a success. American humour can be pretty
basic at times and I think people were expecting at least
Laurel and Hardy. Instead they got undigested Parisian
Existentialist *Weltschmerz*. Some asked for their money
back. But in Baghdad we would have triumphed under
the same circumstances. Laugh hit? They were rolling
on the dusty floor; we could hardly hear ourselves
mangling the lines.

As they say in Scotland, you never know the
minute.

4. HAMMAM

The only means of proper bathing in our house in Baghdad was by lighting the Turkish bath and waiting for at least an hour and a half. Hamid it was who saw to the deliveries of paraffin (is that right?) that were needed to feed the dragon that lurked under the floor. He went outside for a considerable period and we heard mysterious bangings and muffled curses in the yard. He would come back in with black hands and say 'Fire lit! Two hours!' and push off to wash in the kitchen.

The result of his efforts was that the dragon would roar for a while and the concrete floor above it would become hot. This was the floor of a windowless room of some considerable size whose only ornament was a cold tap at about ankle level. When the floor had become hot enough Hamid would turn this tap on slightly allowing a trickle of water to spread slowly over the grey floor. Bit by bit this water turned to steam and after a long pause he would announce 'Bathtime!' which meant putting on gym-shoes and seizing a towel before plunging into the Stygian cauldron. One took a chair with one or went in and did exercises but either way one was flattened by heat and sweat after about ten minutes and had to come out and beg for mercy.

A bath usually finished me for the day and I had to go and lie down, but the others alleged it to be refreshing. Among these others was Israel the houseboy. Now he, as those can easily imagine who have followed events in Iraq in the 21st century, had not been dealt the kindest of hands by fate. He was a Christian, which was only partly OK in the Iraq of the 1960s and of course became a beheading offence among the mad Sunni brethren of the north of the country when they set up their Islamic State. And then his first name was that of the hated enemy of all Muslims and a fortiori all Arabs, of, that is to say, the 'State' of Israel. The word 'Israel' was for instance scratched out on the surface of the globes that my colleagues distributed when they were trying to impart Political Geography at the school where I was teaching. The Kurdish school secretary saw to that.

In addition to these disadvantages Israel was employed in the house exclusively to act as the catamite of our housemate Richard Wilmott, a man designed by nature to perpetuate the myth about Englishmen and boys. He had come to Baghdad from Ethiopia and greatly regretted the move. Boys in Addis Ababa were a great deal more easily obtainable than in Iraq apparently. However, he was now making do with Israel and every evening one would see them ascending to Richard's bedroom on the first floor (luckily the only bedroom up there; we slept below) whence would issue cries of pain and pleasure during the long hours before midnight.

Israel, anyway, found a Turkish bath invigorating and would emerge from our steam-room towelling his astonishingly-coloured hair and grinning. 'Feel good' he would say in Arabic. As Richard was I think largely innocent of the native tongue I assume that their evening *pourparlers* upstairs were conducted exclusively in the language of love. Although, towards the end of our time together in that house, Richard did tell me that he had been teaching Israel to say 'I love you' when necessary.

CHAPTER 6. ALGIERS 1967 - 1968

1. ATTACHMENT

Talking of love. I have a high regard for the psychoanalyst Miriam Stoppard, one-time wife of the very intelligent playwright Tom, which reveals something. During the 1980s one of the Sunday papers ran an article on happiness in which they lined up a team of shrinks to pass opinions on the human capacity to feel *well*, to be happy. La Stoppard was one of these and she came up with a striking summary of the situation we all face: in general, psychologically at least, the Worst Thing in the World is separation. Separation from the mother, from the welcoming other, the meaningful, the loving, the safe, this is the pits. As well as being essential of course. This may not be how she put it but it is what I remember of it: Separation is unhappiness. As François Mauriac puts it in *Le noeud de vipères* : '*On cherche des yeux maman dans la foule du monde.*'

    I found myself in passionate agreement with Miriam, 'Mary' as we might call her, standing in for the mother of all mothers, lodestar of a Catholic boyhood, above the high altar in peaceful blue, haloed by stars, smiling and open-armed; and in agreement with Mauriac. Once, years later, on a return to Belmont Abbey, alone in the abbey church, I came upon a new statue of the Virgin, slightly raised on a plinth, an Our Lady of greater beauty and conviction than most, wreathed for a feast in tasteful flowers, looking at me. I smiled at her. She made a tiny movement, gesturing with her body and head minutely towards me. Then she smiled back. You may smile too, but there she was, smiling at me. I nearly struck up a conversation, wondering what the etiquette would be for talking to the Queen of Heaven, but caught myself just in time.

Separation is the necessary fate of us all and also the worst thing in the world. A conundrum to be handled delicately. We must all leave the womb and yell; we must all leave the everlasting arms and learn to run about; we must all leave home; we must all integrate into the world, accept it, establish ourselves, be grown-ups. Of course. But it is still potentially the worst thing, and that's delicate.

I once asked John Fowles (remember him? *The Collector*? *The French Lieutenant's Woman*? - see 'Regis' in 'Stirling', above) to write a piece for me about Hardy. His first reply was 'If it's only for the eight-and-a-half Tenure Points for your academic career, don't bother,' in spite of which he did comply, convinced somehow that I was not a don-con and, additionally, I think, needing to get something out psychologically. He wrote an essay for my collection *Thomas Hardy After Fifty Years* (Macmillan, 1977) in which he describes himself being psychoanalysed at a distance, mostly via the *French Lieutenant*. His remote Californian analyst proposed that he had a particularly vivid repressed memory of the separation from his mother such that, like many novelists including Hardy, he wrote to revisit the painful place and to try again to get the reward he needed – the heroine's attention and love. Fowles as Clegg then, or as Charles Smithson.

Perhaps nobody ever seriously writes adverse criticism of Proust (other than the Gallimard editor who rejected the first volume of *A la recherche* on the grounds that he found it intolerable to read a book in which '*un monsieur*' takes 'fourteen pages to tell us how he turned over in bed') because Proust is entirely open about his need to repair the breach of separation

161

which is the indispensable if uncomfortable part of becoming what we later come to call our selves.

Falling in love occurs, it seems to me as it seemed to Proust, when the '*yeux maman*' strike us in synchronic symmetry with physical desire of the simplest kind. "She looked at me so *warmly*!' just about covers both bases – she's warm, she's *hot* - and the eyes here represent both the heart's warmth and the breasts'. Try Dennis de Rougemont on this in his *Love in the Western World* of 1939 where passionate love, as invented by William IX of Aquitaine and his Provencal troubadours in the 10th century, is defined as a desire of such re-absorption into the body of the mother that he calls it Death. As Ronsard put it '*L'amour et la mort n'est qu'une même chose.*'

At all events I was frightened when I was 'sent home' from Egypt – that is away from *home* but 'home' to England. I thought that I was just scared of the flying. The journey took place after all in a converted Lancaster bomber, one of the very chaps who had pounded the Hun in his lair only eight or nine years before (did you know that they made *thousands* of them and that there are now only three left?) These slow heavy grinding air-machines, took us from the Canal Zone (Suez) to Malta in four hours and there, after two hours for an English breakfast (at three in the morning) and a warm stroll about the airfield another seven hours to Croydon (was it really?) 'Feeling icky-picky?' asked a brigadier as I staggered off the plane into the Maltese night retching and diminutive and quite ready for death myself.

But what must really have frightened me was the disappearance of my mother. How can any child spend seven years with its parent full-time and then accept without a qualm the prospect of an *infinite* separation?

162

Especially when the separation has been voluntarily put in place by the mother herself? Ye gods.

2. SAND

Jasmine rather contradicts the usual smell in the backstreets of Algiers. One evening, having been caught up *à la* Omar Khayyam with the astonishing scent of those little white flowers, on my way back to my flat off the Rue Didouche Mourad, after dark, I thought there was a flood in the street ahead of me. The tarmac, such as it was, was moving, flowing away from me in the middle-distance under the weak yellow lamplight. I looked more carefully and, as the flood moved off, I saw that it was in fact a huge pack of rats undulating towards some drain or hovel, as scared of me as I, recognising them for what they were, suddenly was of them.

From the paradise of jasmine to the hell of a whole Black-Death's worth of rats. In an instant. In the same street.

I walked more slowly, thinking on these things. And of the existence, and the current absence, of my new Latin lady, Carmen. In the flat, its balcony above my head now as I shuddered towards my door, there was nobody. This sadness forced me to concentrate on my work teaching EFL in a private evening school. All work is a bore but this way of earning a living is at least an absorbing one: you can't teach English to foreigners without entirely losing your personality for a couple of hours and trying to get inside the straining monolingual skin of Ahmed or Marie. Which was useful because it does appear that at the time I was suffering from what, years later, a friend would call 'bloody love.'

The evening school, though called the '*Centre Anglo-Africain de Langues*', was, I now realise, just a large old flat, surely abandoned by some recently-departed *pied-noir*; no doubt I taught in the very bedroom where *he* had loved, snored, despaired. This was Algiers in 1967.

Now I had to cope with the Lower Intermediate Class: 'Look, Omar, it's better not to say that you approve of world piss.' 'But sir, I believe in piss!' Here there was enough to distract me from Love: the usual thumping energy needed to get people talking a foreign language and the tangible tension in the room among the ten men (Men Only was the norm at the school – not our norm - theirs.) Unusual this tension, this time. At coffee-break I took the most silent student aside, a middle-aged man from the embassy of some non-English-speaking Arab country – Syria perhaps. 'Is everything all right Mr Saleem?' He looked embarrassed but sounded determined: 'I do not like the students in my class.' 'Oh, OK, what is the problem? Is it with all of them?' 'That man' he began, 'That man opposite to me. He is – how do we say? He is *tekrooni.*' I got it at once. His unfavorite fellow student was from Djibouti or Niger or somewhere, and he was black. '*Tekrooni*' – a wog – a nigger. I couldn't believe it. 'But Mr Saleem', I remonstrated, 'as far as I'm concerned *you're* a *tekrooni.*' He looked at me.

I think I was popular enough with my fellow teachers, and the boss, to get away with this. I sometimes even got paid for hours I hadn't taught. They certainly weren't going to take seriously the ravings of a Second Secretary from the Syrian embassy who claimed that I had called him a nigger. I hadn't of course, not quite. I had just seen red; how dare he complain about the colour of a fellow-student's skin? I mean, *him.* I had

164

flipped, like a Zen monk I hope; you know, the one who, seeing a man kicking his dog, goes up and himself gives the dog a good kick. When the man remonstrates the monk says 'Now you know how much you value your pet.' Saleem never came back to the school. We didn't mind that much. He had paid in full.

Carmen was scheduled to come out to visit me, overcoming separation for once, and that weird insecurity which wreaks havoc with all good sense got going inside me. She wouldn't come! She would be prevented; she would die! Or I would die before she got here! The plane would crash; she wouldn't be able to sort out an Algerian visa (in *London*, for a *Colombian* passport). I had imagined her; she didn't love me; it had all been a joke – 'Oh did you think I *meant*...?' She *did* joke, after all; laughed a lot. When the Sugar King, her name for a fat countryman of hers, had come to her flat in Kensington she wouldn't let him in. 'I have a contagious disease!' she cried through the door; and: 'Yes, I can still speak in Spanish, but one of my symptoms is to prefer English... No, I never go to the doctor.'

I had bought a small Turkish trunk, wooden, green, and put her letters in it. When she came she admired it; I said I had carried it back from the shop in the centre of town on my head, half a mile. Nobody had commented. She touched my head to see if it was all right. I smiled, 'See, it's OK!'

When we had Abdurrahman and Melika to dinner there in Algiers (that's another story) Carmen talked about food the way people from different cultures do at first in default of better topics. 'In Colombia' she said, 'you can't give your husband a steak for dinner. The cooking is too easy. If you do you will become known as a bad woman. He will be thought a...' But she

165

couldn't remember what the husband of a faithless lady
would be, either in French or English, so she raised her
hand to her hair and with two fingers made the cuckold
gesture familiar at least since Shakespeare's time ('He
should have worn the horns on his head' those courtiers
say in *Midsummer Night's Dream* during the Rude
Mechanicals' play, making yet again the weak joke that
had them rolling, we are told, in the Globe mud.) Then
she found the word: '*Cocu!*' Abdurrahman snorted
humorously; Melika continued not to be there.

It has only just occurred to me: Carmen was
known as Cuqui ('My mother called me *la cucaracha*.
You know – one of those beetles.' God, a *cockroach*.
Ugh. 'Why?' 'Because she loved me!' OK.) And
'*Cuqui*' sounds a bit like '*Cocu*.' But I didn't see it
before because there wasn't time. She laughed at it too.
Her visiting cards had 'Cuqui' on them, just that. This
was one degree more minimalist than the visiting card I
once got from Samuel Beckett. It had printed on it,
pretty uselessly, just the two words: 'Samuel Beckett.'
On it he asked me to give my dog a bone. The dog,
admittedly, was called Godot. I bought an expensive
and tasty-looking bone and Godot chewed it for days.
He was the only existentialist animal I have ever known.
Unless they all are.

"I will be there when you get married!' Carmen
said to me. 'And then you will be happy. And later I
will be a wicked old lady – very thin. I want to grow old
just for that.' Jesus, I thought, she wants me to marry
someone else. Why? She was only a few years older
than me - I was 21 and at 29 she had had a couple of
husbands, and an invisible child resident in Barcelona
with her *cocu* of a first husband. Though she was no
adulteress. Astonishing word. I would have married her
in a taxi, under any law or by any religious or satanic

means. 'Look', she said, 'I can't just stay in Algiers
with you – it would be too like a marriage.' 'Oh of
course' I said trying to sound grown-up and in
agreement.

***

To jump forward a bit. I was the only one of the four of
us to survive the accident, or so I thought at first. The
lined French doctor, Gauloise in the side of his mouth,
strong grey hair, a cliché of himself, looked down at me
as I lay strapped immobile to the iron bedstead. *'Et les
autres?'* I asked. He looked at me a bit more before
taking the cigarette from his lips. *'Eh bien'* he
answered, *'pour eux c'est déjà fini.'* I liked the *'déjà'*.
    But Françoise had survived too, as I soon
learned. Unfair that. Her man Michael was killed but
Françoise was unharmed. My Inca Extravaganza was
killed too but I escaped with a broken neck. One from
each pair. Actually Carmen's family wasn't Inca (in fact
you can't be – it isn't a race) as they traced their descent
from the Chibcha tribe – 'So stupid!' she would say,
'they didn't even have the sense to eat each other.'
There was quite a lot of gold in her back teeth – pale
Inca gold after all. Françoise, who had gone whizzing
out through the windscreen, took her two enormous
black eyes back to Algiers.
    We had been going, the four of us, to the
Saharan town of Ghardaia for Christmas. We never got
there. In fact we ended up an oasis short, being taken
into Laghouat in a number of pieces and by a number of
means. I was unconscious for a good day and paralysed
from the neck down for two. Several times in that
second twenty-four hours an Arab orderly would come
into my room with a large hypodermic and cry

167

'Préparez les fesses!' Of course I couldn't, but he injected me anyway. Slowly the sensation returned, starting at the top. At the end of that second day I could just feel my toes. Then I had the worst pins-and-needles of my life.

The weirdly-coincidental thing was that just after the crash (large lorry coming the other way, poor steering by Françoise) on that empty desert road there had come along a person who was both one of my students at the English-language school in Algiers *and* a doctor. He had seen the hopelessness of Michael's case and Carmen's and had concentrated on the survivors. In the event, as a broken neck trumps black eyes and bruising, I was the one who needed attention. He pulled me around the desert by my ears, put me in his car, took me into the hospital at Laghouat, tied me, with the assistance of Daniel Cazenave, the French doctor to the oilmen in the place, to an iron bedstead and put ropes round my ankles. The idea was to create what is known as traction, pulling the compression-fracture of my seventh cervical vertebra out again so that the spinal cord would no longer be under stress and I would be able to, well, *walk* and play squash again for instance.

As it was Christmastime the gallant doctor had been called to my rescue from a party where the French oilmen were jugging it up as only those inhabiting a desert a thousand miles from home can. He therefore went straight from my bedside back to the party and asked the assembled company for blood, 'Lots of blood! There is a young Englishman…' The oilmen to an oilman rolled up their sleeves without waiting for anything like an explanation and, crowding round him, offered their inner elbows with cries of *'Prenne! Prenne!'* Thus it was that I was topped up with equal parts of French blood and *pastis*, and awoke, when

168

awake I did, feeling on top of the world. A little later I was surprised to find that in addition to a broken neck and other injuries I had a monumental hangover.

When I was a bit more *compos mentis* after a couple of days in Dr Cazenave's contraption he paid me a visit, presumably one of many in a series of which I had been unaware. He said 'Can you laugh?' 'Well' I said, 'the English are known for their sense of humour...' 'No' he said, 'I mean your body. Does it hurt when you laugh?' 'Try me' I said. I had been rather short of jokes in recent days. 'You know Ahmed?' asked the doctor. Ahmed was the Arab orderly, he of the *fesses*. I did know him. 'When we first got you in here I needed weight to tie to your feet and I thought of wet sand as an idea. I got two canvas bags and I said to Ahmed "Get some sand please." Ahmed took the bags and looked at me. "Where shall I get the sand?" he asked.' Dr Cazenave's face crinkled as he raised his eyebrows, also his smile, shoulders and hands. 'You know... he wanted to know where to find sand... here... in the middle of the Sahara.' Laughing did hurt rather a lot as it turned out.

The family rallied round and sent Piers out, for the efficiency that is in him, to try to get me home, and with him came Celia, selected by Arnie on the spurious grounds that her knowledge of Spanish would be helpful to us in Algeria. This was extremely trying for Piers.

Let me have another go at this, this *thing*. It won't take long.

It's London in June 1967 (the 'Summer of Love', no?) newly-met Carmen agrees to come out to dinner with me and I book a table at Martinez's, the old Spanish restaurant on Swallow Street, off Piccadilly. I arrive three-quarters of an hour early just in case; she arrives three-quarters of an hour late because she is

South American and that is manners down there. During this *hour-and-a-half* I drink sherry (but not too much, for God's sake, not too much) and chew the end of the Evening Standard like some dog in its basket. After five minutes I am anxious, after ten incredulous (she isn't able to come), after fifteen certain (she doesn't *want* to come), and after twenty traumatised (she has been run over by a bus.) This all before the moment when she could possibly have come at all. After the hour-and-a-half I am hallucinating and wheezing gently from the back of a dry throat, unable to speak. In a fit of some emotion I cannot identify I suddenly stand, pay and leave. In the hallway there is a blur of scarlet silk and a huge Inca smile over Colombian gold and under glossy black hair and other clichés. Clichés don't matter now. None of this corresponds to anything objective.

'Oh! Were you leaving? Oh, I'm so sorry, I came at the South American time!' We laugh, we sit. More sherry and, I suppose, a meal; I suppose talk. This is a disaster. The better it goes the more of a disaster it is. Why? Because pride and the good stuff go before the inevitable fall and the bad stuff? Because I can't cope? With her? Without her? I have no idea what I am talking about. We laugh a lot, some of it at things hard to identify as funny. I would immolate myself cheerfully under Eros a minute after she told me to. Except of course that that would mean not seeing her again, so I don't suggest it.

'Your place or mine?' she asks in the taxi, playing another cliché with the irony of a poststructuralist undermining his own discourse (they hadn't been invented yet of course although Derrida was presumably beavering away at the *three* fat books he published that year). 'Yours' I say through thick cotton

170

wool. For a sheep as for a lamb is what I'm thinking. Sheepishly.

Everything follows that should, I suppose. I may have inadvertently kissed her shoes. She may have inadvertently had her feet in them at the time. She served up, as a bedtime snack, honey into which she put rose-petals (no *really*) and which she fed me from a spoon. There may have been Mahler. Morning came too soon. Dull London morning with added angels.

One runs around a lot at 21. I had to go to an interview, to visit my stepmother in Sussex, to get some light trousers for North Africa. All sorts of trains and taxis took me about southern England when they should all have been going to Carmen. But there was another evening with her, two, three, before I took the train to Paris, to Marseilles, thence the boat to Algiers. In London she came to the station, kissed me, watched me disappear as my train drew out; her white dress became a blur against the dull colours of Victoria Station – an Impressionist splash of diminishing significance.

In Marseilles I stayed in the cheapest hotel I have ever known; in the boat the next day I shared a cabin with three Frenchmen going over to be *coopérants techniques* instead of doing their military service. I didn't quite puke. In the morning I looked down on the quayside at Algiers harbour and saw again the Arab dress and style of my childhood in Egypt and of my time in Baghdad, felt the warmth. It was very intriguing and faintly attractive. It meant nothing. I knew I was set to count the days. Tough stuff this love.

The days passed. She came to Algiers for a week, then went to Rome to see a friend, an Italian Baroness no less but I didn't mind. She could have gone to see the Pope or visited Mars for all I cared in comparison to the other side of the equation which that

171

she wasn't with me. I remember, during our week in the white city before she went to Rome, walking with her in the *Jardin d'essai*, shabbier now, I suppose, than it had been five years earlier when the French left. Gide calls it 'the most beautiful garden in Africa' but how would he know? Had he visited all the others? For myself I would have given it freely in exchange for the average cottage garden in my native Dorset in July. A day with Carmen in Gehenna. But it was of no significance. I still cannot see a picture of Algiers, or of the *Jardin d'essai*, without thinking of that afternoon when delinquent boys threw a stone at us as we walked among the neglected species and where we touched hands.

She came again for Christmas. I waited for her at *Dar-El-Beida, Maison Blanche*, the Algiers airport, in the cool sunshine of a North-African winter. She asked me if I was drunk, which I wasn't, as I kissed her. But the woolly mammoth that rose and shook itself in my insides when I was in her company was having a field day in there, tusks and all, and that sort of thing rather limits one's coherence. Once again I noticed in the taxi that I had partially consumed the end of a newspaper – *El Mujahidine*, The Freedom Fighter, organ of the ghastly corrupt government of the FLN. But I didn't mind.

My flat seemed very small and humble with Cuqui in it. But let's cut from cliché to chase *s'il vous plait*.

We wanted to spend Christmas in the Sahara and we set out on December 23rd, the last day of Carmen's life, with another couple, a young fellow-teacher from my language school called Michael Drake and his girl Françoise. I forgot to lock the door of the flat. We left the city easily enough that morning. We lunched when we had got over the hills south of Algiers, at a nice little

172

restaurant at Djelfa, where it begins to become deserty. I
drank some red wine, felt sleepy, gave the keys of the
car to Françoise to take us out into the Sahara; she was
uninsured for sure, perhaps licenceless, certainly
inexperienced. We drove for twenty or thirty miles. I
fell asleep on Cuqui's lap in the back seat. Then
Françoise panicked and drove into an oncoming lorry.
Françoise's man, Michael Drake, and Cuqui were
killed; Françoise survived with two black eyes; I had
my neck broken. Appropriately the Renault 4 was
entirely undamaged on one side and utterly crushed on
the other. So it goes.

3. COCKROACH

Love is by some distance too much for us, its
dimensions beyond our scope, as if nature is
exaggerating. But then we talk it even further up,
inciting ourselves to greater exaggeration. And then we
wonder why it defeats us.

When we are 'in-love' we feel too strongly for
comfort and we are inclined to say too much for sanity:
'I'll love you *forever*', 'You are *everything* to me'. Or
we resort to poetry: a thousand ships, ten-thousand
years before the Flood. Some of this discourse is funny,
some touching, but all of it is also the background music
to inevitable failure. And there we have the paradox:
there are many good *expressions* of love but not one
successful love affair. Perhaps the telling is better than
the loving, though that works best if you are a genius:
Marvell or Auden, say, Donne or Hardy, Petrarch or
Dante.

Love in this sense was allegedly invented by a
medieval kingling, William IX of Aquitaine, and
became fashionable, as *amour courtois*, among the

173

castle-dwelling small-time country-owners and relatively bad barons of southern France in the eleventh century. In a world where everyone had a target for their adoration and obedience – God, say, or the King, the Virgin Mary, the Abbot, the Head of the Knightly Order, your apprentice-Master, your patron saint, your schoolmaster, your husband – love, for men, had to be directed to the Domina, the lord's wife, the only lady at dinner with you, up there unavailable on the dais while you stewed analphabetically in the reek of the hall. So much so that some of the first love poems were to a 'Dominus' (*sic*) who was the 'Lord' of your love, though actually female. See Dennis de Rougemont's *Love in the Western World, passim,* again.

Pope Gregory X had set up the conditions for the massive, fruitful, disastrous overbid of love even before William of Aquitaine had got his lute out and set the troubadours going. Despairing of the behaviour of the knightly class – the princelings and their hangers-on - Gregory proposed that the old Roman knightly order, all arrogance and family pride and fighting, should be revived and remodelled according to Christian principles. It was one of the great moral reforms of the western world. Knights, now, were to be crusaders defending the Christian passage to Jerusalem, *preux chevaliers*, unselfish, preferably unmarried, protectors of women, semi-monastic, establishers of God's kingdom on earth (an aspiration seen as hopeless but worth a try), kind, polite, brave, good. This must have come as something of a shock to the bold bad persons who had enjoyed raping and pillaging across Europe since the fall of the Roman Empire but, astonishingly, it worked, in part at least, and as a result the chaos and brutality of the tenth-century gave way to something slightly better.

174

This would lead in time through Chretien de Troyes, Troilus, the Romance of the Rose and Malory to some of the best aspects of the Renaissance: to Sir Philip Sidney, to Don Quixote, to the idea of the Gentleman, to a (historically very rare) respect for women, to Jane Austen's Mr Knightley (note the name) to responsibility and courage, to Captain Oates, to some of the best people the planet has ever had in a ruling class, especially in the modest English version.

Anglo-Saxon poetry has no love, indeed almost no women in it at all, because it pre-dates this revolution and came into little contact with it before the language vanished. But in the later Middle Ages love became fashionable at the top levels of society, in royal and less-royal courts, and by the Renaissance it had begun to penetrate the ever-aspirant Middle Classes. There's a whole history here, recounted by Laurence Stone among others. If you try to think of an Elizabethan or a Romantic or a Victorian in love you find them only slightly differently in the grip of what is pretty obviously the same passion as your own. You may need to revise your thinking if you go back too far - to Ancient Greece say – I mean the *shock* of your first reading of the *Symposium*. But 'love' is alive and well in mainstream Western culture, and has been since Petrarch; there is a direct line from his sonnets to Iris Murdoch's *The Black Prince*. I think love may be under threat in the modern world (that was Lawrence Durrell's opinion at any rate) but in the mid-twentieth century it was still alive and very well, in its known modern fashion. Certainly it was fully operative when I was a young man in London in the 1960s. We read poems. We wrote them.

I don't know how love, the *coup de foudre*, happens – nobody does. Passion has some definitions

175

but no satisfactory explanations. It is like the Black Death (before they thought about the rats and the fleas), like a general outbreak of pyromania, like a revived mammoth, like the end of the universe. When you meet it you know it, but what the hell *is* it? And what's it *doing* there? It is worth pondering a little about the moment of innocence *before love*. That imaginary, later-to-be-looked-back-on-with-yearning moment when you *could have stopped*, when it *didn't have to happen*. In theory. But in reality when it comes it is always-already too late, as you soon realise; like death, love is always-already-there, like something out of Heidegger.

I loathe cockroaches. But anything *right* by any name smells right enough. My *Colombiana* could have been called Satan or Doreen and it would have sounded like Mozart to me. And, yes, I wrote poems. Teaching literary structures at university years later I had no difficulty in seeing the deep generic ties that bind all texts together. It's not just a matter of verbal echoes. All love poems say the same thing by slightly different means. But this 'same thing' is nothing concrete, nothing definitional or essential. Instead they are all trying to say what they *cannot say* because what they want to say is that what they have to say is beyond being said. It's like religion. It's like Derridean deconstruction. You can't say it.

And the detail of this, when it happened to me, you can supply yourselves. Carmen? She was beautiful, brilliant, funny. Of course. And very special, and all the other true nonsense. H.L Mencken defines love as 'the illusion that one woman is different from another' and from this distance I find I can't even say who Carmen actually was, even what she really looked like. She was a South-American millionairess who was drifting about

176

the world in the aftermath of those husbands. And that child. Doing what exactly? 'Being herself?' Surely not *waiting for me*? I realise now what a frightful farrago of essentialisms this love thing generates in us. 'I am really *me*, I am *myself*, when I am with you.' 'I *am* you.' 'You are the *world* to me.' Carmen was no more 'herself' than anyone else. In my flaming eyes *less* perhaps.

That was love. I blame William IX of Aquitaine, testosterone; also myself. Ask Proust.

4. CODA

I was flown from Laghouat to Algiers strapped to the floor of a medium-sized propeller aircraft in a sand storm. Driven to the air-strip in an open-backed pick-up truck I was left lying by the plane while assorted officials turfed several bona-fide fare-paying ladies out of their seats to fit me in. When an employee of *Air Algérie* saw me looking a bit dubious about this he said 'Never mind! There is another plane in a week!' Piers, to keep me amused, told me how he had spent the previous night in the only bed available in the oasis with both Françoise and Cousin Celia. This was a mixed experience that marked him for years afterwards but whose details remain obscure to me.

In the capital I was put into a clinic largely the province of the remaining French expatriates. Piers slept in the room with me and rushed out every morning returning at stated intervals in the day officially to see how I was but, as I was always the same, in fact to regale me with the latest adventures of our cousin Celia who, naturally, couldn't let a near-death in the family put her off the main business of her life which was... well, however you would define it, it involved clothes, men, expenditure and a great deal of show. Especially men.

The first morning in Algiers she had set out in a taxi for somewhere. Piers saw her off but the taxi suddenly screamed to a halt while he was still watching its departure. Celia's head appeared through the window. In piercing tones she shouted back 'Take the number of the cab. I don't want to be raped and murdered.' Piers hoped that the taxi-driver didn't speak much English. Mark you, the Algerian who took on Celia for the best of three rounds in almost any department would have had his work cut out. We never really worried about her in the family. Not like *that* anyway.

Whatever else happened in the clinic, not all of which I can remember, I ended up on a Swissair flight from Algiers via Zurich to Heathrow. This was in January and the plane was grounded at Zurich by a snowstorm where the passengers disembarked, the crew left, and the lights and heating were all switched off. Silence descended. I alone, strapped onto a stretcher fixed between two special seats and forbidden to move, remained in the plane enjoying the falling temperature and the almost total darkness. I spent some of my remaining time and energy wondering what the chances were of anyone, let alone someone recently almost left for dead in the Sahara, freezing to death in an undamaged stationary aircraft parked neatly at a Swiss airport.

Needless to say someone remembered me in due course and before actual hypothermia got going a couple of pairs of high heels were to be heard coming up the steps which were muffled in snow but still metallic enough to catch the unmistakable sound of stilettos. The heels were the signal, in those days before

178

Low-Cost travel, of the suavity of the airline and the desirability of its hostesses and, sure enough, two sweet Swiss girls entered the cabin, switched on the lights and spent half the night playing cards with me and telling stories. They were infinitely patient and went totally without sleep. Just for me. The kindness of women.

Eventually I was carried and manhandled all the way to the Middlesex Hospital in London. On my back, as I lay on various stretchers and beds in this process, I was wearing a large plaster shell lined with cotton wool from neck to waist which had been put on me in Laghouat and which I had been wearing for nearly three weeks. You can imagine the effect this had on the matron in charge of the orthopaedic ward: 'Off with that filthy thing!' she cried, 'Come on nurse!' In a trice I was as shell-less as a turtle about to be eaten and convinced that my spinal cord would snap at once. But the nurses had a good grip on me and all went well. One of them washed my back which was, I think, after so long a period of sand and sweat, the most simply delightful physical experience of my life.

This section has been a strange one, reflecting the strangeness of the whole Carmen episode. She seemed to have floated down from another sphere to me and she left to go back to that sphere. I led her to her death. So unusual, to use a calm word, was her presence in my life that I felt some very strange things about this horrible fact. For instance I was a good deal more concerned about Michael Drake's death than I was about Carmen's. I felt in his case that I had contributed to the ending of a life that would have been normal, fulfillable, familiar. In Françoise's case I felt that her luck suited her personality. But Carmen? I really did not feel her to be dead, not *dead*.

But to such thoughts there is no conclusion this side of the grave and I think I should be concerned here with a life. Bits of a life. It is time to turn to that again.

In the Middlesex in those days the orthopaedic wards had eight beds. Once I had been confined to mine, shell-less, I was forbidden to sit up and was limited to verbal communication with my fellow-patients. These turned out to be a genial crowd who all had something in common which I discovered on my first morning as I called out to each of them in order to introduce myself. 'Hello, I'm Lance. Who are you in the bed furthest to the right opposite me? What are *you* in here for?' That sort of thing.

The first chap had been in a lift whose cable had snapped. He had plunged down a few floors and broken some legs. The second chap had stepped into a lift that wasn't there. The doors had opened and he had reacted as one does with that slight movement forward, enough to propel him into the void. He had broken ribs and bits of his shoulders. The third bloke had been trying to retrieve something from the bottom of a lift well when the lift had come down on top of him crushing parts of him not, luckily, including his head.

So the inquiry went on, each fellow-patient presenting a lift story that became, as I went round the room, increasingly funny. The poor victims themselves found the whole thing amazing and amusing and there was much sniggering as each misfortune was recounted. But I felt there to be an increase in tension as we got to the last story and I noticed that everyone had fallen silent when I addressed this seventh cove. He seemed reluctant to begin his tale and I waited wondering. Eventually, with a sigh, he said in none too loud a voice 'I am a lift engineer.' This was greeted with laughter and hooting from the assembled lift-victims. Cries of

'You'll do a better job next time, won't you Jim?' and
'The biter bit!' rang through the air.

Besides that there was the incident of Carla. She
was a nurse at the Middlesex who took something of a
shine to me, as far as I could tell, and who went off on
leave after I had been in the hospital a week, leaving her
telephone number. During her absence I had
physiotherapy, sat up for the first time, then got out of
bed, then started walking and so on. Eventually I was
discharged without seeing Carla again. A few weeks
later, thinking that life had to go on, I phoned her and
made a date. This involved my picking her up at her flat
in Portman Place which I duly did in a taxi from
Knightsbridge. Her building had an intercom and she
told me to wait downstairs for her. She wouldn't be a
moment. And in due course I saw a light come on in the
stairwell and some feet appeared on the stairs. I could
see them through the glass door. Down they came,
followed by the legs and all the fixings - Carla in fact, to
the life. But oh! What was this? She seemed not to have
descended the last step yet here she was opening the
door! Horrors! She was a head taller than me.

Be advised, then, that it is very hard to tell how
tall someone is when they are lying down. Place no bets
on their size until they are standing up.

It was a grisly evening. Carla went through the
motions as I took her to Bentley's, strolled a little, got
back to Portman Place. I noticed her shuddering as she
glimpsed us in shop windows. Outside her flat she said
'You can come in for a coffee but I'm not sleeping with
you.' In all the long annals of the relations between the
sexes this seemed to me to be a low point, something
with nothing whatever to recommend it. Rather
ungallantly I still harbour a mild resentment at Carla
and her… vulgarity.

181

But see how heart, mind and body go on! Within weeks of the death of the first great love of my life, if that is how to describe it, there I am back on terra firma up to the hocks in sexual humiliation. In fact, in spite of the resentment, I am grateful for this experience. After the sublime must come the ridiculous.

CHAPTER 7 LONDON 1960s and 1970s

1. DEATH

Less than seven years after the night near Oswestry when I saw an apparition of my father (see 'Ghost' in the 'Prep' section above) my mother died of cancer. In her last months and weeks of life she lived with her sister in Knightsbridge not far from the Spiritualist Association headquarters in Belgrave Square and, perhaps because of this, was visited by a fairly well-known healer from the Association named Gordon Turner who comforted her greatly. When we sat round my mother's bed in a circle holding hands with her it gave her some relief, but the relief was much greater when Gordon was part of the circle. Then she felt, as we all felt, a tingle of electricity running though our palms and fingers for as long as he was in contact with us, a tingle that stopped when he let go. Came the day that she died he was luckily present. He stayed focussing on her until she was definitely dead and there was a silence. This was broken rather unexpectedly by Gordon, who was by now looking at the ceiling of the room. He said to my aunt with great clarity 'You never told me that Diana had red hair!' Now my mother Diana was dark-haired and, indeed, by the time she died, was going grey; I myself have no memory that she had red hair. But my aunt, who was four years older than her sister, immediately confirmed that as a girl and young woman my mother had indeed had very dark red hair; so she asked Gordon how he knew. He at once replied that he had seen a young man come down into the room and take Diana (not her corpse of course, but her 'astral body' to pick up the term used in Spiritualist circles) by the hand and lead her up and away. This astral Diana, who had emerged from my mother's dead body, was young-looking and red-headed.

In other words my mother, on dying, assumed, at least in the view of the psychic healer who was 'gifted' to see such things, the appearance she had had in her twenties. Why, you may ask, should we believe the healer? Aren't they notoriously frauds? Couldn't he have seen a picture of my mother as a young woman? Well, I could go into great detail, but briefly: there was no picture of her in my aunt's flat and Gordon Turner, anyway, had only recently been introduced there. Plus I don't think there ever was a colour photograph of my mother *anywhere*. My aunt swore that she had never mentioned my mother's hair-colour to him – and indeed she had never mentioned it to me either, though I was of course in a much closer relationship to her than a newly-met healer. It was a fact I didn't know myself.

So one has to pause for thought. Gordon Turner was a good healer with many inexplicable cures to his name. He refused any payment for his treatments; he died a few years after the incident with my mother at the age of fifty-six following a heart-attack partly brought on by overwork because he tried never to refuse to see a patient. What on earth would he be doing making up or pretending to see things in the death-room of my poor mother? Human nature is strange and people do strange things, and if this were the only story of its type it would have to be dismissed as an inexplicable anomaly or an odd fraud, but, as we tend eventually to see, if we are open-minded enough and as patterns start to emerge and evidence mounts, explanations based on fraud or

184

fantasy seem a little thin. Gordon, anyway, was no fraud.[14]

A footnote: my mother managed to die at home, in the flat in Knightsbridge, where Arnie looked after her in the most devoted manner. Mutti had also managed to have her children at home. In the intervening years a strong contrary current set in and, in the days before 'natural' childbirth, the doctors managed to medicalise birth and death to an extraordinary degree, but she mercifully escaped all that. Unless there are very special reasons it is nicest I think to have babies born in their parents' houses and not in the horrible glaring antiseptic atmosphere of a harassed hospital. I am also certain that dying at home is the best thing for the soul. When our friend Margaret Greive, an expatriate neighbour in France, died in 2013 I was impressed by the ease with which she was allowed to do so at home. The nurses and doctors visited her and made sure that she had a good supply of morphine but she faded peacefully away in her own bed surrounded by her own family in a manner that came to seem almost inviting.

---

[14] Another astral body episode from this same period, the 60s: a friend of mine took a flat in London with a chum. In the way of these flat-shares among the young they slept in the same room. On the second night my friend saw his chum rise from his bed surrounded by a blue flickering light and walk about the flat before eventually returning to bed. The blue light was odd enough but worse was the fact that the chum *also* remained in bed throughout his wanderings. My friend could see him clearly still in bed sleeping soundly. This was repeated on the next night which was too much for my friend who packed up and left the next day at great personal expense and inconvenience.

2. GHOSTS

My father when he appeared to me as an Apparition of the Living[15] was younger than he should have been, the age in fact that those people regressed to the Bardo Plane often claim to be. Neither he nor I knew then that, if he was in some sense temporarily 'on the other side', he was 'supposed' to be younger; indeed modern Past-Life regressions had not even been attempted when the incident happened. Then my mother seemed to appear the same way (see above) that is, younger than she should have been, immediately after her death in 1963, at a time when again I had read nothing of the Bardo Plane or Spiritualist theory and neither had my aunt.

Of course, this might mean very little. But when we ask what has happened in cases like these the small coincidences of detail, the apparent emergence of a pattern, begin to make one wonder if one can simply go back to saying that, sorry, *nothing* has happened, nothing abnormal at any rate; nor does it seem adequate simply to assume that there is a normal scientific explanation available even if we can't quite see it yet (this is known as Promissory Materialism.) If we take that line we are like people confronted with a mystery who have no explanation of their own and who, when offered an explanation that they do not like but that at least shows some promising regularities, stick doggedly to their own absence-of-explanation in the hope that something will turn up to enable them to fit the problem into their usual mode of thinking. There is only one way of going here: taking a few steps further down the

---

[15] Again, see 'Ghost' in the 'Prep' section above.

promising-but-unpalatable road is surely the *scientific* way to proceed.[16]

If one comes at the two stories I have told from the open-minded position (that is, we assume that they are not hoaxes or lies) my parents' 'wrong' ages mean that there is something odd going on that science needs to explain. But it can't. So then it seems sensible to allow a little light to be let in from a position that might have to be called paranormal or 'non-linear' and see whether anything fits a bit better. We don't know what these 'spiritual' positions might really be based on (although I think it is only fair to point out that we don't know what a 'natural explanation' of these events would ultimately come to either) but where there is regularity there just might be meaning. Once is happenstance, twice coincidence, but three times? It isn't much, but it just might be something. Regularities, after all, are the very life-blood of, oh yes, science itself.

Here is David Fontana, one of the best-informed investigators and theorists of the field of afterlife evidence. He is speaking of the 'astral body' which, he says,

> is said to resemble the physical body in appearance but to be free from its imperfections, and to be even more susceptible to our thought processes than is the physical body when we are on earth – thus it may in due course come

---

[16] For those interested: the first modern account of past-life regressions seems to have been published, coincidentally, in 1956, the year in which I was ten and saw my father's younger self. It was Morey Bernstein's *The Search for Bridey Murphy*, an account of the regression of a young woman who claimed with some evidence to support her that she was the reincarnation of an Irish woman born in 1798. The next important books in the area date from the 1960s and 1970s.

increasingly to resemble the individual's ideal image of him or herself.... communications through mediums... suggest... that in appearance people in the next world, whether they die young or old, either go forward to a time or revert to a time – usually in the early twenties – when they look their best.[17]

Fontana is summarising hundreds of years of spiritual tradition but he is also, more to our point, summarising his enormous reading in the literature of modern investigation into the afterlife through mediums, Near-Death Experiences and so on. If I had seen my father looking his correct age that night or if my mother had been described as looking her actual age at death my small stories would thus be less interesting. As it is, they happen to coincide exactly with what anyone knowledgeable in the field would expect – my parents appeared 'free of... imperfections', 'looking their best' and perhaps as the 'ideal image' they might have held of themselves in their 'early twenties' or a little later. Fontana suggests we consider the 'astral body' as something like the 'body' we seem to have in our dreams: real enough even if not 'physical'. I myself am follically challenged (i.e. bald) but in my dreams I have a good head of black hair, as I did when I was twenty. However, *other* people appear in my dreams *as they are now* (or randomly modified according to the oddity of dream processing) while I appear as a somewhat idealised image of myself. So if I had been *dreaming* my father, or if Gordon Turner had been dreaming my mother, that is if he or I had been dreaming *other*

---

[17] David Fontana, *Is There an Afterlife? A Comprehensive Overview of the Evidence.* O Books, 2005

people, it would be a considerable coincidence for them both to appear at their peak of physical perfection.

One still feels uncomfortable thinking these things through. If they can't be accounted for by science they must belong 'elsewhere', in another dimension of explanation, perhaps of reality. But isn't it quite simple to make that awkwardness go away? The apparition of my father was his 'ghost', seen by me while both my father and I were in 'this' world; the ghost was also in 'this' world. I don't think parsimony allows us to multiply worlds irresponsibly. It looks a great deal more likely that my father's 'spirit', operating in a field usually closed to our senses, made a brief appearance in my life not from 'another place' (though that expression is acceptable as a metaphor) but as part of an unexplained dimension of *this* world.

3. SERPENTINE

It must have been June 1968 and the night was hot. Wanting to entertain ourselves we wandered about Knightsbridge looking for a jolly. My brother Piers and I, together with my pal Johnny, he of the Puking fame, had a couple of girls in tow whose names, I fear, I am unable to recall, but these young ladies were jollies too in their own anonymous right. We came after a while to Hyde Park and its railings, pulled down by the Chartist demonstrators in 1848 in the closest England has ever come, allegedly, to a revolution. I think the Chartists pulled them down after their attempt to pull down the Houses of Parliament had been frustrated by a thin blue line of peelers.

By 1968 at any rate they had been restored and stood as a barrier to our further progress northwards. In those days the gates to the Royal Parks of London were

189

closed at dusk or thereabouts in an attempt, as we will see, to reduce the intense activity of the lower end of the capital's sex-market. So with gates closed it was go over the railings or go home, as it seemed to us. The spirit that had built the Empire was still faintly discernable in our veins, along I suppose with a liberal quantity of mixed alcoholic refreshments, and the challenge once posed there was only one possible outcome. Over we went.

Once in the park we seemed to have entered a sort of fairyland. No traffic, no people, no bicycles, just the lights and the hum of Knightsbridge and Park Lane in the distance. We wandered around for a time in a species of enchantment until we found ourselves confronted by that cold slice of dark water The Serpentine. This natural obstacle immediately stimulated my imagination and I heard myself proclaiming 'We must take a boat! Rowing or nothing.' Rowing it was. At first we were defeated by the fact that the considerable number of rowboats on the Serpentine had been cunningly moored out in the middle of the lake where we couldn't get at them. But the British had climbed Everest for the first time and crossed the Antarctic for the first time only a few years before and we decided not to be defeated – such decisions being a pretty good way of *not* being defeated as it happens.

Beside the water, never before noticed by me, stood a boathouse, one of those Victorian buildings with one end in the water and other on dry land. With the immense cunning that alcohol often seems to give me I led the boys in the group on a traverse out along the side of the building, clinging to the low tiled roof and giggling. Once we had made it beyond land and were above mere water we redoubled our courage and went on to the end, rounding the corner and climbing in over the water-gate. Then we set about trying to open the gate from the inside, which proved impossible, and subsequently attempting to sink the rowboat that was inside the boathouse in order to get it out under the water-gate. Johnny, with surprising coherence, managed to persuade us that the method needed for this was not by pressing down equally on each side of the wretched craft. 'No no' he cried, 'One side only!' We all went round to one side and pushed down and, behold, the boat sank easily enough and we could push it out below the wooden paling of the gates. We dragged it round to land and emptied it of water with a certain amount of cursing. The girls were then invited aboard and we set out for the main flotilla fifty yards out.

As we arrived at the main body of boats several things happened. First Piers took off his trousers with something of the air of Charles I moving his beard to one side in order that it not be chopped off with his head ('*It* has not offended' Charles said). Then Johnny declared 'There are a hundred boats!' which sounded like a challenge. Then I leapt from our damp craft to the relative comfort of the leading boat. The others scrambled after me and we got the oars into the rowlocks and were off in a trice, if such an expression could possibly apply to five drunken youngsters heaving gamely at a couple of low-grade oars and attempting to tow a hundred rowboats at once. Our progress was imperceptible.

Slowly and with much giggling we drifted and splashed towards the further shore to some extent and, after a few more heaves, paused to consider our position. But at this point lights flashed and voices were raised in wrath from the direction of the boathouse whence we had come with such effort. 'Come back!' they cried, but we were too cunning for that. Oh yes, with positively naval presence of mind we cast off the painter which had attached us to all the other craft and, making better headway now, bore down with excited shrieks on the further shore.

Alas. On the further shore, more cunningly positioned than we could have imagined possible, was a solitary peeler. As we sprang onto the quayside tarmac he emerged from the trees with a soft 'Evening all' and I whooped with relief, saying to my companions in one of those bursts of inspiration that only substantial drink can give one, 'If we run in different directions he'll only catch one of us.' We began to scatter, but as we did so the policeman gave a little shake of his left arm, to which a chain was attached. At the other end of the chain was an unexpected Alsatian who said 'Grrrr' very loudly. 'So', said the plod, 'would you mind accompanying me to the police station?' And, d'you know, we didn't mind at all.

Now perception is all. In a hundred visits to Hyde Park it had never occurred to me that there was a police-shop there; but so it was, and within five minutes we were inside it. We blinked in the light and smiled ingratiatingly. 'Well now' said the chief rozzer, 'what have we here?' I really do think the police watch too many cop shows on television. We stood before him in various poses of contrition and indignation. To our surprise he went on almost affectionately: 'Look, you aren't in much luck lads, and I'm very sorry about this but I'm going to have to take this seriously. You are going to be charged with theft.' 'Theft?' Piers asked. 'Yes' said the chief, 'theft of a rowboat.' 'Just one?' I asked a touch naively. 'Oh yes' said his blueness, 'yes, we can say it was only one, but even then I'll have to charge you.' 'But', I said, sobering slightly, 'but you *can't* steal the boats on the Serpentine. I mean, how would you do it? Where would you take them?' 'Aha' said Roz, back on his script, 'that's not the point.'

Apparently the point was that new legislation had just been brought out to prevent car thieves and joy-riders from claiming that they had not 'permanently intended to deprive' the owners of stolen cars or bikes of their property. You know, Nosher and Mincer nick some wheels and go for a burn-up or use it for a robbery. When they are caught and prosecuted the theft of the car should count against them; but apparently wizard lawyers had begun pointing out that, as Nosh and Mince were only taking the car for a brief robbery or a joy-ride, they could not be permanently intending to deprive the owner of it, so it wasn't real stealing. The law had now been amended so that any taking and driving away of any vehicular conveyance would be treated as out-and-out theft regardless of the time-scale involved. All police stations had been informed and no exceptions were to be made as everyone got used to the new law.

'So we'll be charging you with theft then', he said. I was appalled. Thoughts of Arnie and Dick, not to mention a criminal record, flashed across my brain. But the fuzz was at its softest that night and we began to strike up a warmer relationship with them as the paperwork went on. One was called Ginger, another Fred if memory can stretch back that far. They asked us what we were up to in the Park; Piers said that we were celebrating the Queen's Official Birthday and everyone slowly realised that it *was* June 2nd. They offered us bail, and when it turned out that we only had five pounds between us they let us off that and had us sign a form that said that we would turn up at court as instructed *as if* we had posted bail. They proposed the following Monday morning. I was booked in to have my hair cut at Harrods that day so I suggested Tuesday, which they at once accepted.

With many expressions of goodwill and much schoolboy banter they escorted us to a park gate and bid us farewell for the time. Their narratives as we crossed the grassy expanses before saying goodbye were a response to my questions, asked in accordance with my usual softening strategy, and they concerned the daily life and work of the Park Copper. 'Well', said Fred, 'we spend most of our time trying to get on top of the Hands-Across-the-Sea merchants.' 'And who are they Fred?' 'Well' he said again, 'there are men who, er, meet other men in the park and hide out inside here after gate-closing time and then have, er, parties... if you see what I mean.' In those days homosexual activity was not what it has since become – a sentimental theme of liberation and true love among the *bien-pensant* liberal contingent ('Isn't it *sweet* that Elton John has married his partner?') - indeed it was illegal in all its forms but most especially in any public manifestation. 'They get into a ring around one of the big oaks' pursued Fred and then they er...' 'We call it Hands Across the Sea' said Ginger. '*You* know...'

The next day we decided that the situation we were in, not to mention our forthcoming indictment, were too good not to exploit socially. The five of us agreed that on the Tuesday in question at 8am we would meet for breakfast at the Cadogan Hotel in Pont Street before proceeding to the place of justice, Marlborough Street Magistrates Court in Soho as it turned out, 'in memory of Oscar Wilde' as Johnny put it. We met, we breakfasted, Piers paid as usual (what *was* it about my twenties?) We then took a taxi and announced our destination, slightly to the surprise of the cabbie, and drove into Soho. We got out of the cab, Piers paid, and

194

we went into Marlborough Street Mags. Once we had announced ourselves we were at once escorted into a species of very large cell, complete with bars, and *locked in*. I remonstrated with the gaoler: 'We came in a *taxi!*' I said. 'If we had wanted to abscond we could just have *not come...* in a taxi...' I felt I was stressing the taxi too much and the others told me to shut up.

We had dressed for the occasion and I now began to wonder about the wisdom of this. I had given a couple of my Cambridge ties to Piers and Johnny, a Leander and a Hawks Club to which neither of them was entitled, and we were in smart suits; the girls were in summer dresses and hats. Looking about we found that we were in the company of an assorted selection of pickpockets, traders-without-a-licence and ladies of the night, none of them at their sartorial best; and if we were looking at them you may be quite sure that they were definitely looking at us. What on earth could such a selection of posh-sounding young idiots be doing *here*? Doubtless they were further puzzled by the gay cries of 'Hi there!' from the uniformed Freds and Gingers who now appeared and in their turn looked at us through the bars.

After a space we were summoned to appear before the magistrate whose name, we had discovered, was Mr Justice St John Harmsworth. This Christian name naturally encouraged me and he turned out to be a bit of a St John indeed; wearing half-moon spectacles and an old school tie and with an accent like Terry Thomas playing a dastardly squire he was just the ticket for us. He listened to the evidence and we pleaded Terribly Guilty; Ginger had put on his official mask to give his version of events and I wondered for a moment if this might All Go Wrong. But St John was not to be trifled with. 'What do you have to say for yourselves?"

he growled benignly at us. Piers trotted out his ex-post-facto *canard* about the Queen's birthday; Johnny said that he had only thought it all a bit of fun. Harmsworth smiled and remarked that he thought it probably had been. There was a pause.

Then came the decision of this great and understanding man. 'I'm not inclined to take this matter too seriously' he said; 'young people enjoying themselves. But you have pleaded guilty and so I can't Acquit you. Instead I'm giving you an Absolute Discharge.' This sounded definitely good enough and we began to smile and thank him, perhaps a little too effusively, and there was a ripple of low-toned complaint from the public gallery of which the gist was summarised by the protector of some whore or costermonger: his acid tones cut through the muttering: 'Bloody toffs!' he huskily said, 'They always get off.' Immediately St John straightened up a bit and barked 'But two guineas costs!' This silenced the public gallery and sobered us a touch. Seeing our slight dismay the man of justice relented a little and, slumping back to his normal slouch, softened the blow with 'The boys only.'

So it was that we were out among the clerks and coppers after only a few minutes in court and I was reaching for my Coutts cheque book (sign of wealth and distinction in those days) wondering, less wealthily and distinguishedly than I should have done, whether my overdraft would stand six guineas. Then Piers paid.

'That wasn't too bad was it?' bellowed Ginger or Fred as we emerged into the Soho street. 'Where are you going now?' Before we could answer we were hailed by a pack of pals (Cambridge people; my future wife; belated partygoers) and as we were carried off bodily across the road and into the Marlborough pub I called back to our police friends 'We're going for a drink!' Thus the party began. Legal victory, however trivial and hedged about with costs, is always exhilarating and there was much shouting and throwing down of pints and wines and gins and then it was lunchtime but we just went on, unheeding as far as mere food was concerned in our youth and exuberance. After a while four large policemen came in, rather quietening the pub for a while until we realised that they were *our* policemen who had come to celebrate with us. 'Whoopee!' I remember yelling as, overdraft or no overdraft, I bought them all drinks. It was one of the best, least self-conscious parties I have ever been to. Spontaneous, created *ex nihilo* by our triumphant encounter with a benevolent justice system and with just the right balance of friends and strangers, it flashed past joyfully.

Came, therefore, the dread hour of 2.30pm when the pub had to shut for the afternoon (this was London; in the provinces it would have arrived at 2pm) and I saddened. What a pity! If only these licensing laws.... But, well... if it had to be... I stuck out a hand to Fred to say goodbye, certain that this was the end of the only party I had ever really enjoyed, to find my hand ignored. 'Oh no squire!' said Fred as he shouldered his way to the bar. From his jacket he produced his police badge and waved it at the barman. I heard him bellow 'This is a police investigation! You must keep the bar open!' And so, somehow, though I cannot remember paying for any of the many drinks that followed, we got through the long sunny afternoon until it was time, 5.30pm (6pm in the provinces), for the pub to open again when, against the normal tides of a drinker's life, we staggered out blinking into the late afternoon.

There was a coda to this event. One night a few weeks after the Great Boat-theft Trial, in Essex where

197

he was working on some benighted local rag, Johnny
gave a party in his flat. He must have mentioned this as
a prospective fact to our new friends in blue from Hyde
Park because when the party was raided by a couple of
large cops (Johnny had seen the blue light flashing on
their car outside and had thought 'Oh no, I can't
remember where I've hidden the hashish') they turned
out to be Ginger and Fred. 'Just thought we'd pop in
and see how you were getting on' they said, and when
offered drinks 'Don't mind if I do.'

Those were the days before the drink-driving
laws; also before seat-belts and overall speed-limits. We
have won some things and lost some things, like all
societies at all times, and perhaps these developments
are in the end improvements; but I regret
unambiguously the passing of the Freds, the Gingers,
the St John Harmsworths, the drinks before driving.

4. FUNERAL

When Uncle Dick died in the early 1970s Arnie moved
heaven, earth and parts of the Admiralty to get him a
Burial at Sea. As it happens such things are no longer
allowed, but the First Sea Lord, or some other old pal of
Dick's, found out that the Navy didn't have a film of
such a thing and, at Arnie's behest, he used that as an
excuse to fulfil Dick's last wish.

So it was that at 5am on a summer's morning the
family assembled at Portsmouth where a minesweeper
took us out into the grey Channel, turned off its engines
and allowed the last-ever official British Naval Burial at
Sea to take place. It was quite extraordinary.

As guests of the Navy we were of course treated
very well, the dozen of us who were there, all family
except for the faithful Brooks (our gardener from Silton,

198

not Johnny) who stood apart looking sad. Respect was in the air; even the ship we were in was respected: other vessels that passed us did things with their flags in recognition of the fact that our own flags signaled a deceased warrior aboard. A submarine, nosing into the dockyard, lined up half-a-dozen Able Seamen along its shiny spine and we watched them salute.

Out in the chilly Channel this courtesy extended into the wardroom, the officers' mess of a ship. There we were offered coffee and condolences. When the engines stopped we went out on deck and the religious ceremony took place, just the right length. Then, as a Marine bugler blew the Last Post, the lead-weighted coffin, draped in the Union flag, was slid decorously over the side and, in a cloud of bubbles, Uncle Dick's mortal remains were sent down to sleep among the fishes. Wreaths were thrown onto the water and we realized how cold it was. Back in the wardroom we were offered a choice: tea or coffee?

'Ah' said my brother, 'Is there any brandy?' Well, the person who asked this was either Piers who, now that Uncle Dick was no more, was the member of the family most orientated towards alcoholic refreshments, or my cousin Celia who held, and had held for nearly half a century, the family record for impertinence, bad behaviour and getting divorced. The young officer detailed off to look after us paused for a moment, his face a blank, and then, the wonderful manners of the Senior Service coming to his aid, he said 'Certainly. Anybody else?' A chorus of 'Well, er, I wouldn't mind...' rang round the neat little cabin from all of us with the exception of the teetotal Arnie who was heard to say 'Really!'

I looked at my watch, expecting to see a normal after-funeral time of say midday or 2pm, and had to

shake it when it seemed to say 8.45 am. It was 8.45!
Brandy for breakfast! We were upset and cold and
empty; naval measures are large; and as a result within
five minutes there were several plastered persons sitting
about the wardroom shouting about things at short
distance. The transition was astonishingly rapid. Piers at
once became genially explanatory, I incessantly
facetious. You would have thought it was a wedding
breakfast. In fact it reminded me of my mother's funeral
in London ten years earlier when I had adopted the role
of joker in what on reflection may not have been an
appropriate fashion.

Family occasions have been rare in my life – the
family is small, scattered and not altogether in harmony.
But in the early 1970s there were several of them: my
own first wedding, Piers's wedding to 'Tricia, my niece
Emma's christening, Uncle Dick's funeral, each
quainter than the last, each a thing that was different.

My own (first) wedding was at a rather pretty
church in Berkshire. The only events of note, related to
me by one of my ushers months later, concerned my
cousin Celia. She was first caught by the assembled
guests urinating behind a grave whose stone was not
adequate for the concealment she thought she was
enjoying. Then during the reception she made a loud bid
for the large hat a friend of mine was wearing and
wouldn't stop bargaining for it until she had it not only
in her hand but on her head. I seem to remember that the
price was some sum then astonishing: fifty pounds I
think.

Piers's wedding and Emma's christening took
place at the same church on the same day, in Silton
church in fact where a liberal vicar (but do Anglican
vicars have much choice these days?) permitted the
fruits of fornication to be received into the bosom of

200

God's church with only the decorous interval of a nice lunch between the two ceremonies; it was as if little Emma had been conceived with the starter, born with the main course and had reached six months by the time pudding was served, ready to be Christianised at the point at which we should have been having coffee. It was all entirely delightful; the Anglican Church and the Dorset countryside at their best.

During the lunch, at rather a nice pub on the A30, I sat opposite Cousin Celia, she of the bad behaviour. I made my usual small talk (here's the logic of it: Q: 'What do people want to talk about?' A: 'Themselves'. Solution: Ask People About Themselves. This was not a taxing strategy in the case of Celia.) All seemed quite well as she chatted on until, a few wines in, she seemed to be developing an Existential Question and I started to pay more genuine attention. 'I have a problem Lance' she announced with more than usual emphasis. 'Ah, tell me' I replied. Celia was only not as overdressed as she usually was because this was a fairly formal wedding. During lunch she continued to wear a considerable hat, perhaps her purchase from the former occasion. 'Tell me about it Cessie' I said.

'Well,' she smiled as coyly as it was possible for a so ultra-self-confident person, 'What should I do now? I mean in my life?' 'Ah! Well… what would you *like* to do O Coz?' I asked, following my strategy. 'What do you fancy?' 'Oh it's not that' said Celia, 'but you know, when one is beautiful, intelligent and rich what is there left to do?'

I have since then been very clear about problems: some are worse than others. You might even think that there are some people who have it too good or, at least, have misunderstood something pretty important.

Celia, if I may add another funeral to this, solved one widely-known problem in an original way. This is the problem of Where to Scatter the Ashes? Where to dump the residual mortal coils of Grandpa, Aunt Jemima, the dog, whoever. You know the way it goes: it seems as if it's going to be easy, but in truth you need four things that are not easy to assemble in one place at one time: dignity, relevance, open country and a gentle wind.

This episode occurred after the death of Arnie in about 2001 when matters consequent on her demise were enlived by Celia at her best. Arnie had been living in a convent-cum-hospice-cum-old-folks-home-for-Catholic-clergy somewhere in the East Midlands wherever that is. The denizens of this establishment included a centenarian retired Canon who was engaged to perform Arnie's funeral service in the chapel attached to the premises. At the start of the service Celia made An Entrance. She was dressed in an outfit which gave her the appearance of a Moroccan whore of the more expensive variety and provoked a sharp intake of breath from the assembled nuns and family mourners. The Canon looked as if he had been shot, although it may have been a case of love at first sight because, *en route* to the crematorium in the undertaker's limo, the Canon, carrying his ton lightly, pressed upon the cousin a suit which can only be described as amorous. This however was not the end of it.

Cremation produces ashes which the local body-burners make available for collection, supplying a tasteful canister for the purpose. Celia collected this object, whereupon it was proposed that Arnie's ashes be scattered over the top field at Silton, the old Glebe. Celia, who never went to any church at all, declined to take part on the interesting basis that the field was not consecrated ground, but sent the canister by DHL, *in loco parentis* one might say, to the assembled family in Dorset. The Awful Truth, however, was that prior to despatch she had actually scattered her mother's ashes over the garden of her rented cottage in Northamptonshire (equally unconsecrated one should imagine) and refilled the canister with bonfire ash. Why? Goodness knows.

The occasion at Silton was a great success. The burnt offerings from Celia's redundant vegetation were distributed over the ancestral sward amidst respectful murmurings as to how moving it all was, and nobody was the wiser - except, that is, my brother Piers who was privy to the Awful Truth and in consequence suffered moral agonies (which he later likened to having a severe attack of wind when in company - you just can't let it out), especially when it was his turn to do the scattering.

People cried a bit. Which just goes to show that reality is what you believe it to be.

5. REALERS

When I was working in the City, or rather 'working', in the old Ottoman Bank in Abchurch Lane a pal whom I met there, a sex-maniac and teetotaller rejoicing in the name of Jeremy Baer who subsequently became Director of Ship Finance at Lloyds Bank, mentioned that he played tennis. The twinkle in his eye should have informed me that he didn't mean what other people mean by that word but rather Real Tennis, aka Court Tennis, *le jeu de paume*, the game of kings. Our first trip out to Hampton Court was a surprise and a delight and I fell in love with the game forthwith. It is truly called *tennis* while the game played at Wimbledon is a late-nineteenth-century invention for girls properly called *lawn-tennis*. In the small world of the older game we distinguish between these versions by referring to them as *lawners* and *realers*.

I got a lot of pleasure out of the strange complexities of the old game as played by medieval monks, Henry VIII, Shakespeare (have another look at the tennis-ball scene in *Henry V* and see if you can understand it) and nineteenth-century aristocrats. I played all over England and had a hand in keeping alive the two courts in Scotland, one at Troon and the other at Falkland Palace, without becoming as absorbed in it as some people do who then feel they have to travel on a planetary level to play on *all the real tennis courts in the world*. This is a disease that some people catch badly and they end up flying to Tasmania to play on the Hobart court just because it's there. Admittedly there are only nine courts in the USA, four in Australia, four in France and twenty or so in the UK.

Anyway, Jeremy and I drove into Hampton Court Palace, said 'Tennis' to the guard on duty and parked by the Grace-and-Favour residences before strolling through the garden to the court. There the professional Les Keeble, one of the last of the old school, greeted us with deference and that sort of ubiquitous facetiousness inseparable from the status of NCO, Warrant Officer, Flight Sergeant, RSM, that sort of chap. To show the gentlemen how the tennis-racket was to be held in preparation for the stroke, for instance, he would cry: 'Keep it cocked up Sir, and you won't make a cock-up of it.'

The high point of my experience of this sort of salt-of-the-earth fellow came at another air-orientated venue, RAF Cranwell the flight-training establishment for pilots. Visiting the place on behalf of the Military

204

Education Committee (I was the only person at Stirling University prepared to show any interest in things military and so got appointed to the national committee *nem con*) we were given a tour. We were shown round the classrooms, flight simulators and other places of aviation instruction and came at length to a leadership exercise going on in a large hangar. Teams of three or four young men were being set tasks such as re-assembling large pieces of broken equipment, moving heavy beams with limited mechanical means and constructing towers that didn't fall over. Coming to the zone where a team was supposed to get a jeep across an imitation river with two ropes and a baulk of timber I asked the Flight Sergeant who was in charge of us what the secret of success in this case was. 'This one' he said in that special voice such people have, 'This one is impossible Sir.'

Les Keeble, then, also ex-RAF Flight-Sergeant, coached me through the basics; Jeremy and I played. Slowly, then and on many subsequent visits, I began to learn the difficult art of realers. It took about twenty years in fact, but those early days, going to Hampton before Security had ruined everything, playing on a court redolent, as they say, of Tudor history, having a bath, there being no showers, watching the bath being drawn by Les ('Now I want no Man-Fridaying tonight Sir'), going to the old pub outside the gates (orange juice for Jeremy), discussing the game (me) and women (him) was an almost perfect defeat of the modern world. Man-Fridaying, incidentally, was Les's term for gentlemen who would insist on walking around the changing-room before drying their feet. Geddit?

Within a decade Les had retired and been replaced by someone who could actually play realers rather well, the World Champion indeed, one Chris Ronaldson who later became the pro at Troon. He was a gung-ho

205

Australian of no great age, and there were no 'Sirs' and drawn baths with him. Australia is of course the country, according to an English friend who went there for a spell, where if you tell a *garagiste* that you car has broken down he is quite likely to reply 'Well why don't you fix it mate?' It came as a shock but no surprise, if that makes sense, when I learnt that Chris had a wife and that *she* played realers, even herself claiming to be champion. Of course, since then women have taken to playing rather a lot. I don't think Les would quite have understood.

As time went on, getting into Hampton became impossible, Security keeping the gates firmly shut; parking first became *paying* and was then banned altogether. Getting through to the court was an obstacle race and the fees for membership rose steeply in real terms (no pun.) Playing at Lord's meant booking a fortnight ahead and being a member of the MCC (not either easy or cheap). Membership at Queen's Club in Kensington rose to £7,000 a year. So much for democratisation.

But it has been fun. My most recent games have been at the, ahem, multicultural university of Middlesex (aka Hendon Poly) where an enthusiastic millionaire forced a realers court on the powers that ran the university by dint of throwing money at them. These powers now, as I write, are once again trying to get the court and its appurtenances changed into lecture rooms. No soul; no courage.

I haven't played with Jeremy for years, certainly not since he emigrated to the Philippines, sex centre of south-east Asia, after Thailand I suppose. 'You know Lance, you can get a blow-job there during the lunch-hour. Or for a bit extra a 'BJ on the rocks.' 'Golly. What's that?' 'One where the girl has ice in her mouth.' 'Ah.' My last games at Middlesex were with David Ogilvy, a lovely man

206

soon to become the Fourteenth Earl of Somewhere and a friend of the Queen, but unlike me, not a snob at all.

CHAPTER 8. BRAZIL 1969 - 1970

1. CLEONICE

Arriving in Maceio in the Northeast of Brazil in 1969 was like stepping into a warm cheerful version of the world as it used to be. Quite exactly where and when it had been like that escapes me, but there was something unfinished or unplanned about the town and the country around it that reminded me of some imagined past somewhere else. I say 'country' although the farming was patchy and the sugar-cane estates by no means the whole story. As a British expatriate who had been there for twenty years said to me, in his already-brazilianised English, 'The interior here hasn't been *moulded* by man; it's in a more primitive state, no?' Indeed.

Tim Plumptre, my fellow trainee at the Bank, had been panting for company for several months before I got there and, indeed, after we were moved on to other branches the Bank decided not to send further trainees to Maceio as it was 'too tough.' But we had a very nice time. Had Tim not been there it might have been difficult, but, *gracias a Deus*, he was.

We lived in a flat over the Bank and, like all people above the *favela* level in Brazil, we had a maid to help us out. She was large, extremely dark and rather pretty, also as sentimental as a Victorian schoolgirl and as strong as an ox. Her name, obscurely and romantically enough, was Cleonice, in four syllables.

Cleonice cleaned the flat and washed our clothes; she also went shopping for us and cooked an evening meal. After serving it she disappeared to some dark shanty rendered tolerable by the warmth and neighbourliness of the place. But with her background in the black culture of the *nordeste* she had certain lacunae in her knowledge of more European social niceties and a mixture of courage and fear that were different from ours. As well as Herculean strength.

Our first surprise with this lovely lady came when we had, early in our time together in Maceio, a new fridge delivered. Enough of the American style of doing things had penetrated Brazil for this to be one of those monsters that dominate the kitchen and produce ice from a marsupial pouch in their middles. The bank had paid for it. Gazing upon it on the morning it was delivered, indeed standing beside it at the bottom of the steep flight of external concrete stairs that led up to our flat above the banking hall, we decided to invoke the aid of a couple of bank messengers to help us get it up and installed. 'At lunchtime' we told them 'please. And we hope you're feeling strong.' They smiled and flexed at us a bit. But when we came out of work at midday and went round to our staircase our first thought was that the fridge had, improbably enough, been stolen, for there it wasn't.

'Oh hell' said Tim. 'Ahh' said I. We mounted the stairs to find Cleonice at the top of them wearing a slight smile. '*Bom dia*' we said, 'have you seen a refrigerator?' '*Sim senhor*' she answered and led us into the kitchen where the monster lurked massively. '*Aqui!*' But how had it got here? Without either embarrassment or pride Cleonice said 'Oh, I brought it up.' 'Did you get Walter and Jose to help you?' asked Tim. '*Nao senhor.*' She had carried it up thirty steep concrete steps unaided.

'Why', we asked later, 'are you so strong?' Well, she looked pleased: in her family the men strode about with machetes making their living by cutting cane, a dangerous, swashbuckling sort of business, very *macho*. But sugar-cane *roots* have to be pulled up after the cutters have passed, and this was her job. If you give them a very strong pull indeed they will come right out, but you need muscles like *uma gorila* to do it. These Cleonice had. Looking at her shoulders when she wore sleeveless dresses made the point pretty clearly. 'Wow' said Tim.

One never knows what the next chapter of anything will hold. In this case the second chapter came as soon as our return to the flat that same evening when we found our maid in tears sitting on a chair in the living room. She stood up when we came in and we forced her to sit back down and talk to us. 'What is it Cleonice?' 'Oh *senhor*!' 'Well?' 'There is... [sob, deployment of Kleenex] there is a devil in the fridge!' 'OK' said Tim. 'Um' said I. 'He burns me!' she said. Tim approached the white monster gingerly, tentatively touched it. 'He doesn't burn *me*' he said and looked at his feet, then at the maid's. 'Ah' He reflected for a moment and then decided: 'Do you know how to jump?' 'Jump *senhor*?' 'Yes. To defeat the devil in the fridge you need to jump into the air, open the door, let go, then land. Can you do that?' Cleonice looked dubious. Tim demonstrated. Reluctantly Cleonice imitated him. She remained unburned.

Needless to say Tim was wearing shoes with thick soles and the poor girl was wearing bare feet; worse, *wet* bare feet. We learnt a few months later, when she went down to Belo Horizonte to work for some other Bank people, that although she was a great success in all other respects they couldn't get her to explain why all white goods provoked a regular jump response from her. Freezers, dishwashers, washing machines, all got her leaping like a young gazelle. But she never got another shock.

210

We had a shock of our own when we invited the manager of Maceio branch to dinner. He was not a tremendously amicable sort of chap but we thought it best to get him on our side for various venal purposes such as Good Reports and Days Off. Normally, when it was just the two of us, Cleo would come into the dining room with the supper which consisted of two plates heaped with meat, a kind of couscous called *farofa*, and vegetables. Not at all bad, actually, though the morning ritual that produced it became a little tedious. 'Would you like meat tonight?' she would ask. 'Yes please Cleo.' I should say that 'meat' in this context is (or was) known in Brazil as '*bife*', pronounced 'beefy.' So the maid's next question was always '*Querem bife de porco*? [pig beef] *Bife de frango*? [chicken beef] *Ao bife de bife*?' – the last possibility being self-explanatory. There was never mutton. And whatever *bife* it was it had come up from Bahia frozen in a substantial rectangular block, always the same size.

When the platefuls made their appearance, carried one in each large hand, Cleo's thumbs were always stuck well into the *farofa*. This simple, even touching style of service was rather pleasing to us but we realised that the manager, and even more the manager's wife, might not fully appreciate such rustic manners. So the evening before The Dinner Party we asked our high-class slave if she would be prepared to forgo her usual method and bring the food in on a tray. '*Sim senhor*' she said, looking a touch puzzled.

The following evening the manager arrived, rather spick and span with his wife smiling quite elegantly alongside him. Once the *cuba libres* has done their work conversation became a little easier, and at the due moment Tim said to Cleo, 'OK Cleonice, we'll have dinner now.' '*Sim senhor*' she said and exited stage left. We went and sat at the table. From my rather low chair I was happy to see the large tray that Cleo brought in – thumbs well stuck-in of course, but what harm could that be? Then she lowered the tray and, behold, not a plate in sight, not one, not even a saucer, just, directly on the tray, a large steaming pyramid of *bife*-de-something, *farofa* and vegetables. With thumbmarks. Tim gasped. But nobody said anything until I suggested, very humbly and to Cleo's obvious surprise, that in spite of our instructions of the previous evening we would, in fact, like plates. 'Oh' she said, 'OK' and looked at me in a puzzled way: these *ingleses*.

A few days later I found this lovely person sitting on a bed in the spare room again crying quietly, this time over a *fotonovela*, a sort of comic, very popular in Brazil, where the drawings are replaced by photos and a Mills-and-Boon plot unfolds with considerable predictability and stereotyping. The print equivalent of a television soap opera I suppose. Her *fotonovela* reminded her, she said, of her boyfriend, whom she missed and whom she hoped one day to join in Belo Horizonte. For a moment, a moment of extreme clarity and simplicity, I was jealous of him, whoever he was.

I hope Cleonice, wherever she is, let's hope in Belo Horizonte still, is as happy as she deserves to be. If she is as happy as that, she's happy.

2. JORGE

After a short time in Maceio and some other towns the bank sent me to the equatorial region of Brazil to learn about Foreign Exchange of which, as I was soon to learn, there was little to be had up there at the mouth of the Amazon. The town of Belem ('Bethlehem' in

Portuguese; as my friend Paul Williams, another old Brazil hand, used to say, the Portuguese are the only people in the world capable of saying 'Tottenham Court Road' as one syllable), Belem, then, where the branch was, on degree Zero of latitude, aka the Equator, seemed in 1970 to be past its best days. As in the best days of the town of Manaus, hundreds of miles further up the river, the good times had been during the Rubber Boom of the mid-nineteenth century, before the advent of modern plastics and the competition from Malaysia.

Brazil's history was one of exports from its earliest colonial times – sugar, coffee, rubber – so at one point Foreign Exchange must have been of some importance, but by the time I was taken up into the bank's attic to meet Jorge not a dollar, not a pound, not a franc, indeed not very much of anything that was both monetary and from abroad had been seen in Belem for decades. This would have some slight bearing on my Amazonian experience and had certainly had an effect on Jorge (two strong syllables) the poor fellow detailed off to train me in the mysteries of FE, known in Portuguese as *Cambio* and now of course, internationally, as Forex.

Our encounter being run with the slightly old-fashioned manners of some South Americans, Jorge could not be dumped on me, or I on him, without ceremony. So the Manager of Belem branch, having greeted and interviewed me on my first day ('Do you like Mozart?'), passed me on the Accountant ('Do you like football?') who took me up two storeys to what he optimistically called 'Our Cambio Department' and introduced me to the Head of Foreign Exchange, Chefe Branco. I realised only later that 'Chefe' was not his first name.

213

The Cambio department took up the entire top floor of the substantial old building where the bank was housed. On the ground floor real, sweating transactions were taking place under some form of lighting. On the first floor there was some activity and a faint effort at air conditioning as well as a little natural light. Here on the huge top floor there was pleasant warmth, almost no light at all, and two men, just two: Chefe Branco and Jorge.

The Chefe's desk was at the extreme right-hand end of the room if you looked from the stair-head at a central point where the Accountant and I had emerged into the tepid gloom. We turned right and walked for what seemed about a hundred metres across dark-brown floorboards through almost complete darkness to get to the enormous piece of polished teak behind which Branco sat in state. The Accountant introduced me to the Chefe ('Senhor Branco - Senhor Butler') and groped his way back to the stairs. I was gestured into a seat. 'You will be working', said the Chefe, 'with Jorge', a piece of information he accompanied with a wide sweep of the arm towards the invisible distances of the vast attic. 'You will find him interesting.' I looked round and saw nothing.

A few formal questions seemed to bring the Chefe's welcome of his new trainee to an end. He rose and, leading me by putting his hand on my arm in order not to lose me in the tenebrous spaces, took me across the warm dark tundra of that attic, managing to steer me finally to a desk right at its far end that was apparently the only other piece of furniture in the room. There, facing away from the direction in which Branco's desk was orientated, that is to say with his back to his boss and staring at a wall over his slightly smaller piece of teak, sat a tubby Brazilian with a moustache and a wide smile. He rose. 'Senhor Silva – Senhor Butler.' The Chefe then retreated back into the darkness leaving me to grasp the damp paw of my new friend, trainer and confidant. 'Call me Jorge' he said. 'I'm Lance' I said, but giving it two syllables to rhyme more or less with 'Fancy' because I had despaired of getting any of my Brazilian friends to make it rhyme with 'France.' I once tried to help them by asking them to think of the word they knew that most resembled my name (*'Lanche'*, a snack') and to say it 'without the H.' But the second of these suggestions had fallen on deaf ears and only resulted in their calling me *'Lanche'* with the H, which was hardly an improvement, or *'Lanchezinho'* – a little snack – which was no better.

'OK *Lancy'* said Jorge, 'Let's get down to work.' I saw that beside his chair, warm and waiting, was another, lesser chair – lesser in proportion to Jorge's chair as his was to the Chefe's. Fair do, I thought, and sat.

In front of Jorge on the desk was a substantial ledger, the sort of thing you could stun a lion with provided only that you could first lift it and raise it above your head, a thing unwise for anyone to attempt without serious gym time behind them. The ledger was open and in its central rift was a nicely-sharpened pencil; next to it lay an outsize ruler. The pages were entirely bare, innocent of the slightest mark.

Jorge asked me which branch I had come from, what I thought of Brazil, whether I played football. He gestured freely with his right arm, leaving the left planted on his desk. After a while I became suspicious of this immobile left and looked at it more closely. Jorge saw the direction of my glance and smiled. 'It's false', he said, 'it's one the doctors gave me.' And in truth it was, as I saw when he showed me his prosthesis,

215

a hard pink plastic imitation of an arm. I gulped a bit.
Jorge went on talking. 'Have you been to the market?'
'Do you have a girlfriend?' 'Do you play football?' I
began to weary of saying No and wondered how big a
disappointment I was being to my happy soft
companion. 'Luke played football' he said with some
reproach, referring to my predecessor. 'Are you sure
you wouldn't like to try?' 'Do you like Brazilian girls?'
'Have you been to Rio?'

These polite skirmishes over, there was a pause.
Jorge went down for some coffee and came back; I
asked where the loo was. Another pause followed.
'Well', I said, beginning to wonder about my learning
curve in Foreign Exchange, 'when do we start doing...
er... whatever it is that we do up here?' 'Ah yes' said
Jorge with perfect composure, 'let us begin.' He picked
up the pencil and the ruler and began talking again,
about the roads, the river, the football team, the other
people working in the bank, people I had known further
south, what was happening in Fortaleza branch, who
was going to be sacked.

But at last something had to give. I had arrived
in the early afternoon and after two hours there was still
no sign of any Forex activity; how long could this go
on? In the dusky distances of the attic, as if from
another planet, we occasionally heard faint noises such
as that of Chefe Branco blowing his nose or from time
to time the clink of the bottle that he kept in his desk.
He may even have started to sing at one point; certainly
as the afternoon wore on he became quieter and quieter
until sleep seemed to have overtaken him, or the inertia
of terminal boredom. But as the afternoon transfigured
itself outside into a chenille Brazilian evening and
Branco relapsed into coma we couldn't just make small-

talk. Could we? Jorge seemed in no hurry to get on with anything that might be work.

`'Is there much, er, *cambio* in this branch?' I eventually asked. Jorge had exhausted one of the stories from his extensive fund, one involving the covered market that we could see if we went over and looked out through the small grimed window. 'It's called '*Ver-o-peso*' he said without explanation, though that apparently meant 'Watch-the-weight' which didn't seem encouraging. Jorge went to *Ver-o-peso* every day and always had another anecdote to tell about the scoundrels, who also seemed to be his best friends, lazing about in there selling things to each other and if possible selling them for three times the normal price to any non-locals who might stray in. I would learn over the course of the coming weeks that Jorge's other source of conversation was the television. In all my time in Brazil I don't think I watched a single television programme myself, but if you want the basic plotline of the most popular soap opera of those days, '*Gabriela*', you only need to ask me.

'A lot of *cambio*, Jorge?' I repeated. 'Well', he said after a pause for thought. 'You have to understand that the new legislation means that it's more expensive to sack me that to keep on employing me on my rather small wages' and he plunged into a multifaceted explanation of the calculations that the bosses of the bank must have made when they were deciding what to do with such stalwarts as Branco and Jorge. It began to seem that he had a point and that this point would lead to a less-than-entirely-satisfactory answer to the question I had in fact asked viz: *Was there any cambio here?*

Some minutes later, when I repeated my question for the fourth or fifth time, Jorge fell silent,

217

scratched his head a bit and said '*Bem, talvez nao, Lancy*' which is literally 'Well perhaps not', but that 'perhaps' in Portuguese is often used merely to soften an outright '*Nao*' so what he meant was 'None at all.'

He saw me glance at the ledger and he said '*Ooo*', one of the most useful sounds in the Portuguese-speaking world. 'OK, I'm going to tell you what we do here' he said as if revealing the secret of the whereabouts of the Holy Grail. 'Watch.' With his right hand he picked up the nice pencil and waved it about just above the crisp virginity of the ledger's pages. Then he looked at me and smiled. 'You see the ruler?' he said. 'Yes.' 'Pick it up and put it across the page at the top-left there.' This tremendous task was not beyond my capacity. Once the ruler was in place Jorge drew a line across the page; above it he wrote the date and with great care the figures '000,00'. He then asked me to place the ruler diagonally across the first page, below the horizontal line he had just made; he drew a line across both that page and then, with my help, across almost all of the right-hand page. Then we drew a horizontal line across the bottom of the right-hand page. There, below that line, filling the bottom space so that nobody could insert anything untoward, Jorge again wrote '000,00.'

'Now' he said, 'You see! At the beginning of the day there were no cambio operations and no cambio balance. No cambio operations have occurred today so it is the same at the end of the day. And it balances. We have done our work correctly.' 'Oh good' said I and, indeed, I saw it all. With only one arm it is very hard to draw straight lines across large pages in an acceptable manner whereas with a Trainee from England, sent out with his degrees and his training course in London gleaming all over the self-importance of his face, the thing was laughably easy.

This went on for six weeks. In the flat the bank had provided my maid brushed all of my clothes every day – the mildew accumulated fast enough to be greenly visible every twenty-four hours. At 3.15 every afternoon there was a tremendous thunderstorm but apart from that the place was hot though humid, and the sun shone merrily. In the evenings I drank Cuba Libres with the other trainee, a sour Ulsterman who could be heard in the shower singing a song of which the burden was how his forebears had 'Kicked five-hundred papishes right over Dolly's Brae.' When I attempted to divert him with a friendly competition involving recognising well-known quotations from English Literature he became sourer and proposed instead a competition involving the history of Association Football (that again) including all known results of all known games since 1880. 'It's only fair' he brayed, 'You use all of literature, I use all of football, but the history of football is much shorter so I'm giving you an advantage.'

But during the day I held the ruler for Jorge.

3. REATOR

Brazilians are very nice people who don't like to say No. This is charming, but it was a problem for us up in the depths of the Nordeste, the poorest part of the country, in 1970 when quite a lot of things were unavailable and the negative was often needed by shopkeepers and the suppliers of what are known as Goods and Services. One solution to the problem which people adopted when you asked them for things they didn't have was to say '*Tem*' (= 'There is some', pronounced like the name of a supplementary Chinese

Dynasty, 'Taing') but followed by '*Mais esta faltando*' which unfortunately means something like 'But it's not available.' The long for No in fact.

We used '*Nao tem*' in the bank a lot, sometimes trying to amuse customers asking for cash or their chequebooks. Rarely, as you may yourself have experienced, does humour translate across languages. 'For God's sake' barked the manager, 'just give him what he wants and don't try to amuse him. Why do you always have to make everything a joke?' We didn't like to say 'Because we're British' but I think that that was the reason.

But very often, in all honesty and simplicity, our Brazilian friends and acquaintances used the most obvious expression, '*Nao tem*', without the further dimension of '*Mais esta faltando*.' It became another element in that strange bilingualism of the expatriate that we indulged in. You know: 'Have you got the *cerveza* cold?' 'Give me the *bolsa negra* darling.' 'Are you going to see the *immobilier* today to talk about the *acte finale*?' Every day, often many times, we had reason to say or to hear '*Nao tem.*' A nice Brazilian girl we knew, returning from a holiday in the US, said how much she had liked it, in part because '*Ahi tem tudo!*' – 'There there is everything!' She also added '*E tudo fonciona!* ' 'And everything works!' No *Nao tems* in the US of A.

If you take a holiday in South America and you start in Brazil and you want to go abroad you obviously have to stop speaking Portuguese and take up Spanish for the duration. This happened to a few of us when we had a month off and decided to go more or less round the continent. Buses figured in our itinerary. I remember a bus in Peru that couldn't get round a sharp bend in the Andes (no tarmac then) and had to back-and-fill to continue its journey; I was sitting on the back seat and looked out of the back window; as the bus reversed to the apex of the bend I was able to see down about 500 feet and there, small and squashed below me, were the remains, alas, of a bus. You could sort of see how it might have happened.

And planes were another source of raised arterial tension. One flight I took in Bolivia was on a plane which, my neighbour cheerfully informed me, was a Lockheed Electra, the most dangerous aircraft currently in service. During the flight we hit an electrical storm and at one point in its midst we dropped an unexpected 5000 feet in one fell swoop. My neighbour crossed himself incessantly during this stomach-emptying descent, muttered prayers rather loudly and, finally and least acceptably, emptied his stomach into his trousers by more than one route.

To go back into Brazil, our current homeland, after our continent-wide peregrination, we chose an unusual route through north-eastern Bolivia where a Bolivian town called Trinidad is separated from Brazil by the Madeira-Marmore river, tributary of course of the Amazon. Our plane landed at Trinidad on a sunny afternoon, clear enough for me to see out of the window the approaching airstrip. Flying over grass was normal, I thought, at 200 feet, less normal at one-hundred and extremely alarming at zero. In short the airstrip was a mere field not altogether pleased to have large aircraft using it and consequently protesting with a stunning series of bumps and hollows. Still, we were safe on the ground and our only question was when to go across the river into Brazil, and how to get home when we did. No hotel reservations had been possible and our antique guide-book to South America became a bit vague about travel arrangements at this point. My friend Paul took charge.

'We'll go across tonight' he said, ' so let's get down to the river.' The airstrip being actually alongside the water this wasn't difficult, and in five minutes we were looking at the wide muddy river and wondering. But not for long: around the corner came a dugout canoe with two men in it. At the same time two women materialised beside us chattering in Spanish. For a small sum we were all taken across. Rather oddly the women, as we reached the middle of the river, switched into Portuguese, as did the owners of the boat. Capybaras stuck their noses out of the water to inspect us and we argued as to whether there were hippos in the Americas. This seemed to me to be of some importance because if there *were* hippos these smallish ones might be babies in which case there could be bigger ones who might enjoy upsetting the boat, whereas if there weren't these might be another smaller and less dangerous species. The boatmen laughed at us in two languages.

'*Capybara*!' they cried.

At about this point Paul resurrected an old bet that we had had going since leaving Brazil three weeks before. Which one of us would provoke the response '*Nao tem*' first. He asked if he could try before me when we landed. Looking at the unbroken jungle that stretched out in both directions on the approaching bank I thought that it might be some time before he had a chance, but I was mistaken. Hiding in the trees, we discovered as we struggled up the sandy bank with our bags, was one of those shacks which you find all over the developing world and which sell many surprising things but *always* chewing-gum.

Dropping his bag Paul marched ahead to the shack and engaged the lady-shopkeeper in conversation.

As we approached behind him he looked round at us to check his audience and then back at the smiling woman in front of him. 'We would like', he said in Portuguese, 'to buy some things.' 'Good' she said. 'We would like', said Paul, 'to buy a nuclear reactor.' Just to be clear: '*Queriamos comprar um reator nuclear.*' The nice lady remained entirely calm. She looked at Paul with an unaltered smile and said, not '*Que?*' as you might expect, or even 'What's that *Senhor?*' or 'Are you insane?' but simply and clearly '*Nao tem.*' There were unfortunately no nuclear rectors for sale that day on the remote Madeira-Marmore River. Fair do. Paul won the bet.

We spent the night in a hotel in the nearby very small town. The manager said that we should be able to get a train down the Amazon. 'No no' we argued, laughing lightly in case her information was meant as a joke, 'There aren't any trains in the Amazon. Bus? Plane? Mule? Boat?' I think that if I had had to bet on the matter in a London pub at any point in my life up to this I would have bet almost any amount that it was certainly not the case that the *Amazonas* region had trains. It's about ninety-five percent water for one thing.

'*Sim, sim Senhor!*' she insisted. '*Tem tren!*' OK, we humoured her, 'Where's the station?' She gave directions and, before turning in, we followed them through some very quiet warm streets and found, hissing and gulping before us, a steam engine in a wooden shack. Getting closer we saw carriages, and *rails*! 'It's a train' I said with exemplary stupidity. 'But', said the others 'it can't GO anywhere. Can it?'

The driver, in spite of the time, was crouched before his beast muttering. We asked him the obvious. Yes, we could get a couple of hundred miles down the Amazon by train. Then it was boat or plane. 'Well', asked Paul, 'When does the train go?' Now I suppose one gets used to the idea in south-eastern England that a dozen trains a day are normal from almost anywhere to almost anywhere else. Making allowance for the complete absence of passengers or goods here 'near' Porto Velho perhaps this would be a go-in-the-morning-come-back-at-night job? Nope. 'On Wednesdays' said the driver. We had a fierce argument as to which day it was 'today' and felt like Phineas Finn learning from Passepartout in *Around the World in Eighty Days* that he had gained a day by going round the world *that* way. The driver put us out of our agony: 'Tomorrow' he said.

We were the only passengers. The train had no windows. I mean, there were wide-open spaces where windows could easily have been, but no glass. Three empty windowless carriages and us, getting black specks on our clothes from the wood-fired steam engine, specks that burnt small but obvious holes in our shirts and trousers. The journey was slow and hot. Beside the track the occasional clearing allowed another of those shacks to sell us chewing-gum and small knives. And warm Coke. Porto Velho felt like arriving in New York when at last we got there. But why the hell are there 200 kms of track in the Amazon rainforest going from Nowhere to Nowhere?

4. ARREST

If you are going to be arrested, be arrested in Blighty. Try to avoid Russia, Tanzania, China, France… I could go on. Oh, and Brazil. As the bank manager said to me when I complained afterwards '*A policia? Nao sao nada gentil.*' And by heaven they weren't.
We had had a small party, just the four of us, my diplomat pal Stephen Nash, he of the blue nose in

224

Baghdad, and I, in the bank flat in Curitiba where I lived for a time while I was learning another hopeless aspect of the banking profession. The other two guests were nice young women we had met in a cheerful bar and invited home. After a time partying was replaced with sleep.

In the small hours of the morning there was a polite knock at the door and I sighed, rose, pulled a dressing gown round me and went to let in so unusually-late a visitor. As soon as the door began to move it burst open and six large shouting Brazilian policemen stumbled into the apartment. The largest, who was also the only one wearing a tie, ordered a thorough search of the flat. After a moment or two my nice young woman was led from her bedroom wearing nothing at all. Stephen and his lady had locked themselves into their bedrooms and emerged fully dressed a moment or two later. I went up to the boss policeman, *'Senhor'* I began, but before I could continue he had seized me by the lapels of my dressing gown and thrown me violently to the floor where I hit my head on the tiles and passed out.

I came to in the lift to hear Stephen asking me something in English. One of the policemen, obviously the thickest of a thick bunch, said *'Falem brasileiro!'* which is *'Speak Portuguese!'* only without the necessary historical knowledge. I said that Stephen only spoke English and Spanish; this silenced Officer Thick, but also us.

In the Police Station Stephen lost patience and attempted to leave, a plan thwarted almost out on the street, slowly and with heavy and rather ineffective violence on the part of the officers. Dogberry and Verges were quicker on the uptake. After an hour or so we were summoned to the Captain's office; he made a show of being more civilised than his men but he didn't ask us to sit. I was still in my dressing gown, you may remember. I asked what had happened to the girls and he dismissed this with something to the effect that they had been sent home. 'And you can go home too now' he said stretching out an amicable hand. Stephen, the professional diplomat (he was accredited to Bogota at the time and so couldn't play the Diplomatic Immunity card) reached over the desk, took the hand and turned to leave. Then the hand came towards me; I kept mine steadily behind my back. The Captain went berserk and started screaming at me: '*Mal-elevado! Xibungo! Puta de todos as putas!*' But I wouldn't shake his hand; not after what his team had done to us in the flat, and especially after leaving one girl naked for so long. He frothed at the mouth but I stood and faced him, curiously serene; I suppose I saw that, having played the 'I am a civilised man' card he couldn't very well back down. But it seemed likely to become something of a standoff.

His solution was a mild form of brief imprisonment. We were put, me still in my thin dressing-gown, into the back of a police-van, the part used for police dogs perhaps, and left there for the rest of the night. This wasn't too bad – we chatted and dozed – but the problem came at 8 am when we were let out and had to walk the mile into the centre of Curitiba. Stephen was all right – his presence of mind had allowed him to get himself clothed the previous night as I have said – but I was an attractive target for street satire of the nicest Brazilian kind: '*Ooo! Rapaz! Estas ainda dormindo?*' (Are you still asleep?) and '*E uma mulher o um homem?*' (Are you a woman or a man?) But we had to stop for a coffee at a street café.

226

We got back to the flat, tidied up, and I dressed and went to work. When I arrived, about an hour late, everybody already knew everything as everybody always does. There was a quietly excited air in the bank and it wasn't a minute before one of the junior staff came to me and told me that the manager would like to see me. This manager was a rather self-satisfied chap called Otto Brauninger, another South-American German, who had once committed himself in an after-dinner speech to the contentious proposition that Curitiba was '*a cidade a mais bela do mundo*' – the most beautiful city in the world – and was now seated on his desk and facing the door when I came in, flanked by his lieutenants, the Accountant and the sub-Accountant, and several other people all looking serious. Otto looked at me and, as has happened rather often in my life, pronounced sentence without hearing a word from the accused. He wouldn't allow me to stay in the branch, for reasons to me obscure considering the standards of behaviour that obtained in so many parts of his officially lovely town. I breathed a prayer of gratitude to the gods that fix these things and tried to look sad. But I wanted to say a word nonetheless. When Otto had finished saying how bad my behaviour had been for the bank's 'reputation' (sic) I observed mildly that the police had thrown me to the floor for no very good reason. He was unabashed and clearly had no thought that his colleague's safety, not to mention natural justice, could possibly compete with a matter as serious as a reputation. '*Sim*' he said, '*nao sao nada gentil*' ('Yes. They're not very polite') as if that was all that was needed.

I left Curitiba under a cloud (I think) and went to Porto Alegre, an even more German town, where I spent my time issuing cheque-books to the local middle-classes for a few months.

5. ALTURAS

In the middle of my time in Brazil I went travelling round some of the other countries of South America, a curious and enlightening experience (see 'Reator' above). In Paraguay I thought at first that the population were remarkably naturally polite, even deferential, until I realised that one of my British travelling-companions, the said Jeremy Baer, bore a striking resemblance to the son of the long-term dictator who then ran the country, one Alfredo Stroessner. The reason for the smiles, the bows, the free drinks, the brethren dodging down alleys to avoid entering The Presence became clear to me: I was in the aura-zone of a man who could get anyone bumped off at short notice should he choose to do so. Thus my Shangri-La, the perfect country that I thought I was looking for in my twenties, eluded me once again (other candidates for this status, which also fell away on contact, were Monaco, Portugal and the Lebanon.)

In Argentina I liked the people but avoided Buenos Aires. In Bolivia we went by open-backed truck around Lake Titicaca and felt cold but happy until we got to La Paz where the altitude made me vomit. On the landings of the hotel staircase there, where I enjoyed my *sirroche* (altitude sickness), the red things that looked like fire-extinguishers were in fact oxygen bottles for those overcome with my complaint; it was hard not to make the contrast: the very thing that says 'I put out fires' at sea level means 'I will save your life, but don't spray me on fires!' at 12,000 feet. And the fire station in La Paz – for there is one – is a museum containing a single 1926 fire engine, never used of course, complete with hoses and shiny brasswork. Lovely but useless, there not being enough oxygen for a fire at that height.

In Peru we visited Cuzco, one of the old Inca capitals, wondered at the stonework and bought lama-wool sweaters. But from there we decided to go to the now-widely-visited 'Lost City of the Incas' Macchu Pichu, no longer very lost at all.

The word 'Macchu reminds me, once again, of my cousin Celia. Her penultimate visit to me (there were only three in fifty years of adulthood) involved her arriving at my house near Pau with her entourage, at this point reduced to a Lurcher dog and an illitcrate Spanish maid. She had at that point given up, after a very great deal of trying, on Men. For a while she had had a horse called Richman; 'it's the only rich man I'm ever going to own' she would say after a series of more and less disappointing experiences with *los hombres* including one in which she must surely have felt that she was scooping the pool when she married a Rothschild. What could possibly go wrong now? Well, his other name should have given her a clue: he was, in full, Henry De Wolf Rothschild. At all events their wedding night was interrupted (at which precise point I was too delicate to ask) by a visit from the bailiffs who barged into their bedroom demanding the return of her magnificent engagement ring which De Wolf had somehow forgotten to pay for.

Anyway, come Celia's visit to Pauline and myself in our village near Pau, no man rich or poor was in tow, or indeed horse however optimistically named. Only the big dangerous dog called Macho and the silent Spanish slave called Machu. 'They will stay in the cabin' announced Celia, because Celia, of course, had managed to offend the owner of the hotel near us into which we had prophylactically booked her (no, dear spell-checker, not '*prophylactic ally*') and had retreated to a group of log cabins above our village where she was at least theoretically able to run the dog (a possibility of which she didn't avail herself) and allow her slave some freedom (ditto.) Thence she descended to offend, in our turn, Pauline and myself over dinner, but without benefit of either dog or maid. Now the point here is that these two animal creatures had approximately the same name and she treated them just the same. This was odd enough but odder was Celia's insistence on keeping them away from us. 'Machu has 'flu' she said to excuse the absence of one of them. 'And you have cats' she said, in reference to the other.' We didn't enquire but accepted the decision of the court. Pauline sent a thermos of soup up to one of them, we never knew which, and Celia drove on northwards to further offences.

Meanwhile, back in South America, we did what one had to do in those days to get to Macchu Pichu. From Cuzco we took a taxi that got stuck in the mud and whose driver, later, fell asleep *in medias res* and drove gently into the banking on the side of the dirt road. Then we took a train without glass in the windows but with a huge contingent of Peruvian women wearing many skirts, greasy pigtails and bowler hats. They had a number of babies with them, stowed among the chickens and goats and string baskets, and from time to time babies did what they seem so often to need to do and yelled to be allowed to urinate. The mothers would take off their hats and use them as potties after which, really quite often, they handed them to me (I was closest to the non-window) for emptying onto the line.

It was fortunate that the train travelled so slowly and that there were few foot passengers alongside.

Eventually we got to the station below the ruins. At all events the train stopped and we got out along with a gaggle of Americans. The Americans got into a bus that had been provided and ground away up the steep hill. We walked rather second-class-citizenly up the red mud road that led interminably upwards. Luckily we were joined by a very jolly and extremely Alpine young Austrian with excellent English. 'You aren't expecting to pay to go into the ruins are you?' he asked. 'Well yes' we said, having read the guidebook. 'Oh I never pay' he said. 'Just follow me.' When, panting, we got near the enclosure that delimits the considerable space taken up by the huts and temples of the Lost City, he said 'Here' and plunged through some undergrowth. A brief struggle got us through and into the huge enclosure. We were then able to wander round all evening and bed down in one of the empty huts, restored enough at least to have a roof and four walls. During our wanderings two of us went up the immense peak that dominates the deserted town, a narrow track, almost a staircase, that goes up and up into the sky. At the top you are standing apparently looking out over the whole Cordillera de los Andes (though of course it stretches for 3,000 miles down eastern South America so you're only seeing a small part of it) on a space of grass and rock about the size of a small outside loo. It is terrifying and exhilarating in equal degrees.

When we got back to the hut it was almost dark and we settled down to sleep pretty exhausted. But at dawn (5am I think) Paul woke us up. 'I have always', he announced, 'planned to read a poem by Pablo Neruda at this point. It is called 'Las Alturas de Macchu Pichu'. And, stepping outside the hut, he faced the rising sun and began to declaim in loud Spanish. I snuggled in my sleeping bag and listened. It was astonishing.

231

An hour or so later, stiff and cold, we were all up and dressed and the mist had risen. Going out of the hut to answer a call of nature I bumped, quite literally, into a llama. It turned and spat at me, luckily with limited accuracy, and disappeared into the mist. We decided to pause in our activities for a while and regrouped in the hut. But when the mist lifted, which it did with great suddenness, we all realised that we were extremely hungry. Man does not live by poetry alone and we could feel the pull of Breakfast. Being almost without supplies we decided to see if we could find the hotel that has been built among the ruins; the Austrian with his unerring instincts took us straight to it but we found, rather surprisingly, that it was deserted. The staff were all still in their huts round about we supposed, and the Americans all still asleep in their bedrooms. Fritz, if that was his name, led us into the kitchen and started, without hesitation, to make breakfast himself. He found eggs and bread and coffee and got on with it. He was amazing, a sort of good magician of the culinary world. But even he could not keep the Bad Wizard away and behold, there in the doorway, an angry hotel manager. 'Vat are you doink?' he asked. We tried to explain, we offered to pay, we suggested solutions, but he was having none of it and we had to leave. Outside we mooched around making plans and after a while the Americans began to get up. Within an hour they were all outside, breakfasted presumably, and looking about them. I befriended a large Dakotan male who explained that they were now simply waiting for the bus.

We were tired, cold and hungry and a bus down to the station sounded like a very good idea. When it arrived we attempted to board but the hotel manager, who obviously looked after everything on the mountain, stepped forward and stopped us. 'You did not pay!' 'No, I

232

know' we said,' but we are willing to pay now, just for the bus down the hill. You'll earn more that way, something extra.' He shook his head with a sadistic smile. 'No!' he barked, 'You can walk!' At this point the Austrian, seeing that all was lost, took immediate and amazing revenge. Switching from English-with-bits-of-Spanish to loud clear German he asked the following subtle question: 'Why did you leave Germany twenty-three-and-three-quarters years ago?' I stood there calculating on my fingers in a bewildered way (my calculation came to late 1945 or early 1946) but went on watching the manager bloke. He had turned entirely white and was beginning to froth at us with a contorted face, like an Angry Man in an inferior cartoon. He broke into an astounding tirade in German which Fritz gave us the gist of afterwards: we were rude, we were intrusive thieves who expected something for nothing and whom he would report to the police and he had Friends Who Would Deal With Us.

The tall American, my Dakotan pal, stepped forward in that All-American Benevolent-but-useless way and intervened 'Now see here', he said, 'I'm sure we can sort this out' only to be immediately rounded on by Fritz and his Germanic countryman who simultaneously started to shout at him in several languages. With a puzzled smile the American stepped back.

We walked down the hill quietly and were soon overtaken by the bus. The train was mercifully empty except for the Americans and us. We talked of the Vietnam War, then in full swing. 'You did well' I said to the Austrian; 'but how did you know? 'Oh you can always tell' he said, 'they behave just the same now as they did under the Reich.' And he sighed.

CHAPTER 9. SAUDI 1970 – 1971

1. ADULT

At a certain point one realises that one is more or less
Grown-Up and had better see about getting a proper job.
'There is a career in English-Language Teaching' said
the head of the English-Language School where I
worked in Algiers. He smiled. I smiled. But there isn't.
So what else was there? I wanted to be a university
lecturer but couldn't get the support of my Director of
Studies at Cambridge ('You're not a research man
Butler'). I had tried banking which was intolerable and
EFL which is a dead end. So what about the Army? A
gentleman's profession with good pay, nice clothes and
an obvious purpose; anything not to like?

Waking up one morning to this realisation I
made enquiries and got invited for a military interview.
This was to occur in the MoD recruitment section for
officers, then housed in Berkeley Square in a building
which would in due course become flats, offices and the
Stringfellow Club. There a moustachioed Major quizzed
me a bit about myself, seemed moderately satisfied that
I wasn't completely barking and then moved on to what
was clearly his most important question: Which
Regiment? I mentioned the Guards at which he
immediately and, beating around no bushes at all, asked
me what my private income was. As my reply was
pretty negative he suggested the Gunners and I felt the
ghost of my father looking over my shoulder. But,
perhaps because of the social ambition implied by my
choice of the Guards for whom I was too poor, he
tactfully added that I might be best suited to the only
posh Gunner regiment – the Royal Horse Artillery.

So it was that I found myself in Colchester a few days later spending a day with this splendid regiment wearing khaki overalls and trying to look soldier-like. Along with two officers and a collection of men the battery to which I was attached drove out onto a large expanse of scrubland with our guns and were told at a certain point that we had urgently to get to certain map coordinates and set up a firing position. The sergeant who was in charge of my gun stood silently for a moment and then said 'Oh, that'll be up in the trees above the village' and off we went. I asked him why he hadn't even looked at the map to find the coordinates and, wily old gunner that he was, he told me that there were only about six possible firing positions in the area and he knew them all by heart. That's the sort of thing that sergeants do and without it where would we be?

The day went pretty well and it all seemed, indeed, rather familiar to me, up to and including Dinner in the Mess which was formal but seemed easy to me, ever one ready to dine for his country. After that I was invited by the young subalterns of my Battery to go out for a drink. There had been a rather forlorn figure sitting at the end of the table during dinner and I faintly gestured towards him as an obvious person to be invited along too. 'No, no' said Lieutenant Vaughan quite loudly, 'He's an Engineer. Deadly dull.'

Those two stages of interview having been negotiated without substantial mishap I was bidden to Woolwich, Gunner HQ, for an interview with a General of immense status, the Master Gunner or some such, and in due form I was marched into his extensive office overlooking the parade ground. I came to a semi-military halt in front of his desk and he looked up with a nice smile. 'Sit down, sit down, er... Butler... So! Why do you want to join the Gunners?' 'Well sir', I began,

235

'my father was in the regiment and...' General
Important interrupted me: 'Son of a Gunner? Good.
You're in.' And that was that. The final interview had
lasted less than a minute.

But my hankering for academia was too strong
and I decided to turn the Army down and get hold of
any university job at all, at least as a start. I didn't have
the backing for a lectureship in UK so I applied to the
British Council where I was simultaneously interviewed
for two possible posts abroad – one in Hungary and one
in Saudi Arabia. I chose, purely for the money, the
ghastliness that was Saudi. My interviewer looked a
little blank when I made this choice, stuck his head out
of the door and called in a middle-aged chap who had
been waiting in an outer office. Turning to me he said
'This is Hugh Shelley, he's the Head of Department in
Jeddah.' Shelley looked at me like the doctor in
Brussels who checks the sanity of Marlow before he
goes out to the Congo in *Heart of Darkness*. 'Are you
sure you want the Saudi job?' he asked.

But Saudi did not put me off universities at least,
even if it did make me question Islam, kingship and the
lure of the desert. In the event I found that my
experience of English at Cambridge was enough to
enable me to do something with the nice spoiled young
Arabian men who had been obliged to become my
students. It also made for me the crucial contact, with
Tommy Dunn of Stirling University, who as we have
seen decided there and then in Jeddah to appoint me to
his new department where I started in 1972.

2. MAYOR

The mayor of Jeddah was one of my students in the
evening classes that we ran at the university out on the

236

Mecca Road. Accompanied by various pals and cronies, all of middle age and all perfectly charming, he would pitch up at class and do a great deal of smiling while I took them through the difference between Some and Any (Some for positives, Any for negatives and interrogatives – try it some time – it works.) He must surely have been something of a chancer, or related to the royal family, or in bed with the current top religious trend or something, because he was fat, cheerful and rich while never exerting himself too much, indeed never apparently doing a stroke of work. I remember him grinning from ear to ear when the dangerous topic of Islam was raised. 'Oh yes!' He intoned. 'I am too much Muslim.'

Whatever the lights and darks of this tubby enigma with the smiling teeth, he was a party animal. This wasn't an easy role to fill in Saudi where alcohol was forbidden entirely and the women all completely veiled. But human beings can make what they want out of very little, and as the Mayor wanted parties he had them. This was brought rather sharply home to me one night when he rather coyly asked an English colleague and me if we would like to go out to his 'desert house' on Thursday night, the Arabian equivalent of Saturday night. Intrigued, we agreed that we would like to go and that we were free (we were always free.) At the appointed hour on Thursday a gleaming Mercedes drew up outside our villa in the dusk and whisked us away into the velvet Arabian night. The Merc stopped in a sort of lay-by at the edge of Jeddah and the driver got out to say a few words to the other cars which, complete with our fellow-guests, were waiting. There was a certain amount of shouting.

Then we were off. At first the sand was quite smooth but as we got away from the town it became bumpier and the cars began to have their sides scratched by camel-thorn and I began to hit the roof every two or three bumps until I learnt to do as the others were doing and more or less lie down. After a good deal of this all-terrain stuff (though these were saloon cars) we stopped and the warm silence started in on us as we got out and looked about. In the starlight all I could see, besides sand dunes and sky, was a high breeze-block wall. White figures emerged from a door in its middle and came towards us. The shouting started up again and much embracing and some introductions occurred as we were led towards the fairly small doorway from which light struck out onto the sand. Once through it we were blinded for a second and then we saw a very curious architectural sight. The wall enclosed a sort of large roofless compound on three sides; one side had the door in it, and then at right-angles the two sides that went away into the distance before us sloped gently down for about a hundred yards and ended in the Red Sea, which shimmered. Dark but silvery water beckoned to us out there but in here there were carpets and cushions spread out on every concrete step that stretched away towards the water. Lamp-posts like trees sporting neon branches, all brilliantly alight, stood about on the wide shallow steps and servants rushed among them carrying trays; kitchens, perhaps even bedrooms, lurked in the recesses on each side, perhaps a whole house was in there somewhere. We drank it in.

But this was no mere aesthetic visit. After a few greetings from our host and his henchmen (well, they stood around him rather protectively and spoke little) we drifted into one of the groups of loungers who sprinkled the compound where we were pursued by the servants (the *ferrashin*) with the trays. Expecting the worst I picked up the glass nearest to me and was about

238

to take a long swig of what I took to be ice and fruit juice - Arabia is a thirsty country after all - when one of the Mayor's other guests touched my arm to stop me. 'No no!' he said with a big smile as he reached out and caught the *ferrash* by the arm, spinning him round tray and all as he tried to move away. 'Look!' said my new friend, 'Johnnie Walker Red Label!' And so it was. The tall glasses full of ice were simply filled up with neat Scotch; the effect was stunning.

Within five minutes I was absolutely plastered as was everyone else present with the possible exception of the servants who had to remain upright to keep pouring. Someone turned up the music – a mixture of Egyptian Pop, the Rolling Stones and noises from early Arabia. The stars swam above us, the Red Sea glittered in the moonlight and we were suddenly kings of the desert, of the world! 'Yee-hee', I remember thinking, only to realise that I had said, or rather yelled, the two syllables aloud. Everything was entirely marvellous! Where was our host? I *loved* him! What a chap!

At this point in the development of the evening the dancing started. I was sitting next to my colleague John Roe, a quiet bearded fellow several summers further along the track than me. A pair of portly Saudi men in white dresses approached us; would we like to dance, please? I looked at John who remained enigmatic though, I think, nervous, and then back at our prospective partners. 'What do you think?' I asked John. 'S'pose we'd better' he grunted, manners after all being needed here. We rose. In an automatic gesture of the mind (O humans!) I found myself wondering whether his tubby Arab was 'nicer' than my chubby Arab and hoping that mine was the bel of the ball (note the masculine.) What *is* it with men? Women do this too I suppose, but that night my psychological observations were all-male, perforce.

I have a hazy memory of dancing a bit, falling over a bit, laughing a lot. At one point I bumped into our host the Mayor ('Enjoying?' he beamed and leant heavily against a lamp-post) and was just able to enunciate this question: 'Where do you get the whisky?' I mean, I hadn't seen a bottle of whisky in six months; people got flogged for having it! 'Ah!' said the mayor. A side-kick of his manifested himself by magic in the warm night and took on the answering. 'You see my friend' he said, 'Mayor's office in charge of Coastguards; very many bad people try to bring drink into the kingdom in boats' (he didn't know the word for a smuggler, but then would you? In Arabic?) 'we stop them; Mayor's office stop them. But what then to do with whisky? Only one thing! Drink it!' and with that he and the Mayor danced away together shrieking like schoolgirls.

Of course, in a country without any alcohol tradition at all there is no measure, no control, literally no ability to measure how much, or when or with what. Scotch fifty-fifty with an equal number of fast-melting rocks is almost the quickest way to get drunk and that is how, I suppose, they imagined the thing was done. Instantaneous smashedness.

I remember little else until the journey home was announced. We found ourselves singing and belching outside the main gates of the compound, surrounded by Mercedes of all kinds. 'Take any one!' somebody cried and there was a dirty rush for the nearest or the shiniest. The drivers, I realised, had not been excluded from the confiscated lake of Johnnie Walker and had had a considerable party of their own. They roared off in all directions yelling like banshees, regardless of any

supposed track or direction. If the journey coming here
had been bumpy, this was like crossing the Somme
battlefield just after the guns had gone silent. It is
astonishing that nobody was killed; the velvet night
rushed past as a free-for-all race developed and we
screamed and puked and held on for dear life. Next day
was Friday, Allah be praised.

3. OLDER

My students at the King Abdulaziz University were all
older than me. They were six in number and very
charming in their white dresses (they took off their
head-dresses for lectures). They all drove cars much
better than mine; they all drank and smoked like
chimneys when they were in Beirut or London. I did
like them all. Five were languid and amused Saudis, one
a perplexed Palestinian of great humour and almost zero
capacity for university study. He was called Zohair; one
of the Saudis was called Hamid-Ryad, a name that
caused some hilarity when my boss, Professor
H.B.Shelley, lecturing on the pastoral, came to nymphs,
including Dryads and Hamadryads. Another of the
Saudis was called Mohammed Daf'a a surname which,
he said, meant 'Pay.'
    Shelley and I taught these charming Second
Year individuals Eng Lit. They were the senior class
and would become, in due course, the first Third Year.
The First Year, now numbering about forty young men,
were taught English Language and, had I stayed in
Jeddah for second year, would have had a choice
between Eng Lit with H.B.Shelley and me and
Economics with a man called Leggatt and his Sudanese
side-kick who always brought his daughters to work so
that their grandmothers wouldn't inflict FGM on them.

241

There was no Third Year, '*yet*' as everyone said. Personally it seemed to me doubtful whether there ever would be as our six Eng-Lit chaps were intending to leave in a body and go and make money somewhere else.

This they hardly needed. Saudi was awash with cash and these chaps all had rich fathers anyway. They would sit in my lectures (Shelley had chosen the poetry of Yeats and Joyce Carey's *The Horse's Mouth* as our set texts) and occasionally raise a slow arm to interrupt with great *politesse*. 'Yes Ahmed?' I would say, pausing in my exposition of 'Sailing to Byzantium', 'You have a question?' 'Please sir' Ahmed would say, 'Is it true that Englishmen like boys?' 'Well.... Some do, some don't. Like Arabs of course.' Or: 'Please sir, are you a member of the Anglo-Irish gentry?' 'Well... Up to a point.'

Or we would argue about Israel. 'Please sir, Palestine was not a land without people to be given to a people without land. Do you agree?' 'Well.... The Jews had nowhere to go in the middle of the Twentieth Century, did they?' 'Let them go somewhere else, not onto Arab land.' On the whole I was wrong about Israel and they right. After all, were a bunch of wandering Celts to take over Hampshire and impose Druidical law, the learning of Erse and writing in Runes on the existing modern English population as well as occupying all the best land and behaving with arrogance and brutality it might cause a little resentment.

At all events I meandered, with Zohair, Mohammed Daf'a and the others, through a highly-selective syllabus involving literary, political and personal matters in a heady mixture interrupted by cups of hot sweet black tea brought by the *ferrashin* who sat about in the corridors outside the lecture rooms awaiting our orders. They were transparently the modern equivalents of the slaves whose social status had only been abolished seven years earlier, in 1963. Nobody said 'please' or 'thank you' to them, except we Englishmen of course.

Other departments were emerging from the sand. There was a Biology section for instance, the province of a villainous-looking Syrian who was worth visiting from time to time both for the chat (*'Monsieur, je vous assure, qu'en Syrie c'est pas comme ici. Il y des bars, des filles... imaginez!'*) and for his enormous fridge. In this latter he kept an unending supply of Coca-Cola, useful on the hotter days, and half a leopard. The unfortunate beast looked out at one from the fridge (it was his front half) in gelid gloom as one sipped one's Coke and listened to the lubricious fantasies of the biological mind. Then there was the new professor of history, fresh from a PhD in the States, who had gone completely native over there and would greet me with 'Hi there man! How's it goin'?' before launching into weak accounts of American culture ('They always called me Abdul, but you know man, that just means 'Slave of' and I used to say 'complete the name man, complete the name, for God's sake.' If I didn't laugh enough he would persist 'Get the joke man? Slave of.... *God*, for *God's* sake!' 'Ha ha' I would reply.) Of this split person my cleverest student Mohammed Ishqi used to say 'He is a king without a crown' because, for obscure reasons, the History Department kept on not being established and he had nobody to teach. But of course he got his salary.

We were paid in cash. The entire staff, academics, administrators and *ferrashin*, would gradually start to mingle on the *meidan* outside the hut that was the Finance Office fairly early on the last day of the month. It was the social high-spot of university

243

life and involved much childish jesting, but it was not a short-term matter. For an hour or two, that is to say an hour or two after the official time, we waited for Ahmed to get back from the bank. Here, in a country where people get their hands cut off for theft, he simply took a car to the centre of town and withdrew huge bundles of notes and brought them, unescorted, out to the campus. But the *craic* in the bank must have been good because he was *always* two hours late.

Once he arrived he made a palaver of carrying his large bag into the office and lighting up an immense hookah while smiling at us milling hopefuls a subtle smile. Greetings and ribaldries ensued for a space then he suddenly got down to business. He would call out a name and brandish a wad of notes waiting either until the person appeared or for the moment when it became apparent that he wasn't there. A few sucks on the hookah and he would move to another name, clearly selected at random. When it was my turn he would shout 'Butlerrr!' and I would elbow my way forward like some medieval serf hoping to be given his only turnip of the season. Cash, always perfectly accurate in amount, would be thrust into my hand, Ahmed's smile would broaden from subtle to conspiratorial and I would back out from the presence a happier and a richer man. Everybody enjoyed this process including I think me. There was no tax payable of any kind.

The secretary of the English department was an Egyptian of the genial variety, a sympathetic widower who brought me my post even when I had gone home, going out of his way to do so. He suddenly developed uxorious tendencies and announced that any minute now his 'new wife' would be arriving from Egypt and showing me not only her photograph (young and stunningly sexy although he was a gap-toothed diminutive Egyptian secretary of some fifty summers; I wondered what I was doing wrong) but also a picture of the new sofa he had bought to furnish their new flat (hideous.)

It was this secretary, Nazih by name, who supplied me with my most curious moment in Arabia. When I went into his office one morning he rose at once and said 'Come with me.' Taking my hand he strolled us through to a sort of large hall at the back of the partially-built main university building. I played along in memory of Sheikh Sultan of Abu Dhabi. When we got to the hall there was a small but excited crowd gazing into a large glass-topped chest freezer of the kind they use for frozen goods in supermarkets. He pushed me to the front of the group of chattering starers and there, looking up at me from the ice, was an enormous fish. 'It's a fish, Nazih' I said; the man next to me turned quickly and, turning out to be the Biology bloke said, '*Ah, Monsieur Butler! Permettez-moi,*' with which he took my other hand and started to explain this vision in several languages.

The 'fish' was it appeared a manatee, a sort of dugong if that helps, a sea-mammal of great size that swims in some of the warmer seas of the world. This one had got stranded on the shores of the Red Sea and died there poor thing. Some public-spirited individual had arranged to have the large corpse brought to the university as being the place where, presumably, Science could be performed on it. But, being a mammal and a female, the creature had strong signs of its gender about it; indeed, it lay looking at me from atop a pair of decent breasts and, lower down, complete and unmistakable genitalia. The biology bloke, for it was he, sniggered and pointed with his free hand. '*Cela ressemble... ah... hee hee hee, n'est-ce pas?*' Nazih

245

grunted appreciatively on my other side. '*Une femme!*' said the biology bloke. 'Yes' I said. '*Oui. Aiwa.*'

But this was not all. The next morning I picked up a copy of a curious weekly expatriate publication called *The Jeddah Times* on the front of which there was a grainy black-and-white photograph of the beached manatee with its story tediously detailed beneath. I sensed that there was something amiss. And so there was. Peering at the poor-quality reproduction, I was able to see that the censors had contrived to have a black bikini added to the image: strips of opaque black covered the offending parts. Censorship of course achieves, like most things, the opposite of what it intends so that this strange image took on, for a microsecond, a faintly erotic charge. Which is about as close as I have ever got to fancying a fish.

4. TAWFIQ

In the evenings one was a bit pushed for entertainment in Saudi. A guide to the place for travellers, under the heading 'Night-life', had told me that the solution was 'a good supply of paperback fiction.' This suggestion, though it combined intellectual snobbery with the prospect of terminal boredom, had its merits. But when I was asked if I would like to set up an evening class for adults at the university, that is for people even older than my daytime students who were already, as I have said, older than me, I rubbed my hands.

The classes were great. It isn't clear to me that anyone learnt much English but the middle-aged chaps who strolled into the classroom in their white dresses were charming to a chap. There is much infectious smiling and laughing in Arab culture and a free childish spirit that suits my own at times. The slightest tease went down like a piece of brilliant wit and any errors in the language exercises (there were plenty to choose from) brought the house down.

Stars of this show were the Mayor of Jeddah (my friend from the 'Mayor' section above) and *his* close friend, a handsome extraordinarily clean-looking cove of some forty summers called Tawfiq. His head-dress was absolutely *dernier cri*, his sandals a riot. He wore these and the other bits with an insouciant elegance that would not have worked very well in Walton-on-Thames but which placed him in a higher aesthetic category or camp than his pals lounging on their seats around the room. His entrance always caused a slight ripple of attention and his scent was delicious. Think perfumed Arabian George Clooney in early middle age.

It may have been because I too noticed his charms rather openly that he started to react, conversely, to my own charms such as they were. He smiled. Well, I always smile when teaching, grinning like a jackanapes trying to encourage another jackanapes to jump through a hoop, so I smiled back. It never occurred to me that his assiduity, his smiling and even his scent were due to an ever-increasing longing that was mounting in his Semitic bosom. Looking back I now see that he must for weeks have suffered the pangs of an unrequited passion of which, astonishingly, I was the object. He brought me small presents, looked coy, tried to engage Teacher's attention, made impenetrable Arabian remarks.

Now any half-bright girl knows about this sort of thing from an early age. In the playground (I assume, I was never at a mixed school) and ever thereafter the slavering male fool, the white-lipped sudden declarer of All He Feels, as well as more sinister masculine characters beset her path panting and clutching at her. In

247

short, a girl learns the signs and learns how to stop the onslaught, how to say no, how to scarper (though I think that's rhyming slang and should be Scapa, as in the Floe, but there we are.) We poor chaps on the other hand, prompted by both our nature and our nurture to do the slavering and the panting, are unused to turned tables. We are easy meat, at least in the first stages before we Know What's Going On

So it was that I must have been Playing Hard to Get while all the time congratulating myself on the quality and popularity of my teaching and the good personal rapport I was building up with my evening class, especially the star among them.

But Tawfiq was no beginner on the battlefields of love; he played a long game, stalking stealthily. Thus he began to remain behind with the Mayor and myself for little extra talks and charming chats after class, well into the soft Arabian nights. There were of course no bars or any other such places to go to so we just sat on where we were as the weary *ferrashin* brought more and more tea. And then, as he must have foreseen, one night mayoral duties prevented his pal from coming to class and the moment had arrived. We sat for twenty minutes of extra time, the two of us, me thinking what a nice chap he was and how I wished that everyone I knew smelt like him, when the tone and tenor of our exchanges changed subtly and he leant towards me with a new glint in his eye.

'Tell me Mr Butler' (they all called me that, having small idea of the moment when to pass to Christian-name terms or the significance that that could hold; they rolled the final R something rotten) 'Tell me... do you have girlfriend?' I at once knew the reply that would show me in the best light.

'Yes' I said.

'So do I!' His eyes shone upon me in delight.

'Good!' I said, wondering what would come next.

'Well' he said, 'I have plan.'

'Oh?'

'Why you not bring your girlfriend to my house and I bring my girlfriend? Bringing... and we will...' and, running out of words, he made an amazingly graphic gesture by rubbing his two index fingers together, outside edge against outside edge (try it, you'll see) and groaning salaciously.

'Ah, er, OK Tawfiq but' (the way out came to me in a flash; I seem to have natural cunning) 'there is a problem. *My* girlfriend is in London.'

'Never mind!' he beamed back, using an expression I heard a million times in the Middle East - they *love* it. 'Never mind!... you do not bring your girlfriend, OK, then... I do not bring *my* girlfriend.' He paused. 'But you come to my house and I will be in my house and also you and we can...' the graphic gesture, with fingers even more enthusiastically rubbed together, was displayed before my eyes again. The half-Riyal coin finally dropped. 'Oh!' I said, 'Er, look, NO! I mean, that's not me at all.'

Tawfiq, remembering no doubt those moments of pedagogic tenderness when I had winked at him when he got something right (oh God! Had I?), my smiles and my laughter, stayed coolly unrejected. He didn't sit back or look grumpy or pretend he had suggested something else. He smiled on, evidently thinking. A moment passed and then he stood up.

'Come!' he said and walked towards the classroom window. 'Look out.' I looked and there, just outside, shining in the campus lamplight was parked his new powder-blue top-of the-range Mercedes, a thing of beauty that everyone, not excluding me, had coveted

249

since we had first seen it a couple of weeks before. 'It is yours' said Tawfiq and fell silent, allowing the Object of Desire and Result of A Successful Marketing Strategy do its work.

For a short but terrible moment I wavered. I mean, how bad could it be? But then sense kicked in; I turned to the yearning scented fellow beside me with a prayer to the goddesses who look after Girls Who Have To Say No and said 'Sorry Tawfiq. It just isn't me.' But I still get a pang when I see a really nice Merc.

5. VISA

In some of the less-developed countries of the world one is amazed to discover that one has to have a visa to *leave*. You might have thought that fleecing people who visit a country for *going there* would be enough; but no, *leaving* also has to have its price. So it was in Saudi.

A few weeks before leaving the country after my year there I was sent an enormous water bill. Most things in Saudi are cheap because of the oil and the strength of the Rial but water is of course a thing they sorely lack. Nonetheless, this was absurd, eight times higher than it should have been. I thought at first that I would simply leave without paying it (I prefer to pay bills, but not a monster like this which bore no relation to my actual consumption) but then I learnt about the exit visas. To get one of these one had to go round the ministries that controlled the electricity and water, to have an attestation from the bank, from one's employer, all the useless *paperasserie* that Britain, by comparison at least, is blissfully free of.

I managed to get all the right approvals, signatures and stamps on the exit-visa form bar the aquatic one and then, when all the others were in place,

I braced myself to beard the water people. Their office was in a suburb of Jeddah hard enough to find and, when found, hard enough to enter. Eventually I penetrated the ground floor of this newish office block of three storeys. A large notice told me this was the '*Ain al-Aziziyah*' (rather touchingly '*Ain*' means a well) and that bills could be paid here. So far so good. I approached the payment *guichet* on the ground floor by dint of engaging in a considerable barging match with about a hundred Saudis (and some foreigners like me) all of whom were shouting simultaneously in the heat. The air-conditioning couldn't cope with so many bodies. Behind the glass was a harassed-looking young man (no women here of course) who spoke as though I was his personal, specially-selected enemy. He more or less opened the conversation with '*La*', Arabic for No.

After much to-ing and fro-ing he must have begun to see that I would not simply pay up or go away so he said, with a dismissive gesture, 'Pay three-quarters and I will give you the paper you need for the exit.' This would have seemed tempting except for the truly enormous proportions of the bill. '*La*' I said in my turn, at which he said 'Go upstairs.' I looked around and saw a staircase to which he gestured with a flick of his head before turning to the next sweating protestor.

I mounted the stairs and found myself in a room equally as big as the one below but with a mere twenty people in it, mostly behind desks, with just a handful of quiet customers. The air-conditioning worked up here. Phew. Someone came forward and ushered me to a seat where a fairly human-looking person asked me what I wanted. We went through the same rigmarole, to which he listened with grave attention before doing some complicated sums on a piece of paper. 'Pay half' he said. 'No!' I said again, mindful that that was still a ridiculous sum. We kidded back and forth for a while until he said. 'Go upstairs.' By this time I knew the drill and up I went.

The top floor was also the familiar size but in it there was only one person, if you don't count a *ferrash* padding about in the shadows; it also had first class air-conditioning and for furniture just the one desk with a large chair either side of it. The person, large and pale and beautifully turned out in Sheikh kit, sat behind this desk and on it there was one letter, unopened. He gestured to me sit before him. I told my tale again. He looked at me with a smile, ordered tea for me, asked about the cricket scores (in English) while I drank it and, twenty minutes later, dismissing me, said 'Pay quarter. OK old man?' There were no further storeys to go up to and although I briefly fantasized about appealing to Allah up there... I came back to earth. I paid a quarter. It was still rather a lot.

Thus are things managed in the Mystic East. You need patience but it sort of works out, in the end. I left Saudi when I was twenty-five. I learnt in 2013 that scientists have now established that the human brain doesn't settle down into its 'final' configuration until about that age. The modern tendency for children to stay with their parents into their early twenties is thus perhaps not as unnatural as it may seem. In any event I can think of few people who have really fully 'become themselves' before twenty-five. So perhaps that was a good age for me to come home and 'settle down.'

So I may have been as *finished* I was going to be when I was 25 and as I married, bought a home for myself, got a career under way, took on a dog. It was quite a moment. Was this, one asked for the first but not at all for the last time on such occasions, who one was? What more might be expected?

And in a sense, why *should* one assume that there would be lots more? Did a medieval peasant expect 'career development'? Did an Egyptian slave of a 1000 BC worry about pension prospects or self-fulfilment? Were cavemen expecting enlightenment, a 'complete' life, fun, 'freedom', *days off*? Have we got our assumptions upside down? There is no natural basis for us to undertake any special pleading after all: we don't *have* to become any particular thing and we have no right to *expect* to be something special or pre-ordained. Existentialism was accurate in this respect: there is no essence up to which one must live, nothing compulsory, no life plan we had better conform to or else.

So one makes do; there is no choice but to indulge in a sort of *bricolage* with the elements available in our culture. In our present case, since about 1960, we have adopted a rather Californian hedonism and feel that we have 'rights' including, laughably, the 'right to happiness.' Human-Rights lawyers should be making a fortune. We think it 'natural' to expect food, fulfilment, health, comfort, sanity and paid holidays. I am not a misanthropic spoilsport, but it seems just a matter of fact that these things are not givens and that for every advantage humans obtain in this direction there is a corresponding price to pay.

In this great book-keeping act two really good things came along some considerable time after I was twenty-five: my daughters Alice (born 1984) and Miranda (born 1989.) As these memoirs are partly for their benefit I shall spare them the narrative of their own lives, but I cannot resist saying here that these two wonderful girls – young women now - have lent meaning to my existence as nothing else could. Try it some time gentle bachelor – it's amazingly

253

extraordinary and as fulfilling as every cliché will tell you.

CHAPTER 10. STIRLING 1972 - 2001

1. LECTURES

The art of lecturing is to start a few moments late and to stop a few minutes early. It is also to read as little as possible from a prepared script, to talk as much as possible to the people in front of you and to speak as if you mean what you say. These, anyway, were the rules I learnt to work by in the lecture-hall and I think that sometimes it more or less came off.

Be that as it may, my time at Stirling University gave me a lot of scope to observe the lecturing behaviour of the species *homo academicus* and his congeners. We attended one another's lectures in the English Department and very entertaining it sometimes was. It was also on other occasions excruciating, as for instance when the colleague whose rather dull voice had filled all known space for a good hour looked at his audience and, ignoring the surging and baying of the crowds of students outside waiting to come in for the next altogether-different lecture, said to our incredulous ears 'This next bit is quite important. It won't take long.' And this *at three minutes past the hour*. Five minutes since, books had been ostentatiously shut, pens put away, and the air was loud with the click of ring-binders closing; people were putting on their jackets as the poor sap maundered on. I vowed never to do likewise.

Equally at conferences, where lecturing is known as 'giving a paper' and where, famously, academics present material that is going to become an article or a chapter of their next book, most colleagues *read what they have written* with flagrant disregard of the laws of Register (Written Register is not the same as

Spoken Register in any language) and wonder why the audience is asleep. I have even seen otherwise-sensible dons *taking out their biros* while reading a paper and *correcting a typo* as they read. All this at British conferences and American; I prefer to draw a veil over the awfulness that is the French academic conference where for more than one reason one finds oneself unable to understand anything at all.[18]

Nonetheless the lecturing stars I have heard have delighted me. I remember for instance Gustavo Gutierrez the Peruvian Liberation Theologian. He spoke, commanding absolute attention, to four-hundred of us in the big Lecture Theatre at Stirling while we listened rapt. Gutierrez had of course a large halo to back him up coming as he did with the credentials of being the saint of the slums of Lima and the cleric who actually believed Jesus' suggestion that some preference should be given to the poor. His delivery was guttural, as befitted his name, and he had a heavy Spanish accent; you could have eaten his sentences with a knife and fork. He did not speak from notes and he did not rant.

The audience remained spellbound for the duration, but Question Time revealed that some had been present in a different way from others. If you carry a large hot bag of presuppositions into a lecture you may not be able to listen properly on account of your burning desire to unload it *coram populo*. So it proved

___

[18] An exception: in 1986 I shared a platform in the Centre Pompidou in Paris, where the Beckett world was gathered for a conference to celebrate the great man's 80th birthday, with Alain Robbe-Grillet inventor of the *nouveau roman* and director of *Last Year in Marienbad*. Alain spoke for precisely the allotted twenty minutes without a note. His intervention consisted of one immense pyramidal sentence, it seemed, as he moved towards his point for ten minutes and then moved back to his starting place for a further ten in a perfect chiasmus. Brilliant.

now. A shiny young man in the back row who had held his counsel explosively for an hour could not restrain himself from rushing in with the first interrogation: 'Father Gutierrez!' he cried in ringing Glaswegian tones 'You talk about the life of the poor today and the need for justice here and now.... But what about *Eternal Life*?' One could see the priest thinking about this, pondering perhaps the literal meaning of the question covered as it was in a thick layer of sporran or porage; then he looked up. 'Eternal life?' he asked rhetorically, 'if life is eternal... it IS now.' There was durable applause. Neat, I thought, and one of the few occasions when I have heard any theologian taking seriously the orthodox doctrine of the Eternal Present.

On the other hand another speaker who obeyed some of the rules of lecturing but who didn't impress much was Edward Heath the former Prime Minister. During a lecture at Stirling he spoke without notes all right and engaged his audience pretty well, but both of these advantages slowly revealed their origins to the audience and in a way that made them wither to nothing, for absolutely every sentence, nay clause and phrase, that E. Heath spoke was directly related to... Edward Heath.

The egoism was breathtaking, pre-requisite perhaps of a successful career as a bachelor politician. He spoke not of De Gaulle but of 'De Gaulle and I', not of Mao Tse Tung himself so much as a version of Mao interred in phrases beginning 'I said to Mao' or 'When I told Mao.' Like the name-dropper Mr Brooke in *Middlemarch* who manages to pull up just in time not to claim acquaintance with the Ancient Greeks ('He remembered that he had not actually known Socrates') Heath just managed to stop himself from beginning a sentence with 'I told Hitler' (though who knows? Heath *was* born in 1916) but he had put an astonishing number of people right including Churchill, Macmillan and Stalin, some of these corrections being administered, if administered they were, when Edward was a surprisingly young man.

So another rule: no egoism. Yet paradoxically you must involve yourself in another way by showing that the material in question has touched you, altered your thinking, meant something to *someone* other than in an abstract manner - and the only candidate here happens to be yourself. Treading a fine line between these desirables I think the secret of lecturing to consist in exposing who you are and your own feelings while also trying to seem as modest as possible and not going on about it too long.

2. BOTTLES

Ambition, vanity and a dislike of socialism got me interested in what came to be known as the Thatcher Revolution in the 1970s. My contemporaries, at least in university circles, were inclined to see themselves as Left-inclined and to wear badges with Lenin or Che Guevara on them, but that always puzzled me. Left versus Right? Let's see: Adolf H: 6 million Jews gassed; Josef S: 6 million Ukrainians starved to death; both of them impartially including women and children. So not much in it really.

But as nobody was actually under a Fascist government any more by 1960 why on earth did my generation go on saying they were socialist anti-fascists when, *even if there had currently been Fascist governments*, the scores of atrocity were roughly even? And as I say… there weren't any. Attacking a deceased straw man they failed to notice the bloody monster in the room. For there were certainly lots of horrible *socialist* governments in many parts of the world in the 1960s, notably in the Soviet Union, Eastern Europe, China, Cuba and North Vietnam; and there would soon be some record-breaking horrors such as the regimes of Pol Pot, Enver Hoxha or Kim Il Sung, all explicitly of the left, some even educated at French universities. And my contemporaries had posters of Che Guevara on their walls! Che was romantically shot by the CIA in Bolivia, yes, but everyone forgets that he was himself notoriously a top-of-the-range killer when Castro gave him a little power in Cuba.

So this strange leaning towards the left wing was all a bit confusing to me. I remember tangling with one champagne socialist on the subject; when I modestly pointed out that leftism currently wasn't doing itself many favours in the Gulag Archipelago he countered with Caligula, which was fair but rather beyond its sell-by date.

Anyway, while I was in Scotland and being a Tory of sorts[19] and my colleagues and students were supporting political movements even further left than a party that sang the Communist anthem 'The Red Flag' at their conferences (Labour, if you've forgotten), I got on to the Candidates' List at the Edinburgh central office of the Conservative Party and put my hat in the ring for parliament and for the local council elections.

In the end parliament was a step too far. I worked hard, with many others, to make Stirling a winnable Tory seat and succeeded; but it became clear that I would not be the candidate. At the internal selection meeting there were two or three hopefuls (I

---

[19] People like me were known as 'wet' Tories by Margaret Thatcher, but I preferred Richard Ingrams' self-designation: 'Tory Anarchist.'

had bowed out in favour of a pal earlier) including a squirearch rejoicing in the name of Something-or-other Maitland-Mackgill-Crichton which was at least one name too many for the Conservative activists of Central Scotland. Then there was my pal Hugo De Burgh who was a handsome broadcaster of great plausibility and a nice smile. He looked pretty hot stuff and seemed to me likely to make the grade if he played the correct cards. In this spirit I organised a dinner party for him at my house to introduce him to the great and good of the constituency.

Unfortunately a weak head, or nerves, or some nameless complaint meant that, unbeknownst to me, he became totally plastered early in the evening and I had to switch from efforts to make him shine to efforts to keep him quiet. He concealed his state manfully through several courses but fell at the final hurdle. Let me describe the scene, rare enough in all conscience.

We lived in an isolated farmhouse on the Carse of Stirling, five hundred yards of bumpy drive from the road, and the dinner party was on a snowy November night. We were thus surprised, as we sat over our *saumon-en-croute*, one of my then-wife's specialities, to see the dining-room door open and a large male stranger enter the presence. 'Hellooo!' he boomed at us, grinning from beneath a sort of tea-cosy with which he was keeping his head warm. The hot room began at once to smell of farmyard manure. ''Are you hirin'?' he went on. This was a mad tramp, I thought. Sometimes one gets things spot on. *En effet*, it was a mad tramp. Looking beyond this unexpected person at the moonlit snow without I had a vision, accurate enough no doubt, of his slow progress up our long drive. His shadow must have followed him like a sinister stain on the whiteness and woodland creatures must have stopped scratching at the ungrateful ground and looked up only to flee from him in alarm. In a film he would be a figure of horror and supernatural threat, a *golem*.

Silence broke out rather noticeably in the dining room and our visitor, blocking the moonlight and the hall light shining brightly behind him and becoming a sort of ominous silhouette beneath whom our candlelit guests quailed visibly. Stirring myself to discharge some sort of hostly defence of them I approached the malodorous young giant and ushered him back into the hall. 'Can I help?' I inquired in a stage whisper. 'You're no hirin'?' he asked. 'No' I said. 'Ah wuz tellt there was a farm along the carse here hirin'. Ye ken, I can lift two bales o' hay wi' one hand?' 'I believe you' I said. I believed him, but his strength was not necessarily the thing I most needed at that moment. His hands were, I spotted cleverly, enormous. I could hear Hugo giggling back in the dining room and the sound of clinking glass.

It appeared that the man before me, who was under the care of the local authorities and being rather well looked-after by them, had emerged from his hostel in Glasgow and taken a bus to Stirling asking to be dropped off at a farm near ours – *this late* on a snowy November night. What was to be done? Initiative was needed and I racked my brains. The giant produced some papers of the kind that all vagrant persons seem to carry. I gazed at them and saw an address – in Stirling. We agreed that he should be taken into the town, it only lying five miles away, and I said I would get my car.

When I explained the situation to my guests the plastered Hugo, in a flash seeing the opportunity to show off his gallantry, good-heartedness, promptitude in action and other such qualities and thus to impress the Tory big-wigs sitting at dinner around him, sprang to his feet knocking his chair over and waving his arms. 'I'll take him!' he cried and lurched from the room. 'I'd better go too' I thought. 'I'd better go too' I said and rushed after him. The compromise finally was that Hugo would drive the poor chap in his car but that I would accompany him to 'show him the way' and we set off into the snowy night.

I had decided to sit in the front as the giant hay-lifter was too big for anywhere but the whole rear seat and this was lucky because it enabled me to keep a firm grip on the steering wheel and correct Hugo's more exuberant dashes for the ditch or the oncoming traffic. Somehow we got to Stirling, found the homeless hostel where the giant was welcomed in and returned in a jerky zig-zag back the five miles to my house. The evening could yet be saved, I thought, and nothing further could surely go wrong.

As we arrived home however we could see several flashing lights surrounding the building; on closer approach these turned out to be the fire brigade in various guises. Men in yellow boots and those strangely-shaped helmets were running about in the courtyard and garden shouting at each other and my assembled guests had pulled back the drawing-room curtains and were watching the show with evident enjoyment. Taking my own eyes off the scene just long enough to show Hugo where his handbrake was, I jumped from the car and went in.

Contrary to my optimistic expectations, in our absence fires had broken out, allegedly, in the kitchen (toast left to cremate on the Aga for half an hour) and in one of the bathrooms (paraffin stove that had run out of fuel and had been consuming its own wick for an hour.) A guest, Captain the Hon. W.F.E. Forbes of Callendar, had visited first the kitchen where the white smeech was so thick that he was unable, quite literally, to see his hand in front of his face, and immediately after that the bathroom (in search of fire-quenching water) where the black smeech was so thick that ditto ditto. Giving this sudden double smoke conundrum best he had found a phone and telephoned the gallant Brigade who, on a dull night, were only too delighted to come rushing out and run about with their hoses. Luckily no water was in the event needed and the party was the talk of Stirlingshire for some weeks after that.

But Hugo didn't lose the candidacy because of this exciting evening which, on the whole, seemed to boost his standing in the constituency. His failure, in spite of being easily the best candidate, was entirely due to manipulation from Conservative Central Office in London. Margaret Thatcher, always one for a person rather than a theory, had fallen for a hungry young Tory on the Westminster City Council, scene of later corrupt shenanigans involving Lady Tesco (she had a real name that I forget but she was a supermarket heiress; possibly Sainsbury?) This Michael Forsyth character was carpet-bagged into Stirling on the flimsy grounds that he had a Scottish name and was 'Maggie's Blue-Eyed Boy'. In reality Maggie couldn't see any other obvious candidate among Scottish Tory MPs for the post of Secretary of State for Scotland, not one who would think as she did anyway.

So come the great selection meeting Maitland-Mackgill-Whatnot, and Hugo and the other chap did their thing in front of the assembled committee and this Forsyth was put on last, always the strongest position. As he came on the Conservative Agent who was sitting next to me whispered loudly 'It's just chance he's on last! It isn't rigged!' So I knew it was rigged. Forsyth made an adequate speech and then the constituency Chairman stood up to give a résumé of proceedings before the vote.

He spoke in a mixed fashion about the first three candidates and then said 'And as for Mr Forsyth whom we've just heard, he seems to have the right sort of fire in his belly.' And you can imagine how a crowd of political activists reacted to that. They voted to a man and woman for Maggie's ringer. But I voted for Hugo in memory of our epic drive.

Forsyth went on to be Secretary of State for Scotland while that post still existed in its old form and got the inevitable knighthood out of it. This made his wife 'Lady' Forsyth and the last I heard she was still using this entirely unearned distinction to further her career in whatever big-business operation or semi-quango she ended up in. 'Oh she always insists on having it on the door, and on the lips of the secretaries' everyone said.

At a much humbler level I myself stood for the Regional Council seat representing the village of Bridge of Allan, next to the University where I worked. Deciding I'd do the thing properly I visited all five hundred houses in my constituency. This was a revealing experience.

The owner-occupied houses *up the hill*, made of stone and surrounded by rhododendrons, were pretty solidly behind me. 'Good old Maggie!' they cried as soon as I had begun my little speech. 'Don't worry, I'll be voting for you!' That was as expected; but in the lower-end bungalows and council housing *down the hill* there were some Tories too. One older chap came to his door and interrupted my *spiel* with a surprising proclamation: 'Save yer breath son' he said. 'I'm a Mason and a member of the Orange Lodge and I've been a Tory all ma life.' 'Ah' I said, slightly nonplussed; 'really?' That wasn't quite what I had in mind when I declared my own liberal Conservatism to the horror of my academic colleagues. It was true though that when I was given the index cards of paid-up Conservative Party members in my patch I was equally nonplussed to see that they had printed on them 'Stirling Unionist Association.' I just managed to prevent myself from asking what that meant and, cudgelling my brains, realised that I had signed up in 1975 for a party identifiable by its opposition to Home Rule for Ireland in about 1880.

In another council house a large young man looked a little intimidating at the door as I stammered through my patter. But like all of my supporters he interrupted me, though this time it was with 'I'm a policeman. I always vote Conservative.' That wasn't very complicated when you come to look into it, policemen being better paid under right-wing governments, but the lesson seems to be that people's choices are highly various in their motivation.

Only one potential constituent had a question that related to the actual competences of the Council for which I was standing. In one of the up-the-hill rhododendrony houses she came to the door and, in answer to the last part of my pitch ('Is there anything you think the council should be doing?') flummoxed me by answering, as no-one else had done, with a piercing 'Yesss!' 'Ah' I said, as I have so often in life. She fixed me with her glittering eye and said '*Bottles*! I seem to have a HUGE number of bottles. Bottles everywhere! I can't get rid of them. What we need is a Bottle Bank!' 'Yes' I said, though Bottle Banks were new then and rather rare; in fact I don't think I'd ever seen one. 'Yes of course.' But the fact was only too horribly clear: this good lady, swaying and peering at me on her doorstep, was entirely under the influence of the electric soup, stone plastered at eleven in the morning, stotius, hammered, fleeing as they say in Scotland. Bottles played a large part in her life and she wanted a Bank for them. Fair do, I thought.

3. COUNCIL

Once elected to the Central Regional Council[20] I found that being a member was quite enlightening. We were thirty-four councillors all told, mostly Labour but with eight Scottish Nationalists and six Tories. Labour ruled in a fairly humane way and certainly didn't play party politics with local issues. There were mutters about corruption of a mild sort – a few quid changing hands for planning permission for an unusually-positioned house, that sort of thing; but nothing proven. On the whole I was fairly impressed.

What was different from my expectations became clear only slowly. First, I discovered that I was a raging leftie. One day as we were chatting in the corridor outside the Council Chamber the subject of Capital Punishment came up. A large contingent of old Labour war-horses weighed in with cries of 'Bring it back man! We should bring it back! Hanging's too good for some of these people. And what about the birch now? It was a real pity when they abolished that!' I reeled and bleated something about miscarriages of justice and Hanratty and the rest and was at once swamped in a chorus of 'Noch man, not at *all*.' OK, I thought.

The Labour Majority were also extremely tough, as far as I could see, on trades-union representatives and their demands. There were some issues concerning our own workers' pay while I was on the council and the Labourites almost to a man (for none of them was a

---

[20] A bad name. It was the Council that covered Stirling, Falkirk and other parts of *central* Scotland, but its name makes it sound as though it was more or less the governing body for the whole country.

266

woman) had little sympathy for the toilers by hand and pen who had voted for them and indeed worked for them. So they turned out to be hangers-and-floggers, sexists and anti-union. Like my Orange friend in the council house they gave a passable imitation of being made according to a propaganda image of an old-fashioned Tory. They certainly got on well with the Tory-old-school county members, a couple of landowners who sat alongside me.

We Conservatives were led by one Colonel Frank Saunders, a neat, spry old fellow whose actual age was a state secret much explored by the Labour chaps during boring debates in the Chamber. (Labour bloke: 'So that's the gist of the new proposals for a ring-road to the east of Stirling.' Col. Saunders: 'Would the Convenor be so kind as to tell us the exact statistics on which the decision has been based, considering...' Labour bloke, interrupting: 'Mr Convenor, can we ask the leader of the Conservatives for his own personal statistics? Why should *we* tell *him* about the traffic numbers if *he* won't tell *us* how old he is?' – *roars of socialist laughter* - Col Saunders: 'Personal matter old boy, personal matter.') Rather disloyally I called the good colonel '*Finger-Lickin' Good*' though not to his face, in homage to a fried-chicken restaurant then widely-known and sharing his name.

Saunders, who must have been really quite antique now I come to think about it, had had some nasty experiences during the War and had a bee in his bonnet about the Japanese. I too had read *Camp on Blood Island* and other classics of the Burma Campaign and its aftermath; I too felt that forgiveness for the unspeakable sadism of the Japanese army had been accorded too easily. But for the gallant colonel the slightest mention of our cousins from the land of the

267

rising sun produced an unstoppable reaction: 'Do you *know* what they did to our kith and kin? Have you *met* the survivors? Intolerable, intolerable.' Come the Finance Committee then, when we objected as we were supposed to do to the Labour proposals for the next tranche of expenditure or investment, Saunders would always rise to his feet and start in on the undesirability of putting any money into Japanese shares. He was listened to in respectful silence, no further comments were received on the topic, and the Council went on to invest, inter alia, in Mitsubishi.

During my two years on the Council no fewer than five of the thirty-four of us died. As my colleague and clan chieftain James McNab of that Ilk remarked 'We're all falling awf our perches.' I remember all the funerals. Driving to one in a council limousine we were overtaken by a battered Vauxhall going at high speed; I saw that the driver wasn't even wearing a seat-belt. 'Gosh!' I exclaimed, for something to exclaim, 'he's going it a bit.' 'Ah' said my neighbour, a septuagenarian stalwart from the Labour benches, 'that'll be Jim. It's OK – he's Chairman of the Police Committee.'

But after each funeral an unusual ceremony occurred. On our return to the Council offices from the church or crematorium we were all summoned into the Convenor's Parlour where in spite of the daylight we watched the blinds being drawn. Long faces and dark suits swam around me in the gloom. A moment's pause followed. Then the youngest councillor switched on the electric lights and the Convenor flung open a large cupboard behind his extensive desk. In it was an array of alcoholic refreshments sufficient for a regiment of Crippens to drown their brides in. With cries of 'Thank God for the Council-Tax payer!' and 'Here's to – (*enter*

268

name of recently-deceased fellow-member)' we emptied
a great number of bottles in a very short space of time -
you know how it is – after a funeral… chilly…
emotional stress… that sort of thing… and tongues were
loosened.

One of these instantly-raucous occasions
included a brilliant impromptu lecture by my
(presumably) second-oldest Tory colleague, a retired
doctor from Strathendrick with a chubby face, no hair
and a delightful smile. His topic was The Decline of the
Political Meeting. 'I remember the meetings in the old
days' he said, 'before the only people who came to them
were supporters of the person speaking. You got all
sorts of questions, not all of them entirely pertinent. I
recall a young lad getting up after I had droned on for
half an hour about tax or the health service or
something. Everyone prepared to listen politely to this
lad's question – you know, we must encourage the voice
of the next generation and so on - But then guess what
he asked?' We shook our collective head and held our
collective breath in anticipation. 'He asked: 'Please
mister. Why does boiling water make tatties soft and
eggs hard?' That was real politics.'

4. ABUSE

Stirling University between 1972 and 2001 was a
microcosm of the changes that have occurred in Britain
and the world since the Second World War and, *a
fortiori*, since the 1960s. Like every generation mine
believes that it has lived through more changes than any
other, but might we be the first generation to be right?

At a 'new' university in those days there were
new kinds of student, many of them female; indeed in
departments such as English a majority were soon

269

female thus bringing us in line with Continental universities where it has long been the case that soft subjects like mine are taken by girls who then become teachers of them at school. But it is also in stark contrast to the longer history of universities between 880 AD (Bologna) and 1960; during that millennium-plus the students were either *all* men or, for most of the twentieth century, men in the great majority. There were also during my career, increasingly, staff members who had never done anything except get degrees, do research and apply for lectureships; and increasingly these members were female too. I know that one is supposed to be gender-blind, but personally I have the feeling that only death will rob me of my ability to spot this particular difference.

My first Head of Department and the man who appointed me, Tommy Dunn, had the laudable principle that he would never appoint a candidate who was either without extra-curricular experience or who was a teetotaller. It is also true that he tried very hard never to appoint a woman. So the English team at Stirling comprised a fair old selection of eccentrics and unexpecteds and, in particular, people who had travelled and done things. But almost no women, for better and worse.

This was a very far cry from Cambridge. In a 'new university' (I mean a university conforming to the post-1960 norms by which we all now live) there are no Personal or Moral Tutors; even that pale shadow of such a person, the 'Director of Studies' of my first years at Stirling, was downgraded to a mere 'Advisor of Studies' in the 1980s. There was no Staff Common Room as we were all supposed to mingle with the students, no Staff Dining Room, no Colleges of course. Offices were bare and impersonal, corridors, lighting and carpets all basic.

270

Concrete prevailed as the most commonly-sighted substance. When I started in 1972 we had ashtrays, now vanished long since, and telephones with open access to outside lines – that lasted about two years and then only administrators retained this privilege.

But this is all physical, trivial perhaps, and is not the real burden of what I am trying to say. The deeper change that I felt as I moved to Stirling in 1972 was the change in attitude among all members of the university community. Whereas we made the assumption, at Cambridge in the early 1960s, that the intellectual and academic life was a special and separate thing that we were privileged to be involved in, and that any fellow-student or don would at least be interested in any intellectual problem or proposition that might be raised, in the new university the assumption is that everyone is the same, that really anyone can take a course in anything (indeed that university life consists of 'taking courses', an expression I was unfamiliar with before 1972), that the vacations are 'holidays', that one can simultaneously study, work in a bar, spend the vacations as holidays and come out 'qualified' in something.

Those things are of course possible for a very gifted person, but for the others the result has inevitably to be a dilution of focus and, of course, in addition to all this, everyone now has to pass. The attitude behind the new arrangements is what worries me though: there is now a *suspicion* of cleverness among undergraduates, a desire NOT to be too intellectual which seems to me only too likely to achieve its object.

I set myself, from the beginning, to ignore these changes as much as possible. I preferred to refer to those I taught as 'undergraduates' rather than 'students' and above all I always spoke to them, and to my colleagues, as though we were all engaged on a joint intellectual enterprise in which quality of reading and thought were all-important. I was never reluctant to quote in Latin or Italian or French (OK, with a crib for those innocent of those languages; this not being intellectual snobbery but a desire to expand horizons), to suggest books of considerable length and complexity, to speak as though everyone in the lecture-hall had read most of Shakespeare, Milton, Swift, Tennyson, Dickens (you know: 'As you remember, T.S. Eliot calls this the violet hour', or: 'This character could be compared to Parson Adams whose name will be familiar to you.') This was of course bluff, a desperate effort to right the ship of the intellect before she went down with all hands. I hoped that the pretence of a life of the mind might produce a life of the mind in my students. I can't say whether I succeeded at all in this enterprise; sometimes students said nice things (and sometimes less-nice things) about my teaching but never, ever has anyone asked me to tone it down a bit; *au contraire*. But, whether it was a successful ploy or not, I felt I had no choice; I just could not slide down towards the attitudes and intellectual expectations of a schoolmaster. Or what's the point?

The key interchange with our students, in English anyway, came when they wrote essays for us (six per semester in 1972, five in 1982, four in 1992, three in 2002.... deduce what you will.) There were some nice surprises as one encountered occasional students who could *write*, or who had *read some books*. Overall I'm quite sure that they were all doing their best, and the problem wasn't personal to individual undergraduates, it was more a matter of simple change: five percent of the population (the rate in 1960) might conceivably be expected to engage in the life of the mind but fifty percent (the current rate) surely cannot be or we'd all be on the flying island of Laputa.

Things could go a bit wrong with essays of course and one of the things that kept one reading them was the hope of some startling titbit just round the corner of the next page. One moment that I particularly enjoyed was when a stern young Scotswoman was writing for me on Hardy; she had been studying *The Mayor of Casterbridge* (not just 'reading' it of course, but attacking it as a 'set book' – another revealing phrase that I had never heard before) and she wished to express the idea that Mayor Henchard, the novel's hero, is frequently highly self-critical. What she wrote however was this: 'Michael Henchard lived a life dominated by self-abuse', which is not quite how Hardy puts it.

We used to invite weaker students, and this was one of them, to 'come and discuss this essay please.' Duly invited, young Fiona came along to see me; I started to go through her lamentable prose with her. Arriving at page three I saw a vast red exclamation mark, my own, put there in the heat of my hilarity on the subject of poor old Henchard's habits. Oh dear I thought, we've got to get across that hurdle too. I ploughed on with my criticisms until we reached the offending sentence. Fiona was blushing beetroot several seconds before we got there. 'You know what that word *means*?' I queried. 'Oh yes' said the scarlet girl, 'I collected ma essay with ma boy fren', an' he explained.' I had a vision of an agonized pink youth, twisting his hands and saying 'er' until he suddenly blurted out, in front of everyone present, the surprising truth.

On another occasion I counselled a young lady whose handwriting was illegible that she should try a fountain pen. Once I had explained to her what this was

273

she agreed she would try and some weeks later she came to my office to discuss an essay with me. Wearing a light summer dress and holding a wide-mesh string bag on her lap she seemed at ease and the conversation appeared to be going well. She was wearing tights that, though flesh-coloured most of the way up were definitely black at the top where they disappeared. I allowed this thought to flick past as I concentrated on what she was saying about Ibsen or Wordsworth.

But a minute or two later she shifted position and I could not help seeing that the black patch had *grown*. Trying simultaneously to look and not to look at what was happening I scented disaster. Eventually she became aware if not of the direction of my glances then surely of a sensation in her crutch. She looked down and, perforce, raised the string bag. As she did so a small but sufficient cascade of black ink fell from its underside, the ink joining the pool on her lap. She had not closed the cap on her ink bottle tightly enough and this was the result. She stood, which made things worse, tried to speak, tried to mop and failed in both attempts as I sat aghast. Then she stepped to the door of my office, all dignity gone, dripping black. Getting hold of the handle she wrenched the door open and turned a flaming face towards me. 'You and your fucking fountain pen!' she cried and was gone.

Some others at Stirling University were full of strange hatreds too. Not many, but the emotion was clearly very pure. A girl student called Yvonne for instance, a petite beauty who was all sweetness to my face during tutorials, was overheard at one point by a colleague talking about me in a corridor. 'That Tory bastard!' said Yvonne, 'When the day comes we'll know what to do with people like *him*!' So you never know.

Like many of the young people I have known Yvonne suffered from Parent Hunger, specifically Father Hunger, so she must be forgiven. I am not sure precisely why this epidemic of mental distress has silently invaded modern culture, at least in the West, but I suspect it is the reverse side of the new power of the child. If you think about it, until about 1950 children were the enemy, to be tamed, squashed, silenced and if necessary hit with sticks. Then adults became softer, more child-like themselves, encouraged to 'get in touch with their feelings', not to wear ties and to go about in clothes that a previous generation would have regarded as underwear. This may have been a good thing overall, but it left the field of stern demands and high standards open to the children themselves who rushed into the vacated space with glad cries. Placating children now became the precise reverse equivalent of the old task of placating parents. Criticism started to come from below not from above.

You know the sort of thing: '*Child*! Cease being idiotic or I will hit you' has been replaced by '*Dad*, how can you be so *stupid*?' And 'If you are very good for a whole year we'll take you to Butlins for a weekend' has been replaced by 'But we *have* to afford to take them on holiday! What will they *say* if they can't go?' I met this phenomenon one surprising day when some mistresses at Alice and Miranda's public school in Scotland were chatting with me about a thing I had never heard of called Girl Power. At first I literally did not know what this could refer to, but as they talked it quickly became horribly apparent what they meant: for thousands of years the children had been scared of the teachers, now the teachers were scared of the children.

5. FRENCH

Hippolyte Taine attributed the French Revolution to the 'Classicism' of the French *philosophes* under the Ancien Regime; their Enlightened thinking, he assumed, made people yearn for rational government. John Morley in an essay of 1870 or so contradicted him, preferring the suggestion that the world-record poverty, corruption, inequality and hopeless organisation of the country that the King Louis ran were enough to explain some rather cross people. When I say 'the King Louis' it isn't a mistake: what I mean is 'the King *Louises'* in the plural, though that gives a strange impression of ambiguous gender ('Hello! I'm King Louise.') But the plural of 'King Louis' is a bit tricky: in French it would just be *'les rois Louis'*.

Perhaps it's appropriate, talking of plurals, that there wasn't all that much plurality among them in reality either. It is a remarkable fact that Louis XIII, Louis XIV, Louis XV and Louis XVI ruled France for 180 years between them and that had the last of them lived a normal lifespan instead of being guillotined in 1793 at the age of 38 this figure could easily have reached 200 years. No wonder that the average Frenchman, until revolution finally stirred in him, thought that it was by divine dispensation that France was as it was and that a Louis on the throne was as inevitable as winter.

But if the French Revolution itself was not brought about by the French 'Classical' style of thought as Taine opined (you could substitute 'Cartesian' or 'Rationalist' for 'Classical'), modern France in all its maddening mixture of good and bad certainly was. And it is hard to overestimate the difference between French and English thought or indeed the difference between

276

saying anything in one language and then in the other. Translation comes to seem, the further one plunges into it, almost literally impossible.

Long before I moved to Aquitaine in 2001 I had tangled with France, that most ambiguous of our neighbours, on several occasions. Two of these happened at long distance, from the safety of Scotland in fact. Here they are, 'fleshed out' as they say.

First: In 1986 I organised a conference-cum-festival at Stirling University to celebrate Beckett's eightieth birthday. He didn't come of course, either to that or to the even bigger bash in Paris that had preceded mine. Even *sans* Monsieur B I felt that to be international we needed not only scholars from all over the world (120 of them came, Beckett being at that time the tastiest flavour in literary academia) but also performances, on the 'festival' rather than the 'conference' side, from the UK, Ireland and France. One of these involved the leading French Beckett actor of the time, one Pierre Chabert. This intensely Thespian Froggy cove puzzled me at the time of my invitation to him by insisting that he was going to *bring his own table* for a performance of *Krapp's Last Tape* or, to give it its French title, *La Derniere Bande*. And that he was travelling by plane.

Meeting him at Edinburgh Airport was only very difficult. He had brought a silent female sidekick and spent a huge amount of time extracting his enormous table, wrapped in about a kilometre of Clingfilm, from the special Luggage-You-Shouldn't-Have-Been-Travelling-With office. Then he asked if we could eat. Arriving in Stirling at ten at night the choices were few; only an Indian restaurant was open, and he refused to go there until I told him that it was the only food he was likely to get that night. Reluctantly he wolfed down an enormous biryani and the next morning complained that he had slept not at all. With absolutely predictable Gallic cliché he moaned a bit and said '*les épices vous savez*' as he rubbed his stomach.

Next morning, too, we got him to our campus theatre in time for dress and technical rehearsals, fitted in between the other Beckett productions that were going on. He seemed to hit it off quite well with our stagehands and I breathed a sigh. All seemed set for his epoch-making *Krapp* or *Bande* at 8pm.

Came the hour and the entire conference, together with a multitude of hangers-on, crowded into the theatre, a small, black circular affair with seating almost all round. The black walls echoed the low lighting and the dark play. I felt that this was going to work. The ushers turned the house lights down and we waited in hope. But nothing happened. At seven minutes past eight I felt anxious, at ten past cross, and at a quarter past I saw that the whole thing would be a disaster and I had better just go back stage and see what sort of a disaster it would turn out to be. I walked across the black floor, watched by a couple of hundred eager eyes some clearly already thinking about the bar but still in general full of the will to out-Sam Sam. Somehow.

Entering the scene-dock from the stage door I found myself in the high empty space that a modern theatre always provides. Scaffolding towers loomed at me, black curtains. Minimal lighting made the stored scenery ghostly and huge. And among it all, dressed in an immense Beckettian dressing gown stalked Chabert, hands behind his back, *pacing*. His two-metre height rose ominously.

'*Pierre! C'est l'heure!*' I whispered in a stentorian hiss. He swung round on me and his eyes glittered from about four feet above my own (I have

278

said he was tall; I am not; and he seemed to have grown substantially since lunch; perhaps he was wearing elevator shoes.) He looked, in his grey giganticness, like a character from one of those Beckett television plays such as *...but the clouds...*

'*Non!*' he replied in an equally powerful whisper, '*Je joue pas ce soir!*' And he resumed his pacing. I trotted after him. '*Mais Pierre! Pourquoi pas?*'

It turned out that Chabert had made a deal with the stagehands that they would set everything up and then leave; he would manage the one-man show by himself. But he had asked for the green Exit signs in the auditorium to be switched off for the duration of his performance, contrary to the law that governs theatres; the stagehands were supposed to have done it before going home, but according to Chabert they had not. In a fiery display of Gallic temper, artistic egocentricity and biryani-enhanced halitosis that would have felled a charging yak, he pronounced as if they were his last words before descending into hell, '*C'est de la guerre psychologique!*' '*Oh surement pas*' I replied weakly.

I cajoled, I bullied, I threatened, I begged. Eventually he relented and, saying only that he had never been so deceived in his life (perhaps he meant 'disappointed'), he ushered me back into the theatre and, after a due pause, made his entrance to the applause of the cognoscenti and, of course, of those who had to pretend that they knew that that was how the play was supposed to start. I looked about me: the green Exit signs had all been extinguished as per his request. He just hadn't bothered to check. Neither had I.

Second: a couple of years later I was invited by my friend Colin Donald to help him with the preparation of some programme notes for the Edinburgh Festival. In particular he wanted an extensive note translated from French for a theatre company of considerable intellectual pretension and intense obscurity. I did eventually go and see their play, which wasn't absolutely bad although it went on for four hours, but the immediate task was to make some sense of the small essay, as provided, which was to be included in the programme and was intended, shall we say, to explain the piece.

Gazing at the first sentence I could at once see where I was, namely at the place where the normal mind begins to go numb and the chaps lose the will to read on. Abstraction was piled on abstraction even here at the beginning; enigma was compounded with enigma and by the third line I was totally lost.

What, under these circumstances, was I to do? I was not prepared to parrot the incomprehensibilities in front of me by indulging in that most hopeless of exercises 'literal' translation, but to make sense of the article I would need to tear it to pieces and, guessing at what was meant, reconstruct it approximately along English lines. In translation I have always been a '*cibliste*' rather than a '*sourcière*' – that is, I believe that the translation is *for the reader*, for the '*cible*' or target, rather than for the benefit of the originator or source (there is a pointless pun here on '*sorcière*' which is the French for a witch.) If the target reader is happy and unencumbered by Gallicisms or Hispanicisms or wonky English he has his money's worth, and this regardless of the question as to whether the impossible dream of precise or 'accurate' translation has been achieved. As Edmund Wilson pointed out long ago the best translations are those which differ most widely from the original – *Omar Khayyam* being a case in point.

But reconstructing the garbage, the *ordure*, of this programme note was a tricky business and I definitely diverged widely from the intentions of the author although I have to say those intentions were far from clear. Had I gone for a more source-orientated translation the theatre-goers of Edinburgh would have been treated to a long series of sentences approximately as along the following lines:

> The spirit of theatrical deconstruction of the self undertakes an altogether aleatory circularity consisting of chance encounters. Intelligence and force combine. Passion remains encapsulated. Although the anthropological approach forces stringent requirements onto the psychological element in modern culture there is also another sociology, the sociology of the word, an attitude combining grace and perception. This is not to be taken as freedom. Far from it.

The huge gulf between French and English, and between the cultures carried by those two languages, yawned before me. In short: what the bloody hell does that all mean? And there were pages and pages of it. We are just not like them Frogs, but I did my best to produce something that was at least English and faintly coherent (not at all as above) and I sent it in. Ructions followed.

The French author-director-producer, these roles being fluid in the avant-garde to which he belonged, became immediately and wildly incensed. He called a meeting of the Festival people, including Colin but not thank heavens me, and banged the table loudly. The translation was no good, it didn't reflect the meaning of the original; this was a travesty, a treachery. Colin told me that the meeting went on, if not for four hours then certainly for a very long time. If only people would heed the advice of Sydney Smith: 'Short views for God's sake – short views!' Eventually, since life must after all go on even in France, although a compromise was impossible a decision had to be made. The French bloke wouldn't budge and wanted something far more '*fidele*' to his monstrous original, and the committee, to their eternal credit, wouldn't have that at any price. They threatened him with leaving a blank page in the programme if he didn't become more reasonable, but he didn't become more reasonable. Eventually a blank page was left in the programme. By chance I seemed to have reached the apotheosis of minimalist criticism. Oh, and I got paid my fee. For nothing.

6. REGIS

Like all fields of life perhaps, academia has a tendency towards hero-worship. Some writers, even some critics, become glossy although the reason for this may not be altogether clear. They are mentioned twenty times more often than others around the campus and in the prints; they appear on television, become household names, are the stars at conferences, attract the crowds. This Hollywood-ish tendency is even clearer in France where 'writer' and 'critic' are less clearly distinguished from one another. Who has not heard of Levi-Strauss, of Sartre, of Camus, of Barthes, of Derrida? And beyond these, and perhaps another half-dozen that go with them, who has heard of the others at all?

    The novelist John Fowles, for a while, was one of these charisma-merchants for my generation. People would have that slight intake of breath when they sang his praises, and colleagues and students looked at me with that odd mixture of awe and hatred when I began a sentence, as I did on occasion, 'As John Fowles told me

282

the other day…' That he was a victim of this not-always acceptable adulation was apparent to the novelist himself. He complained of letters from admirers, many of them covering-letters enclosed with the lamentable MSS of their novels, in which aspirant writers more or less lay down before him and asked for him to take over their lives, be their guru, hand down the word of God from on high and answer the riddle of the universe, preferably by return post.

Writers like Fowles for one reason or another develop a kind of emotional-intellectual charisma that can turn the heads of aficionados and, *a fortiori*, university-level admirers of their work. I remember an otherwise quite sane colleague from Chicago telling me that he had prepared a little speech to make to Samuel Beckett when that great man finally conceded him an interview in Paris. The speech began something along the lines: 'There have been three great moments in my life Mr Beckett: the day I married my wife, the day my daughter was born, and today when I have the privilege of meeting you.' Quite how Sam the sardonic nihilist felt about this nauseating *captatio benevolentia* I never learned, but I can't imagine that he just smiled, sat back and said 'Right on pal.'

So it was with mixed feelings that I drove down to Lyme Regis on the Dorset coast one fine day when I had been at Stirling for a dozen years or so, to meet the great man. Was this useless and nauseating hero-worship or academic research?

Fowles lived at the top of the town, overlooking the English Channel, in a nice early-Victorian place called Belmont House, fruit I suppose of the film rights for *The French Lieutenant's Woman* and its considerable success as a novel; also curiously coincident with the name of my public school. A woman answered the door.

Now, if Fowles was not quite in the Sam Beckett answer-the-riddle-of-life league he was, in spades, someone from whom one might expect to receive the glad word on the subject of women, so meeting this lady produced an immediate frisson of emotional interest coupled with a certain intellectual vibration as if here one might be in the presence of the Key to Love. Remember *Daniel Martin*? Remember the first (better) version of *The Magus*?

We late-existentialist readers of Lawrence Durrell's *The Alexandria Quartet*, novels concerned with Woman, Meaning and the Art of Writing, also readers of Sartre, Camus and Colin Wilson's *The Outsider*, were keen to make sense of this new wisdom, to live as these novelists, philosophers and suicides of the great disenchantment lived. So for me to see, framed in the doorway, an actual woman of this ilk, presumably as existentialist and full of the Fowles thinking as it would be possible to be, was like meeting Ste Bernadette of Lourdes on a bus during an intense Catholic childhood.

One reason for the visit, and the first question I had prepared, was about a recondite literary matter. In Fowles' historical novel *A Maggot* of 1985 there are facsimile pages from a contemporary publication, *The Gentleman's Magazine* of 1736. Teaching Fowles' novels one year at Stirling, I felt a strange intertextual presence as I struggled with this *Maggot*. There was something on one of the facsimile pages of the magazine, reproduced rather at random in the novel, which stirred my memory. Then I saw what it was: there was a reference in the *Gentleman's* of 1736 to the Porteous Riots that took place in Edinburgh in that year.

And the Porteous Riots, of course, are central to the plot of *The Heart of Midlothian*, allegedly Scott's most serious novel and the book that would later bequeath its name to an Edinburgh football club.

Scott's Porteous, historically real, was the unpopular government official who decided that a death-sentence passed on the young hero should be carried out. After the brutal execution of this man the burghers of Auld Reekie, resenting the long arm of London government stretching out in this way, took justice into their own hands and determined to show Captain Porteous what was what. They staged an extremely orderly riot with the sole aim of catching this blighted administrator and stringing him up, which they did. Revenge having been taken they went back to their homes. Eventually the news reached London, got into the *Gentleman's Magazine* and provoked anger and retribution from the government.

I was in contact with Fowles at the time, thinking of writing something about his fiction, and wanted to ask him what he felt about this rather random connection with Walter Scott. He wrote back admitting that it was entirely fortuitous and that he had neither intended to include the particular page with the Porteous riots on it nor meant to make any reference to Scott. So much for intertextual criticism I thought, until I realised that this aleatory occurrence actually demonstrated the power of the intertextual rather well. To express it professionally: the parasitic paratext (the 1736 facsimile) cannot but relate fully to its host (*A Maggot*), and if there is an intertext within the paratext it too must be allowed to have its semantic day quite regardless of the intentions of the author.

One thing led to another and, as a result of negotiations, here I was arriving at Lyme to interview the great man. So we get back to the woman at his door. She invited me in, showed me through the kitchen (an Aga, flowers, space, light) to the study. As I followed her across the hall I caught a movement out of the corner of my eye – another woman! Coming down the stairs, young, blonde, beautiful. Dear God! The Fowles harem, keepers of the flame, knowers of the knowledge, vestals but surely not virgins. Scenes from that astonishing collection of Fowles stories *The Ebony Tower* sprang to mind: was this the heroine of the title story? Was she the muse of the old painter who is a thinly-disguised version of Fowles himself? Was the other woman the one who actually has the sex with the old boy while the muse just sits around being a muse? Was I the young man, the 'hero' who visits the painter in his *domaine*, his Bluebeard's Castle of erotic and artistic depths and learns so much? Phew! Was this my chance to be part of a novel?

The two women vanished and I was in The Presence. Fowles looked like his picture, handsome with beard and dark hair, deep brown eyes and all; we exchanged the usual. The first woman brought coffee and we got down to business. Yes, John remembered the essay on Hardy that he had written for a collection I had edited; no, he wouldn't write another; yes, wasn't it funny how the Porteous Riots had slipped into *A Maggot* without his being aware of it? Ah, I came from Dorset too, did I? Up in *Tess* country? Very nice if slightly strange. No, he hadn't heard of Silton. Did I know 'Bill Golding'?

This turned out, after brief embarrassment on my part, to be William Golding, he of *Lord of the Flies* and much else, also of Dorset. *He*'d write something for me if asked (he didn't; I didn't ask; he died.) Then it was time for lunch.

286

To my chagrin the imagined *déjeuner à quatre* around the large pine table in the kitchen with the vestals producing nectar and ambrosia with added flavour of Wessex while the Master discoursed to his promising disciple was instantly liquidated by the announcement that we were going out. Still, a tête-à-tête with the great man over a lunch with much fine wine wouldn't be bad.

We walked down the road and out into the sunshine where some large houses and hotels overlooked the Channel. One of the hotels had a nice shady bar and restaurant and then a lawn going right out to the cliff edge. 'Your usual Mr Fowles?' asked the lady at the bar before I could get my offer in. 'Thank you Jane – a St Clement's please' and, turning to me, 'you know, Oranges and Lemons'. 'How about something a little more interesting?' I squeaked, seeing my second imagined High Point vanishing as I watched. 'Gin and tonic? Wine? Just name it!'

'No no, no thanks'. Doctor's orders I'm afraid – I've got this heart.'

Now what indiscretions, what existential wisdom, what Truths about Women could possibly come out of a sober sandwich? My heart sank. The sunlight was brilliant, the awnings on the lawn inviting, my own gin delicious, but we were like a pair of well-heeled pensioners picking at the whitebait and clutching our wholemeal rolls as we gazed at the sparkling Channel and John held forth… on publishing and publishers and a mutual friend who was starting up a small Wessex publishing house.

I made a few small efforts to get into the deeper matters I had surely come for. 'No,' he said, 'that's my wife. And the other girl's just a temporary secretary. Gosh, I've been married *so* long! You married?' My visions of tales of complex intensities, of group relationships with serious existentialist undertones, vanished into the bright afternoon. We fell back on the publishing numbers for the *French Lieutenant*. After a piece of fruit (no creamy puds for old Hypchondriacus of course) and a de-caff Fowles looked at his watch. 'Better get back.'

The lesson is too banal but infinitely useful: Don't believe. Don't believe that anyone else has the same agenda as you when you are on the make or desiring, wanting, trying to get.

Don't be disappointed in anyone. Don't go Expecting, Looking For, Desiring. Don't imagine that the charismatic don't get old and ill.

I should have read Hardy more carefully. Remember in *Jude* when Jude goes to visit a musician who has written some appealing church music? The young if obscure idealist knocks at the musician's door hoping for artistic insights only to find that his hero has become a wine-merchant. Jude leaves carrying with him nothing more than the former-genius's wine catalogue – a list of wines that the young stonemason can't anyway afford. *Jude* is a chronicle of ill-judged desire and ambition. Though, to be fair, one can't help desiring what one desires, can one?

Twice I had my own opportunities to meet Beckett. Twice I let them go by without taking action. That was the better path, the untaken road to Paris set against this taken road to Lyme. I thought I refused the chances because I was too proud to be an acolyte, but the reasoning may have been more sensible than that.

'John Fowles' are two words that signify the novels and short stories written under that name. They bear no relation, at least no relation that is our business or anything to do with us, to John Fowles. *Que cela suffit.*

The 'reference' to the Porteous Riots in *A Maggot* is of some interest, but there is no deeper reward available; you could be tempted to say that it 'means nothing.' Lyme Regis is neither more nor less spiritual or wise a place than any other. Existentialism was only a fashion. This too shall pass. God is not mocked; be thou not mocked either.

7. CELTIC

Scotland is a curious place for a mild Englishman to live in as I did for nearly thirty years (1972 – 2001.) I loved it but remained unclear as to its fundamental nature and as to what the Scots thought of me. The considerable gaps between the different aesthetic and social experiences available there contributed largely to this kind of confusion. At one moment, for instance, one finds oneself strolling in the heather and gazing at a mountain under a huge sky in perfect peace on a longish October day; at another moment, apparently only shortly after the first, one notices that one is stuck in a traffic jam on one of the ugliest motorways in the world (the M8) looking at hideous high-rise flats of Glasgow in the heavy rain of a November afternoon as the light falls to almost zero *lux* although it is only 4 o'clock pm and the temperature falls to 4 degrees C.

Equally one can at one moment be in a Glasgow pub surrounded by a rough culture that seems unchanged since the Second World War (the first man to whom I was introduced in such a place shook my hand with a couthy grin and the words '*Fuckin' glad to meet you!*') and at another moment one can find oneself just a few streets away discussing opera with some of

289

the most educated people one has known. Central
Edinburgh is definitely delicious but a few hundred
yards away there are some of the most depressing
streets in the world. From some such streets in the two
main cities, or in Dundee or Aberdeen, you can actually
see the heather-clad hills as you walk through the rain
and the rubbish; it seems hard to adjust to.

One of the better myths about Scotland is that
The People Are Nice. I use 'myth' here not in the
pejorative sense but to signal an unwillingness to
commit to too firm an idea of 'the truth' about a place.
And the people of Caledonia are frequently and
impressively nice in all conscience. A pair of drunken
punters, wandering about Sauchiehall Street when
Pauline and I were there shopping one morning at 9.30
(note the time), seeing me in my *beret basque* and
Beckettian long overcoat could not refrain from
comment at what to them was an astonishing sight. But
what were they to say? How discharge the hot burden of
joy, amazement and sartorial criticism that was
mounting in their bosoms? The solution came to the
older one of the two as he swayed into my path to
address me the better. Looking me in the eye and
smiling alcoholically he found the very formula: '*Buon
giorno* by the way!' he cried.

Elements of knowledge of life in continental
Europe had not faded from his much-beleaguered brain
cells, the beret signalling something only inaccurate by
a few hundred miles; and in default of that what did he
have? 'Good morning sir'? 'It's a fine day'? Much
better to plunge in with the Italian. After all, he might
have struck lucky, found himself sharing a cappuccino
with a new friend, been invited to Bergamo for the
summer, who knew? But the accost was hardly
mercenary as such, just a joyful recognition of

something and someone different. The 'by the way' falsely implied previous knowledge, an earlier discussion, years of multilingual relationship. A sudden joke. Pure friendliness in fact.

On that same visit to Glasgow we stayed in the Hilton Hotel where, as it happened, some sort of Football Event was taking place. In the lobby where we sat having a drink there was a flurry of photographers and gawpers one afternoon and people rushing about. Then into the melee came a dozen young men in green tracksuits all looking rather shiny. They posed in all directions and muttered to each other or stared about them glassy-eyed. This, said Pauline, was the Celtic football team, there for a photo-shoot presumably. I gazed at them like any of the gawpers. They were herded about, given footballs to hold, asked for autographs, filmed. Pauline said 'This would be a big moment for any of my brothers' and I saw that she was remembering many a tense evening in her family watching the boys in spearmint shirts being beaten again by Rangers. Coming as she does from a Glasgow Catholic family (Irish ancestry, nine children, council house, salt of the earth) this moment put ghosts in front of her that she had never seen in the flesh, indeed ghosts that she had been trying to rid herself of for her whole adult life.

Her oldest brother, whom I came to know quite well, referred frankly to Rangers, the opposition, as 'the Huns'; when drunk he would alter the target of his hatred from his footballing enemies to the national enemy, singing loudly in public '*I hate the English*.' We the English are Huns too if you look at it rightly. He supported Celtic.

Talking of Scottish sport, it happened that in the 1990s I played cricket in our village in Stirlingshire for a team which one year managed to 'Join the League', evidently a matter of much importance to our Captain and the others who ran the show. This meant that instead of randomly playing other rain-sodden teams in villages around the central Scottish countryside we went further afield and even, on a couple of occasions, into Glasgow. The first of these matches involved playing a team that had risen to the dizzy heights of Having a Professional. This young man had been plucked from the sub-continent and had those physical abilities that only Indians and Pakistanis have of bowling unhittable balls and batting without effort. His tan and his flashing eyes brightened the grey afternoon and he managed to defeat my team absolutely single-handedly. We were all out for 53. So soon in fact that once the opposition, by which I mean the professional from Gujarat, had rattled off 54 runs in half an hour the game was over. We pleaded to go again and our opponents rather gracelessly accorded us this honour, so I found myself once more at the crease. The wicket-keeper from the Glasgow team, obviously miffed that his Saturday evening wasn't going to start as soon as he had hoped, squatted behind the stumps grumbling and 'sledging' in that rather horrible manner that has become part of modern cricket. One of the slips standing next to him asked him whether he wanted to get home. 'Ay' he replied, 'the sooner the better; just as soon as we've got rid of this cunt.' I think that was the first and last time that I've been called that.

Our second visit to the city of Kens and Hens was later that season (we must have been dropped from the League the following year) to play Saint Aloysius Former Pupils. We arrived a little early at their ground, not an uncommon experience as those who have read *England Their England* should know - it's a book about life in England written by a Scotsman called Macdonald in the 1920s and includes a description of a village cricket match that has never been bettered. The drizzle persisted with its usual tenacity and we stood disconsolately in the pavilion porch for a space until the bus arrived with our opponents. As the first one got out I thought 'Gosh! A Catholic Pakistani Scotsman!' Then there was another! And another!! I smelled a considerable rat whose form was completed once the bus had emptied and all the players in the St Aloysius FP team were quite evidently from the Glasgow Pakistani community. My surprise was equalled only by my fear that this team would put us to the sword in short order as, indeed, they subsequently did. My fellow team members maintained absolutely neutral countenances and great dignity as we introduced ourselves to this collection of second-generation cricketing wizards. Only at the tea interval did one of us (well, me, of course, unable to resist as ever) put the question: 'Did you, er, did you *all* go to St Aloysius?' My neighbour, a charming demon bowler with a striking combination of Lahore and Bishopbriggs in his speech, laughed. "Oh no! No no, not one of us at all.' (I cannot begin to represent in print the subtle phonemic combinations of his two accents.) 'We are all brown chaps and that used to present difficulties, so we took over this defunct club. Now no problems!' 'Gosh' I said. 'Oh yes' said Ferouz, 'it is much more fun this way. You have to adjust to the situations of life, no? With the football too! When the Old Firm are playing I wear my Celtic scarf round the town in the Catholic parts, and there's no trouble. Suddenly I'm not a Paki any more, I'm one of the boys. People look at me and smile instead of frowning.'

Truly culture is an arbitrary business. As, I fear, is one's hearing when travelling about Britain with its many accents. There was, for instance, a monster-shouldered son of toil who played in the village team with us whose name I failed to capture quite accurately when he joined. He seemed to say, through a thick moustache surrounded by council-house stubble, that he went by the name, unusual in central Scotland, of 'Gus'. I rather liked that and, once I got to know him better and we had fielded for several long damp afternoons together in the covers, I began to feel free to tease him a little – teasing being a phenomenon that the sports field accelerates of course and is in my case quick to emerge under all circumstances. 'Come on Gussie!' I'd cry as he lumbered after a ball. Or: 'Good old Augustus! Well played sir!' Or, for the amusement largely of myself, I'd call him 'Fink-Nottle' after the Wodehouse character, something to which, I should have noticed, he never responded. As his face, though handsome, was entirely inexpressive, I had no idea what effect this ribbing had on the poor fellow until the day, many matches into the season, that he resolved to make a stand. I had asked him what he thought of the match just played as we strolled off the pitch, prefacing my question with 'Gussie old man...' He stopped and faced me: 'Look Lance' he growled in a deep bass (though that was how he spoke all the time) ' *Chrus*! It's no *Gus*, it's Chrus! I think ye've had ma name wrong.' 'Oh?' I said, 'it's *Chrus*?' 'Erse!' he said, 'Ut's allus bun Chrus.'

CHAPTER 11. BALTIC 1990s

1. ESTONIA

I think I may have been Baltic in an earlier incarnation.
I remember as a boy reading an article in the Times
about a distinguished-looking chap, portrayed above the
article in an extremely pensive black-and-white
photograph, who was still in the 1960s the Estonian
Ambassador in London. As you know, the Soviet Union
ingested a whole raft of Asian 'republics' after the
Revolution and by 1945 had also got Estonia, Latvia
and Lithuania well down its gullet. This is not the place
for a history of that shabby imperialism, made shabbier
because Stalin's discourse was violently anti-imperialist
and even more so because dissent of all kinds was dealt
with by the bullet regardless of justice, process or
morality. But I was surprised to find how strongly I felt
about Stalin's three Baltic victims while I merely had
feelings of political disapproval when it came to
Kazakhstan.

The Estonian Ambassador, of course
unrecognized by Moscow, was a leftover from the war.
Britain, with a slightly furtive sense of honour, had
apparently never recognized the Soviet takeover of his
country so on he stayed performing, presumably, a
merely symbolic role in the London diplomatic corps.
And from then on I was always indignantly interested in
the steady destruction of Baltic identity, despairing, as
we all were, of ever getting the Soviets out of East
Germany and Poland let alone out of their 'own'
'republics.' Then came 1989 and the Fall of the Berlin
Wall.

Within a year Tallinn, Riga and Vilnius were up in arms and the Russian occupiers, what with the confusion back in Moscow, were unable to stem the move to independence. By 1991 there was a proper Estonian Ambassador in London, and indeed a Latvian and a Lithuanian one. I sometimes wondered whether the old Estonian one was still going and what he thought, but I imagine he had pegged out by then, dying perhaps from lack of hope some time before. And the UK, along with the rest of Europe and the USA, were busy binding the new Baltic States to themselves with hoops of steel such as NATO and the EU as well as with softer substances such as culture. As a result there was suddenly Money available from the British Council for academic visits and in a very short time I found myself on a plane to Tallinn preparing to spend a week in Tartu, the Oxford of Estonia, lecturing to their English Department. The place felt utterly alien and yet, somehow, faintly like coming home. I repeated the visit twice more, going on until the British Council decided that Estonian independence no longer needed the close support of Butler-on-Metaphor-in-Thomas-Hardy and the Money stopped.

The first night in Tartu was held under the aegis of the Professor of English at the university there, one Heino Liiv. Me: 'What does your surname mean Heino?' Heino: 'Well... the original Estonians had no family names, so the Russians gave them some in the Nineteenth Century. Most of us are called things like Tree or Lake or River. I'm called Sand.' At Belmont Abbey during Civil Defence lessons – did we really have those? – we were taught how to announce a fire in a public building; one has apparently to address the manager or similar responsible authority with the words 'Mr Sand is present' in order to prevent mass hysteria and stampeding. 'Sand' is apparently the least panic-inducing noun in English.

Heino had never left the Soviet Union – nobody ever did – and had learnt his excellent English in Moscow. I think he had all the right liberal ideas but a lifetime of being told what to do and what to think had rubbed off even on this decent man. One of his reactions to the new order now being developed in his country was, for instance, fear. He believed that Western behaviour was sweeping Estonia for worse as well as for better, including teenage violence, gang culture and the widespread use of robbery involving weapons and physical assault.

In consequence on the night of our arrival he turned up at the flat that had been provided for me and another lecturer with an envelope full of money and a bag of sandwiches. He told us that it was far too dangerous to go out these days and that we had better remain at home; he had brought a colleague and their intention was to eat the sandwiches with us. I took the envelope of money with many thanks and then announced that, youth culture or no youth culture, we were going out and that they were going to be our guests. They exchanged resigned looks and nervously accompanied us to a restaurant where they explained that the other night someone in Tartu had been mugged. 'Just the one mugging?' I asked. 'Yes,' said Heino, but you know…' I'm afraid that we laughed and said that we simply didn't know. But after that all went very well not least because of the vodka.

There certainly is a drink question in the Baltics, and presumably all over the former Soviet Union except where Islam has got its hands on the stuff and broken the bottles (though see my experiences in Saudi Arabia, above.) That night we had several very large vodkas

297

each chased down with a glass of cranberry juice that came automatically to take away the taste of the firewater. The next night we went out to the student pub where, astonishingly, two pints of beer were put in front of each of us *before we had ordered anything*. Then, with the real drinks that we ordered after the free beer, came the delicious cumin-seed bread of the region toasted and smeared with crushed garlic, also free. Within ten minutes, thus, one was fairly drunk (two pints of beer, one large vodka) and fairly full (garlic bread in quantity.) Only an hour later was the question of where to eat canvassed by which time I was alas satisfied with my evening's ingestion and had to pretend enthusiasm for what was served next: a Soviet-style soup-of-seven-pigmeats each of which seven must have come, like those served to Pip in *Great Expectations*, from those parts of the pig of which the pig when alive had had the least reason to be proud; and then Trout in Chocolate.

Mark you, on my second expedition to Estonia I nearly came unstuck in my calculations about the electric soup. I had given up alcohol for Lent and was scheduled to arrive in Tartu on Maundy Thursday. Cunningly I had calculated, however, that the Orthodox Easter, falling that year the weekend before, would exonerate me the moment my plane touched down at Tallinn as *there* it would already be after Easter Sunday, the crucial ending to Lenten fasts. Imagine my surprise then when, as we were crossing the Baltic Sea, I remembered that Estonia, insofar as fifty years of communism had left any religion intact in the country, was Lutheran. Which meant that their Easter would be the same as ours and I still had three days to go. I wrestled with this dilemma and, after forty days without the demon drink, weakened to the point of a beer at the airport bar with my mentor and friend, a stray Scotsman who had also washed up in the Baltics though more permanently than me.

On the other hand all the Estonians I spoke to told me that *the Finns were worse.* I was told to look out for the arrival of the overnight ferry from Helsinki any given morning and, sure enough, happening to be in the Old Town of Tallinn one Thursday at about 9.30 am, I saw the flood of drunken Finns piling out of the port and trotting in small shrieking circles towards the bars. They were all absolutely steaming. Apparently they don't bother with cabins preferring the all-night bar on board the ferry and then really start drinking on arrival in Tallinn because the drink is cheaper. No breakfast was visible but there was a lot of Finno-Ugric laughter in the air. They had christened Vodka-and-Cranberry-Juice a Rolling Estonian but they could have given lessons.

There is a slightly hilly and rather pretty part of Estonia that we visited, my Scots friend and I, around Vilyandi, where the highest point in the country is to be found at all of 415 metres. Allegedly the highest point in the Baltic States, this hill was surpassed by the cunning Latvians a little before my arrival: their hill of 410 metres needed only a medium cairn to become bigger than the Estonian one and so they built it up with much giggling. Near our hill was a ski-jump sticking out above Estonia's magnificent Alpine eminence. I was told that it had been the practice centre for the Soviet Winter Olympics team a few years before. Which set me thinking about the flatness of Russia.

Besides the hills we visited the coast, well-known to the better-off English as a holiday resort in the 1920s before the days of compulsory sun-tans and nightclubbing. Rather nice, it even had some older buildings than is usual where communism has passed. One, a small hotel into which we booked for a night, was called Capiteni Vila and had been a private house before the war. The young woman who ran it had extraordinarily good English, better than Heino's and, when I asked her about that, she told me her story. Not uncommon, her tale made one realise what the ructions of the twentieth century were really like for those not lucky enough to live through them in say Gloucestershire.

Her grandfather, the Capiteni who had built the villa, a keen sailor, had left Estonia with the other Estonian middle-classes and Baltic Barons (all German) when the Red Army arrived after Eastern Europe was carved up under the Molotov-Ribbentrop Pact of 1939. He had ended up in England where this woman's father was born and where indeed he, her father, died having spent his life bilingual between English and Estonian but without ever having been allowed to visit Estonia. The woman herself, the grand-daughter, had learnt the language too and, come independence in 1991, boldly went to Tallinn and claimed back the villa, not to mention a block of flats in Tallinn, as her property. This having been successful she re-activated her Estonian nationality and moved into the Capiteni Vila advertising it as a nice place for English-speakers to stay and so it was.

I heard many such stories of people claiming their property back after the retreat of the Soviets who had stolen it: farmers and their grandchildren who had kept the secret of where their jewellery was, along with title deeds to the farms now collectivized, buried on the property somewhere. Amazing. I wondered whether, after the much longer period of theft (seventy years) that was the communist government in Russia itself there are

300

people who have brought off the same trick there. But even if there are, the Putin governments have proved much less law-abiding and concerned with justice than the rather good governments of the Baltic States so one supposes it has been hard for White Russians to prove their claims.

One strange modern disappointment attended this visit to Estonia. After my first visit in 1991 I had made an effort to learn some Estonian and it was on the way to the Capiteni Vila that I first tried it out in anger on a passer-by, asking him where the hotel was. In the spirit of the new national freedom he was getting into a large BMW when I accosted him and, with a smile, he replied in English with a perfect American accent 'It's down there on the left bud.' Of course! If you were a BMW-owning Estonian you would have some international language at your command – first Russian and now English. Why bother to help a struggling British chap with his three words of your own language? What use is it ever going to be to *him* to speak Estonian whereas practising your English is certainly going to be useful to *you*. I felt the tyranny of being a native-speaker of the world's top language, but then I realized that had I been German or Spanish or Mongolian the same thing would have happened. The educated Estonian would always presume, correctly, that I spoke English in addition to my native Spanish or Mongolian and that his English was better than my Estonian. In other words *nobody can now learn any minority language simply by going to the country and trying to speak it*. Strange.

Estonia has done well. They were the first of the Baltic countries to get their finances in order and the first to recover from the recession of 2007 -2008. The 'Troop-Watch' columns in their newspapers, which recorded the departures of the Red Army in the early 1990s, have long been abandoned as there are no more Russian soldiers on Estonian soil. Their Russian-speaking minority has been offered Estonian citizenship which most have taken; it means membership of the EU for one thing, and thus much less difficulty with travelling. The only criterion imposed on these Russian Estonians is that they pass an exam in basic Estonian. Fair enough I'd say. Some of them, when I was there, were trying to make a case for themselves as a minority who, in accordance with international law, should have their rights, privileges and language protected inside their new country. Estonians are decent and reasonable people but they have not been persuaded in this direction; as they point out, they never wanted the Russians there in the first place and only let them in at the sharp end of a tank barrel and as an alternative to being invaded militarily and generally murdered.

Some years later I met an Estonian woman of about seventy in Scotland, a person entirely naturalized into things British. As a girl during the war she had got out of Tallinn in one of the strange exchanges of power and populations that occurred between Stalin and Hitler, come to Britain and never gone back. She used to say how glad she was that she had never been beautiful; her beautiful friend from school with whom she had been walking home one day had been picked up by some lust-crazed Russian soldiers and: 'We never saw her again. But they left me.'

Astonishingly resilient and good-hearted as they are, I hope the Estonians go on doing well. While I was in their country they suffered their worst peacetime disaster on record: the ferry *Estonia* went down one night in the cold Baltic on its regular crossing to Sweden. In spite of a heavy sea the captain had the engines on full and the elderly vessel wasn't able to take the strain; she just split and sank. Nine hundred people died in the black water. Utter horror gripped the nation. In so small a country everyone knew or was related to a victim of this terrible moment. In spite of just having emerged from half a century of official atheism the television was full of dog-collars; previously-invisible pastors led the people in prayer. I hope they are all right now.

2. LATVIA

My Cambridge friend Stephen Nash, then ambassador to Latvia, invited Pauline and me to Riga for a few days in about 2001. We were put up in the grandest bedroom in the embassy complete with four-poster bed and treated to another side of life. Officially I was there as part of another British Council team of lecturers and I sang for my supper at the university. I remember with affection the Latvian bloke who filmed the occasion and who turned out to have rather good English; as we were leaving he approached me and made a small speech to the effect that he had enjoyed my talk and on the whole agreed with it but wondered if my thesis about Register would work among Russian-speaking Latvians, a question better in quality of both content and expression than those of the colleagues and students present during the main event.

While we were there Stephen held a party in honour of something British to which he invited, with apparent inevitability, the whole diplomatic corps of the new country, which is to say all the other ambassadors in Riga and their wives or husbands. Quite what is supposed to be gained by these affairs has always rather baffled me but they can be fun. On this occasion I was struck by a chap I was chatting to who turned out to be the Canadian ambassador's boyfriend - the Canadian ambassador being male. He made it clear that he was a Kept Man and that the Canadian government paid for him in just the way they would have done had he been the ambassador's wife. Mark you, Stephen himself, a man with a strong propensity to unsuitable marriage, had burdened the British taxpayer over a longish diplomatic career with several wives and many offspring these latter all being educated at private schools in Britain. At the time of our visit to Riga he had with him in the embassy a lovely lady from Georgia (his previous diplomatic posting) and their two-year-old daughter Dolly.

Going out to dinner one night with Stephen and some of his British friends in Riga Pauline was refused entry into the restaurant; by an ungentlemanly chance she had come through the doors last of our party and was addressed by the doorman with suppressed violence in Russian. 'What?' she countered. Someone came to the rescue and all was smoothed over. Stephen explained to us that Pauline's fur coat, glossy black hair and bright-red lipstick marked her out clearly as a prostitute. She found it hard to know how to react to this event.

I had my own species of public *malentendu* when we went to the main theatre in the town for a musical event to celebrate the Latvian National Day. Massed choirs of amazingly high quality sang for us – choral music is big in the Baltics – and musicians played local music under most of which we could hear as a sort of ground bass the theme '*This Is Not Russian.*'

All went well until the interval when, perhaps because of the National Day, there was a buffet supper in a large upper room overlooking the town square. I

304

don't know what the masses in the stalls did during this long interval but those of us attached to the diplomatic circus were invited to this supper along with the country's great and good. I got a drink and chatted to a few people and then decided the time had come to join the scrum around the food. Pushing past several large suits filled with Latvian muscle I managed to get through to the bowls of chicken salad and, seizing a plate, started to help myself. One of the suits, perhaps a little put out by my manoeuvre, remonstrated mildly at me in Latvian but I just smiled and filled up the plate. Turning to push back to my party I saw beside me, on the other side of the suit, a large lady in a fine red dress also struggling to get fed. Without thinking I commiserated with her in English. 'Yes' she said, 'it's a bit of a fight isn't it?' and we stood there chatting for a space about buffets. In the inevitable pause that followed this I said, 'OK, I'm here for the British Week at the university, what brings you to Toyland?' 'Oh' she said, 'I'm the President.' 'Really?' I said, 'President of the Opera House Committee that's running this thing?' 'Oh no', she said, 'President of Latvia.' 'Ah' I said, 'Would you like some chicken?'

And so she was – the President I mean. A Canadian national of Latvian origin, she had watched the arrival of independence in her country with interest from the distance of Toronto and, come the moment, had thrown her hat into the democratic ring. Perhaps tired of professional politicians from the Soviet era (read, I suppose, *toadies with blood on their hands*) the electorate had the enormous good sense to choose a complete outsider who wouldn't do anything nasty or stupid. So there she was, eating supper and talking to me, and she an actual Head of State. I didn't stress my meeting with the gay ambassador from her former country.

Talking of political leaders, Stephen had a Dachshund in the embassy called Maggie, after Margaret Thatcher, who, while all this singing and eating was going on, contrived among other derelictions partially to consume the photocopies I needed for my lecture.

CHAPTER 12. ITALY 2001 – 2004

1. FLORENCE

There is an assumption that Italy is a test of sensitivity. What will Venice with its paintings and palaces do for you, what will Rome? But the place of places for this examination of artistic and historical conscience, all Grand Tour and *A Room With A View*, is Florence. It is hardly imaginable that one will merely visit the city, tick it off and move on. Some reaction is required, some emotion has to be generated out of all that stone, out of all that art.

Foolishly we went there in the high summer of about 2004, Pauline and I with Alice and a girl friend of hers. To compensate for this folly I had hired a couple of flats in a villa outside the city, with swimming pool, so that we could retreat there when the Medici became too much for us. And, *en effet*, the owner of the villa, belonging to some species of elderly minor Italian aristocracy, bare from the waist up and looking like a shiny buffalo, gestured at the sky with the words '*Sole de leone!*' The yellow-maned sun roared from above and we wilted.

The owner's wife, an elegant Italian called Miranda, entertained us with local lore concerning her family, Tuscany and the derelictions of former guests of hers. I became, with my two words of Italian, the interpreter for the American family staying in another part of the establishment. 'There is a large toad in the pool!' I was obliged to tell her one hot afternoon. 'You may remove it' she said helpfully. Naturally Pauline stepped forward and dealt with the offending monster, dead I think from drinking too much chlorine. I stood by and quoted the passage in *Far From the Madding*

Crowd where Gabriel Oak realises that a storm is coming as he accidentally kicks a large toad off the path to Bathesheba Everdene's farm.

That was all right but other small incidents were more taxing. The charming American senior who was in charge of the visiting family approached me after breakfast one day and said 'Could you possibly tell Miranda that there is a smell around our place? I mean it's not at all nice; a bad smell.' He looked at me hoping I would twig, but in vain for all I said was 'Oh.' 'I mean', he tried again, 'there is an odour of, shall we say…' and he cast about for a term at once explicit and inoffensive, 'shall we say of *sew-azh.*' This last word rhymed with '*page*' in French. So '*soo-aahge*' a la francaise, or *sew-age* or, oh yes, *sewage*. Miranda did not appreciate this and was clearly looking for a way of saying 'You may remove it' as I left her to deal with the matter alone.

But worse was to follow. The next day old New-England-Dignified was back on the warpath. 'Oh dear, what now?' I asked him. 'Well' he said, 'would you like to look at my grandsons' intimate parts?' 'Ah!' I said 'er… why?' 'Come and see' he invited and led the way to the pool changing rooms. There the two boys, aged I suppose seven and nine, were gazing disconsolately at their crutches under the supervision of their mother. They were bright red about the midships and clearly in some sort of distress. 'Gosh' I said.

'Do you think your Italian would stretch to telling our hostess that her pool has caused these dermatological conditions in the boys?' 'Well…' I began and was about to go on with 'I don't think so' when I remembered David Niven's story about having his penis frozen during a long and very cold Italian downhill ski-run in inadequate trousers which failed to

protect his manhood very much at all. On that occasion
Niven had been suddenly aware that although he knew
only two Italian words they were, conveniently, the
word for frozen (also ice-cream) and a slang term for a
penis, say prick. Arriving in acute discomfort at the foot
of the run he yelled to the people round the ski-lifts
'*Catso gelato!*' ('*frozen prick!*') and was immediately
given aid in various forms including the bathing of his
affected part in a glass of brandy. This would do, I
reckoned, as I made my way to the main house and
sought out our delicately-nurtured hostess. After a quick
buon giorno I managed a sentence that would have
sounded in English something like 'When the boys enter
your pool they are burning their pricks.' She looked
slightly surprised. This time there was no question of
removal one hoped. Instead 'I will bring the creams' she
said. It occurred to me later that none of my own party
needed creams of any kind. What was it about the
American adolescents?

But the city of Florence was curious too. The
huge forbidding *palazzi* put me off with their immense
grey weight; the queues at the Uffizi made me think far
more of modern life than of the Renaissance; the Bridge
of Sighs was a tourist trap; the cafes absurd in their
greedy pricing.

On the other hand, travelling about with Alice
and her friend was special – that teenage consciousness,
energy and intermittent enthusiasm is a drug for parents,
as long as the teenager in question is enjoying herself.
Alice was. So her friend was; so I was; so Pauline was.

Mark you, Alice's friend had become obsessed
by the soundtrack of the Russell Crowe film *Gladiator*
and I found myself rather irritated after a while as we
drove round the Italian countryside listening to this
dramatic score again and again, so it was not all beer

and skittles. Does even good music pall? Or will there never come a time when I can't listen to Mozart's *Requiem* any more?

2. GENOA

The conference was at the university of Genoa; old-Italian and fairly distinguished. Someone was paying for the ticket and the accommodation nearby in the city. I took Pauline along. Flying over the Alps on the way from Heathrow the pilot decided that there was something wrong with his pressure, or ours, and insisted on going back to London. After a free sandwich and a beer we tried again, this time successfully, and we flew past Mont Blanc which almost seemed within arm's length, perfect and cloudless in the silvery moonlight. One of the few clichés that I've really appreciated.

When we finally got to the hotel it was shut. The taxi driver, in answer to my question as to whether he felt more Italian or Genoese had nearly crashed as he explained to us, with many arm-gestures and maximum emotion, '*Genovese! Genovese!*' (I tried to imagine some English equivalent: 'Are you English or do you consider yourself as first belonging to Buckinghamshire?' How many people, even if they could understand the question, would come out with 'Bucks! Bucks!'?) Banging and telephoning eventually roused the owner who let us in sleepily. The night was short. I think the conference was about Emotion: 'Emotion: Between Ostentation and Reserve' may have been the title and most people spoke in Italian which, after all and a little effort, one can just about understand. The food was tremendous.

The professor of Emotion, or at least of English Literature, was one Romana Rutelli who took Pauline and me under her wing and conducted us around the city as well as out to her house in the country. The high point of her act as guide to tourists was inviting us to her house where her husband, Giorgio, a bearded psychoanalyst of sorts, held court if not sway. In his large study there was, yes, a couch.

But Giorgio was also a Genoese, facing the sea as they all do, and he had, besides a couch, a boat, and Romana took us to it and we went onto it and sat down in the cabin. The wind blew, the lines rattled and we banged steadily against the quayside; drinks were poured. After some general discussion about sailing and much other talk that was I think probably lost in translation, I ventured to suggest that we set out on some sort of nautical jolly across the bay and well into the blue Mediterranean. Looks were exchanged and many opinions canvassed in two languages, but we never got to set sail. Either the wind was too strong or there wasn't time or Romana got sea-sick, no? So I cannot say that I have ever actually sailed in the Med. It turned out too that Giorgio almost never actually sailed either. "This is where he comes to think' said Romana.

Pauline and I walked all the way to the top of the town, some feat on that hillside, and came out onto a grassy patch surrounded by odd scraps of urban chaos. Concrete, broken glass, things rusting, all that seems entirely acceptable to modern *Homo Urbanus* who is a strange character in that his home is very likely clean and warm and tidy and his suburb miraculous, in historical terms, in its order and safety. But his built environment more generally is dominated by aesthetic horrors that earlier generation would never have put up with.

Up there, anyway, above the old city, we looked around the whole bay that fills the horizon with blue and the mind with thoughts of a Naval Power, which Genoa was, and of the scale of the sea. The grass, however patchy, seemed to be in secret league with that sea and to signal to it. We felt warm, slow, easy. Our minds were not those of the north any longer, we had left some anxiety behind. This must be what is behind the idea of a holiday in the sun, but it took more than a beach to find it; it took a stiff walk, height, wide expanses, warmth, a clear view of the dirt and trivia that is 'civilisation.' Also, of course, an education that included a good dose of Romanticism.

At Romana's country house Giorgio was left behind and we spent the day with her academic colleagues, all female because this was Italy where Arts departments are exclusively female, staffed by clever middle-class housewives working for pocket-money. They included a lady who insisted on taking off most of her clothes and sunbathing. This propensity, not in itself to be discouraged, had given her skin that closely resembled Morocco leather in colour and texture.

Besides the Sunbather there was Mrs Thatcher. Not *in propria persona* of course, merely an Italian replica in terms of height, face, attitude, clothes (no semi-nude sunbathing for her) and bolt-on hair. Mrs T was rather chatty and revealed a romantic side that perhaps her double in Downing Street might not have managed. She waxed lyrical on the language of Dante pointing out that a farmer of her acquaintance had visited her recently and made a speech about something that was troubling him in the very language of the great cartographer of the afterlife. 'Can you imagine' she asked, 'Dante – thirteenth century. Can you imagine a farmer in Kent or Devon talking like your Chaucer?' This prospect silenced me for a time. I found myself experimenting with lines from the *Miller's Tale* that could still work: 'Tee-hee quod she and clapped the window to', 'This Nicholas answered 'fecche me a drink'', 'But with his mouth he kissed her naked ers.' That sort of thing, though since the Great Vowel Shift of the fifteenth century it would sound very different.

That bit of Italy is somewhat self-consciously different from France. The train that goes from Genoa along the coast to Alassio takes one past some very Italian villages and an unmistakable Riviera. But it goes on quite quickly to Nice where the great Juggernaut that is French culture has eliminated all hints that the town was quite recently Italian (until 1860). Pauline and I spent a day at Alassio and have sometimes looked back on it as a touchstone in our knowledge of Europe. Visiting Nice much later we felt the difference even more strongly. And then we went and lived in France ourselves for fifteen years.

CHAPTER 13. FRANCE 2001 – 2016

1. VILLAGE

In 2001 Pauline and I moved to the south-west of France. I had been offered a Chair at the university of Pau which I took with both hands.

My generation was brought up on a novel called *Clochemerle* published in 1934 by one Gabriel Chevallier, a portrait of life in a small French town with all its idiosyncrasies. It might have been thought a bit dated by the time Pauline and I moved into a house on the main street (inevitably *Rue de la Republique*) of the Bearnais village of Lasseube, half an hour from Pau, in August 2001. The beginning of a new life. The idea was for us to make this new life *French* in as much as that is possible, for Pauline to learn the language, for us to 'integrate', for Alice and Miranda perhaps to make a few friends and have some nice holidays. But the seventy years that separated our arrival in Lasseube from the novel by Chevallier had, it appeared, only altered minor details of what is known as French Life.

The *Clochemerlean* element was made stronger by the fact that Lasseube was big enough to have a priest, '*Monsieur le curé*', an active local political life centred around '*Monsieur le maire*'; also a rugby club and a pelota club; also a fire station where '*Les soldats du feu*' could practice putting out the blazes that never occurred and a Gendarmerie where a handful of '*Gardiens de la paix*' could practice manoeuvres to thwart the criminals who did not exist in the commune. There was also a Primary School, a Middle School and an Old Folk's Home. Two bars, two bakeries and a post office kept the place from dying on its feet as so many French villages have done.

Around these poles of village life, literally, were the extensive vineyards where the locals grew the grapes for the sweet white wine of the region known as Jurançon. During the *vendange* tractors roared past our front door day and night pulling huge carts on which barrels of grapes bumped and swayed on their way to the *cave co-operative* in Gan. All sorts of traditions and jollities were associated with this and with the other agricultural pursuits for which France is famous and which Lasseube tried often to revivify by, for instance, staging ploughing matches, which are not snappy affairs. In short here we were deep in *la France profonde* with all the fixings.

Among the entertainments were, as stated, rugger and pelota. The former one only observes with any serious objectivity after the age of thirty, and observe it I occasionally did on Sunday afternoons when passionate crowds of fathers and mothers, girlfriends and hangers-on crowded the touchline to a surprising extent and yelled with astonishing conviction. '*Aux jambes!*' was the chief cry when Lasseube were on the defensive (official translation: 'Get his legs!': real translation 'Hurt him to the max!') while when they were on the offensive the cry was '*Alleeeeeez!*' The level of violence can be indicated by the following fact: did you know that in rugger the game has to be abandoned after six red cards? Well, I saw several games abandoned. Enough said.

The latter, pelota, Pauline and I participated in. This involved Thursday evening sessions when I played against the giant sons of the local *boulanger* who were not only huge but also fit and experienced, usually partnering a slight chap from the local cheese factory. I think we never won. Then there were the Wednesday lunchtime sessions when Pauline played with the *boulanger's* wife, the local postman's wife and a random girl whose background escaped me. But when she couldn't play I joined in. I have to say that playing such a game (think tennis or squash) after the age of sixty is best done against women. Not only can one hold one's own but they are also nice to one.

Emboldened by this participation in one of the profound activities of the village I unwisely accepted an invitation to attend the Annual Dinner of the Pelota Club. Pauline felt that her French wasn't really up to it yet, so on a Friday night in about 2005 I pitched up at the *Salle des Fêtes* behind the *Mairie*, all alone and in the grip of a specially-prepared hunger. All of this was a mistake. In the first place there was nobody there at the appointed time, and indeed nobody appeared for twenty minutes, but second and worse was the fact that when proceedings started I became almost immediately and quite definitely extremely drunk. A couple of monster *pastis* did for me, and there were several more of them before any food was produced. This food was, I am sure, delicious but to me unfortunately unmemorable, like so much of the rest of the evening.

The official meeting had taken place, though belatedly and rather briefly, and several doubtless vital decisions had been made about the changing rooms, the calendar for next year and so on. But early in the meeting, in anticipation of its end, the President of the pelota association had thrown open what looked like a large schoolroom book-cupboard which had been lurking behind him against the wall to reveal a massive selection of mixed alcoholic stimulants. I was starkly reminded of the post-funeral drinks at the Central Regional Council HQ in Stirling twenty years before.

So drunk was I by the time we moved (somehow) towards the meal that I could hardly eat it for giggling. I am sure that I declared some species of passionate devotion to the person on my left though this may possibly, on reflection, have been a man, or even a pillar. We had, apparently, by this time left the *Mairie* where the meeting had been held and somehow managed the hundred-metre walk across the road and up to the restaurant. More wine was consumed. By midnight I was definitely flying unaided and in that state I left the party and flew in great loops down the main street to our house where I found the door open (it was never locked there in rural France) and the stairs miraculously before me. Tittering and stumbling I flew bumpily upstairs to the bedroom where Pauline was in a peaceful sleep. She says I made little sense but giggled for ten minutes and then slept for six hours.

I never stood for the pelota committee and, indeed, never went to one of their dinners again. But it is true that the next morning a man whom I had last seen dressed as a nun came and knocked on our door. He had been en-habited at a fancy-dress party to which Pauline and I had foolishly gone earlier in the year and had, allegedly, been present at the pelota dinner though I have no recollection of that. '*Bonjour*' he said with a knowing smirk. 'Oh God' I thought. Then he said '*Tu viens donc?*' What had I committed myself to? Ah! A visit to a Jurançon wine producer where we were (heavens!) to drink again and make merry. I feigned another engagement and he looked slightly relieved. Later he went off to Réunion to work there. For the weather.

All villages have to have Characters. Perhaps they stand out less in towns or perhaps they are attracted to village life where they can expand their eccentricities to more effect. At any rate they were thick on the ground in Lasseube.

One of these characters we knew as Santa on account of his deceptively benign demeanour and a large white beard. He strolled slowly and frequently up and down the main street, past our windows, between his house and the café where he drank and held forth with rigid lack of humour throughout the day and evening. His method of conversation was simple: speak, pause briefly while looking with hostility at your interlocutor, resume speaking by what the linguists call skip-connecting back to what you were saying before, pay not the slightest attention to anything the other person may have said, stop speaking to drink, continue as before.

Santa came from Burgundy and when he actually managed to notice the people he was talking to (in this case us) and found that they drank *Kir* (white wine with sweet alcoholic blackcurrant, *crème de cassis*) as we frequently did, he would shift his large bulk over to the bar and order a 'real *Kir*' for us. This meant a glass of red wine polluted with *cassis* that we had to demonstrate sincere affection for although, come to think of it, had we said it was disgusting it would have made no difference as he of course paid no attention to anything we tried to convey to him. It was I think only seeing us drink conventional *Kir* that had alerted him to our existence as anything other that two pairs of ears.

Then there was Short Arms, our next-door dwarf who had finally, at about 40 years old, given up the unequal struggle with his desired profession which was, alarmingly, that of *camioneur* or lorry-driver. He now worked in the Lindt chocolate factory in Oloron and drove there every day in a large old Audi with enormous cushions to help him with the steering and the other useful parts of driving. The car was an automatic and one hoped fervently that the lorries he had driven were also without too many foot controls. He expressed indignation that his earlier employers had eventually sacked him as a safety hazard. Like everyone else in France he had had a wife from whom he was now separated. From time to time a large fat daughter of about twenty would come to visit him and loom over the poor chap while berating him for his eating habits and demanding financial assistance. One had difficulty in imagining the marriage as lived.

Opposite us lived the Lautes (two syllables, separated after the 'a'), Loulou and Christine. Loulou you must understand was a man in spite of his nickname, indeed a cameraman who had worked in Paris and had only now retired to his native village where he was constantly engaged in doing-up his rather odd little house, being mildly nasty to his wife and talking. He was garrulous and opinionated, something which many Frenchmen and, in their absence, French women are. More than we British I think. They had a beautiful daughter who had become an Air France stewardess and therefore in theory spoke English; she had been a national swimming champion of some sort and Loulou used to complain that her handsome husband, who was a saintly teacher specialising in difficult children but thus not in a high-status career, was not good enough for her. He always said, after we had seen this young couple, '*elle aurait pu faire mieux.*'

Among Loulou's opinions was a very traditional French anti-clericalism. This was made awkward by the fact that he and Christine lived next to the presbytery where *monsieur le curé* lived moved and had his being among portraits of the Pope and bottles of wine donated

319

by grateful parishioners. I caused merriment among my acquaintances in the village by calling him *Père Albert* (his full name, rather wonderfully, was *Albert Majesté*) which seemed to them the height of Anglo-Saxon ignorance. This inoffensive middle-aged man, who married Pauline and me in the non-civil sense in a ceremony held largely in English, a language of which he was entirely innocent, and who had a sense of humour, was the subject of many bitter remarks by Loulou who would certainly have had the poor man done away with in any further instalments of the French Revolution. Loulou was particularly incensed when the Liberty Oak, planted as so often elsewhere in France just outside the church in 1789, decided shortly after our wedding to die pretty finally. It was removed and the debate about its replacement in the *conseil municipal* was bitter. I could not engage Loulou on the topic of the symbolism of its decline; he simply couldn't see it. 'Liberty is an absolute!' he would cry, eyes popping.

Our wedding was wonderful. We went up to what in English would be called the Mayor's Parlour – that is the *Grande Salle* upstairs in the *mairie* – where the mayor, besuited and wearing a large tricolor sash united us in the eyes of the state under a large portrait of Jacques Chirac. Unfortunately he forgot Pauline's name during the ceremony and I think I am technically married to someone called '*Merde! J'ai oublié le nom de madame.*' But Pauline is philosophical.

The other village character who springs to mind is the chap we knew as Roland Jumbo the One-Armed Log-Deliverer. This combination of name-and-soubriquet was perfectly accurate in most of its terms; he was, at least, a monobrach who cut and delivered logs for the winter. He was not, however, elephantine though his name was certainly Jumbo. Roland had taken

320

up the passion of shooting, so common *dans le sud-ouest*, at an early age; so early in fact that he had gone out with a contemporary whose inadequate control of his shotgun while they were messing around had destroyed Roland's right arm. Undeterred, he took up the obvious profession for a one-armed man: tree-feller and log-merchant. When he came to our house with a couple of cubic metres of American Oak in large slices, for Bearnais fireplaces are of medieval proportions, he would stop his tractor and knock on the door. When I answered he would be urinating on the wheels of the tractor, as permitted by French law, because, as he put it, he had cystitis and couldn't control himself. He would then offer to re-cut the metre-long slices of wood to fifty-centimetre pieces with his chainsaw and, if I said yes, would do so in the street with his one hand. I gestured feebly towards holding the end of the piece being cut and offered to carry in the logs as he roared and swore outside. "*Non non!*' he would say, refusing my aid, '*c'est trop dangereux!*'

French rural life is a very mixed blessing. You get more house and more countryside for your money, and you are often somewhere beautiful. The romantic aspects such as vineyards and pelota courts are matched by some very French-textbook elements such as the gendarme in his car, the village communal feast, the annual fair, the weekly market and so on. But then, without wanting to be ungrateful, there is that strange patina of hostility that lies over French life, that intransigence, that decision that the way they do things is the only way, that incomprehension of the foreign, that administrative burden, that inability to make proper friends after the age of twenty. It makes an odd life for the foreigner and limits one to enjoying the good bits and just ignoring the bad. Most expatriates, whatever

321

their original intentions, return home after a certain time.

There was something good about living in Lasseube, but we never go back. And when we left we moved to a remote farmhouse, Maison Garat outside the village of Esquiule, where we had most of the advantages of French country life and fewer of the disadvantages.

2. OUTSIDE

The trouble with France, famously, is the people. There are, most certainly, some very pleasant encounters to be had and a good deal of superficial and even some not-so-superficial politeness. In the countryside of France, which is largely where I have spent my time *outre-Manche*, both pre-Pauline and then with her, farmers and tradesmen have usually responded in a fairly decent manner to my overtures and invitations to chat. And they love to help you with a disaster, going to great lengths to fix your car at the roadside or call in aid. But there is something underneath, something less appealing, that many of the French reveal on closer acquaintance. Its origins rather defeat me and even its psychology, but it is there all right and you know it when you meet it.

One hot night in about 2003, going past the *mairie* in Lasseube, I heard a meeting of the *conseil municipal* going on. The windows were open and, from the lateness of the hour, I would guess that dinner had been had. The experience was sobering, even shocking in our 'nice' village. Voices were raised, names were called, swearing filled the warm air of the meeting room; it was a cacophony of bad temper and lack of restraint.

322

I never discovered what the topic under discussion was but it can hardly have been earth-shattering as *mairies* do not decide much. But power performs its insidious black magic at the lowest levels. It became apparent that evening and on several other occasions that the '*équipe*' that was running the village was being undermined by another aspirant bunch of would-be local politicians who seemed unwilling to reduce the volume of venom they poured out at all points in any proceedings.

While we lived in the village there were elections of several kinds, but the local *conseil* elections were by far the most acrimonious. Tensions, difficulties, anger, marital and political break-ups all simmered below the surface of village life. The commonest reaction, once one had got beyond the superficial politesse, to any serious discussion with a villager about his or her fellow-villagers, was a sucking-in of breath and a few dark hints about the subject in question's derelictions.

Gradually this pattern seemed to become clear. I don't know what the French really think about foreigners, but I do know that they find it very easy to hate each other. And they are scared of each other, as they might well be in the land that invented and gave its name to the *lettre de cachet*; scared on a sort of advanced 'What-will-the-neighbours-think?' basis. And they don't trust each other. For instance: working at the University of Pau I eventually gave up going to conferences because they were too expensive. In all other professions employees go to meetings and conferences at the expense of their employer. In academia, where to do one's job one has to attend conferences, one is expected to pay for a good deal of the travel and accommodation oneself. It's scandalous.

Anyway, l'Université de Pau, chronically underfunded like all French universities, limited itself to €180 per lecturer per conference. The last conference I went to, in 2004 in Versailles, but NOT in the palace as you may imagine, cost me €500 in fares, hotels and fees. So I was out of pocket by €320 for doing my job. Basta! I said.

The point here is not the absurdity of this but the untrusting nature of the French towards each other. Behold: among other humiliations and awkwardnesses I found that I was expected to indent for my air-fare-to-Paris after the event and that my request had to be supported not only by an air-ticket but also by *both my boarding passes*. Ye gods. A tiny example of a chronic mistrust.

The result of this mistrust, and of their fear, cantankerousness and nervousness, is that the French snoop on one another, criticize one another freely and sit in almost permanent mutual judgment. Selling the house in Lasseube was quite interesting in this respect. Several people came to see it merely because they were nosey; many estate-agents tried to horn in on the sale (at 6 or 7 percent commission on house sales, wouldn't you?) and the people who finally bought it threatened legal action over some detail even before the sale had gone through. We had also looked at another house to buy in the village, owned in that strange *code Napoléon* way by a mother-and-daughter duo. The daughter seemed to have some sort of man in tow but he was clearly mere dust beneath her chariot wheels. The mother was a semi-literate peasant who lived in the house we were trying to buy and supported herself by scratching at the soil on her hillside and producing vegetables for sale at the Lasseube Saturday-morning market, along with such ducks she had managed to catch and murder, and some rather hair-raising cheese.

These two ladies were utterly different in a disconcerting way. The mother appeared to have been modeled crudely out of the clay of her dank smallholding while the daughter was elegant in that entirely unsuccessful way that involves skin-tight clothing much of it patterned along the lines of leopard-skin. She had bolt-on blonde hair of some size, huge gold earrings and day-glow lipstick. She was a violent and uncompromising bargainer whom we nicknamed Spitfire and who involved us minutely in the detail of her mother's lamps, farming equipment, old clothes, bank account and personal hygiene, all in a tumultuous rush as we sat down in the estate-agent's office.

He, the estate agent, was called Monsieur Leloup and had indeed a wolfish set of mouth and a look in his eyes that boded badly. In the event he contrived to extract €11,000 from us by way of a deposit and then refused to return it to us when the sale fell through, which it did because a dual-carriageway was to be built, quite unknown to us, a few hundred yards from the farm. Had we not found out about it by accident we would even now be listening to the roar of the lorries going past the village and on to Spain and cursing our credulity.

We got our deposit back with the help of another estate agent who was of course delighted to explain to us the derelictions of Leloup and to shaft his brother-parasite as royally as possible. He wrote a letter for me to copy out in heavy legal French; this did the trick instantly.

One never quite knows where one is with the French, unless one happens to be French of course. Take massage for example. There is a lot of it about and everyone one meets has their 'Kiné' to whom they go with the slightest sprain or discomfort. But when I

325

finally summoned up the courage to go (never having thought of massage as altogether British or masculine although I absolutely love it) I found myself in a small cubicle with a cross fat male thirty-something masseur at the ski-station at Cauterets. I lay shivering in my underpants as he advanced across the cubicle and started stroking me unenthusiastically and commenting on my person. '*Vos cuisses, monsieur*' he said when he got to them, '*elles sont exceptionellement courtes. Je n'ai jamais vu des cuisses aussi courtes*' and he put a finger at the top and bottom of each of my thighs in turn to demonstrate to me the sadly inadequate length I had between *les genoux* and *les fesses*. I realised later that all he was doing was indulging in the favourite French pastime of criticizing others, preferably to their faces or, in my case of course, to my rump.

Then there are Dinner Parties, which the French might lay some claim to having invented but which, in the actual flesh, turn out to be harrowing encounters of the least expected kind. In my experience they are rare and wild. We were invited, for example, when we lived in Lasseube, to some people a few kilometres outside the village for whom I had done a little work. I had spoken the English version of the voice-over for a short film advertising an air-conditioning system that they were trying to sell. They were pleased with what they considered to be my 'amazing' voice (I just talked proper and talked slowly and loudly; they declared themselves ravished.)

With some difficulty we found their farmhouse ('It is not very clean' they had promised) and knocked on the front door. There were the sounds of furniture being moved within and, after a space, a light came on, the door was unlocked and ground slowly open. Inside stood the couple, dressed if anything in garments even scruffier than those they had worn to make the recording. We were welcomed in and as we went down the hall I became aware of someone descending the staircase on my right. I halted and looked into the gloom above me and there, smiling, was a small but pretty young lady. 'Aha!' I thought and, once she had got down to my level, extended my hand. '*Enchanté!*' The smile went on and she managed her return '*Enchantée*' rather nicely. *Then she descended the remaining two steps* which I had not seen. Now she was staring straight into my crutch. Think of it as The Revenge on Carla.

At many moments during the ensuing evening, which was not altogether an easy one, my mind kept slipping back to this minute person. She had vanished into the kitchen after our arrival and now returned to sit next to me on several cushions. I made small talk with her in several senses. But all the time that awful, unpolitically-correct internal voice was wittering away at me: 'She's a dwarf! She's a dwarf!' Why should it matter? I wondered, but matter it somehow did. I felt very uncomfortable at the mean turn my mind kept insisting on taking but after a while I began to settle down and think more rationally about what was being said by the others. This was not easy. The only other guest, who had come an hour late (why does that always seem to happen?) wearing a three-piece English tweed suit and who insisted on sitting next to a blazing fire where he sweated very obviously, was the Librarian of the main library in Pau; his conversation was, to say the least, recondite. Local history bulked large as well as ornithological matters of only faint interest. Nonetheless I managed to keep abreast of his quick-fire French and felt quite pleased with myself. Pauline had only a little of the language at that stage and he would turn to her from time to time and attempt a laborious translation of what he had just said. This made things worse. And still the demon inside me that spots all differences only too uncomfortably quickly would rear his fiery head an inch or two.

Food and drink helped and by the end of the evening I was in better form and the demon, it appeared, had been defeated. But my unconscious mind was not going to let me off that easily. I launched, at a point in the bird-watching conversation that seemed somehow to invite this intervention though I can't remember what it could possibly have been, into a story about Queen Victoria. This went down well and I felt I should add a few titbits to the story's already considerable bulk to keep the company on my side. What else did I know about *La Reine Victoria*? Ah yes! I had it! '*Vous savez, messieurs/dames, que la reine Victoria, bien que l'on ne le dit pas souvent, était…*' here I paused for effect and looked everyone in turn in the eyes. As I got to my tiny neighbour I delivered directly into her face the surprising information that was going to be so amusing to all: '*elle était… une naine!*' (For those who might struggle here let me remind you that '*naine*' is not just the French for a dwarf, it is explicitly feminine too: a lady-dwarf.) I felt my eyes sparkle with glee, and then it hit me. Oh NOOOO! I had let the poor creature beside me have it with both barrels. There was a stunned silence.

One of the few other dinner parties we were invited to was at the Chateau de Navailles, north of Pau. My Belgian connection, Philippine de Limburg Stirum, had a grandmother who had been born there in the late nineteenth century and when Philippine came down to Pau to visit us she asked to be taken to see the old house. We bumped into the new owners who, after much chat about the past and how they had got the place, invited us to dinner. An unusual and welcome gesture. But await the event gentle skimmer.

We set out Philippine and I, smartly dressed, on the appointed evening and arrived fashionably late. The chateau was looking lovely in the summer evening sunshine, the drive was swept, the lawn mown. So far so good. Our hosts were at the door to greet us. We then entered an alternative universe.

Inside the front door were two enormous flower-displays perhaps eight feet tall. OK I thought, some people like flowers. As we went through to the hall we were met by an excellent Renaissance portrait over the fireplace. 'We purchased this' said Pierre, 'Yes' said his partner Louis, 'We purchased this.' 'Ah!' said Philippine, 'It's one of my ancestors.' 'Yes' said one of the twins, 'Now ours.' They then told the story of the Duc de Something and what he had done around the time of Henri IV and Louis XIII. Philippine interrupted from time to time with an alternative version of the story. 'No' they corrected her, 'It was as we have said.'

Passing into the *salon* we were confronted with a raised dais or stage at one end of the room on which were two tall gold thrones and a lot of red rep. Also many more flowers. 'Gosh!' I said, or the French equivalent. 'Ah!' said Pierre, 'It was our birthday.' Now, they weren't *really* twins, I knew, but ... 'We share a birthday' said Pierre.

It transpired that these two *chatelains*, whoever they were, and that was something I was slowly to find out during the evening, had recently if not simultaneously both become forty. Their party had been fancy dress and the guests were all asked to come in pairs as Kings and Queens. Some had come as figures from history, others as playing cards, the hosts themselves had sat up on the thrones as a full-dress heraldic lion and lioness; the photographs, when they were brought out, were astonishing.

The ceiling of the salon had been painted blue and then stencilled over with golden *fleur-de-lys*. The porcelain that sat about on the tables and commodes was heavy with coats of arms and gilding. But the prominent presence in the room was the pile of photograph albums. These, to Philippine's intense surprise, were of many people quite unknown to the owners of the castle, but they included many of *her own family* – there were even some of her own children. Being a perfect lady she showed polite interest in these and helped to identify some of the people whom Pierre and Louis couldn't identify. It gradually became apparent to me that the centre of this wild charade was Navailles, the name of the chateau, the house itself. Every time another surprise was sprung one of the gay brethren would cry *'Ah oui. Navailles!'*

Now these chaps had bought the place a year or two before and had no ancestral or any other connection with it but it filled their entire horizon and all of their joint imagination. I must have heard the word 'Navailles' a hundred times that evening.

'Shall we visit the house while we wait for dinner?' asked Pierre. Louis slipped out to the kitchens and we were taken through the state rooms and around a number of as-yet-unfinished bedrooms. But I can only remember the chapel. It had been done up, obviously *en priorité*, in full Ultramontanist fig. There was a finely-dressed altar, fresh to all appearances from High Mass, open Missals, lots of things in Latin, holy images, more flowers. But the *pièce de résistance* of this *pièce* (*de résistance* too - remember *'pièce'* is a room in French) was the *prie-dieu*, a sort of chair-to-kneel-on facing the altar at the back of the chapel, on which lay a rare and expensive-looking tome. On closer inspection it turned out to be the '*Liturgie pour le Sacre des rois de France*' – in other words here were the words for the ceremony that would legitimately crown a new king of France. Well, one never knows when they may come in handy I suppose, but to get them into position before the spare bedrooms are finished? We went back to the dining room.

This was lit by exactly one hundred tall wax candles. They were all over the table, the sideboards, the floor, the hatches, the window-sill. It gave a fabulous effect in the cool white room and made Louis' delicate platefuls of perfectly-cooked French food seem even more elegant than they were. The first of course was waiting for us as we went in and others followed, Louis doing all the serving. In one of the intervals of Pierre sighing about '*Navailles!*' and Philippine reminiscing compulsorily about her stolen grandparents I more or less exploded with a question. I had felt questions coming on for about an hour by now and the only impediment to my asking them had been the realisation that I didn't know which one I should choose of the hundreds that presented themselves. But then it came out all by itself: 'Tell me Pierre: what do you *do*?'

'*Je suis podologue*' was the answer that silenced me. I was not entirely sure what a *podologue* was. Something to do with feet, but was he a specialist surgeon or a sort of *masseur*? And how much does such a person actually *earn*? He had shown us, lurking in an upstairs room, an enormous roof-decoration-cum-lightning-conductor of the same type as but literally a hundred times bigger than the one I had just bought for Maison Garat at €100. So €10,000 say, for a *roof decoration*? Plus the scaffolding towers for the installation of same? And those wax candles at €10 a go, and there were 100 of them at dinner? And how much does that worst-seller the liturgy for a French coronation cost? These sadly vulgar calculations were forced upon me as I thought of how much money there is in rubbing people's feet. And his boyfriend didn't appear to work at all.

The topic of how to keep up country houses and castles has been dear to my heart for much of my life and the expedients needed have alternately amused and depressed me. But for an ordinary middle-class Frenchman to set about major-league chateau-restoration and *ancien régime* extravagance smacked of something else.

During dinner Louis and I discussed James Joyce, naturally. He didn't seem willing to do much in the way of English conversation but he assured me that he enjoyed *Portrait*, *Ulysses* and even *Finnegan's Wake* in the original. I wondered how this fitted in with his activities in the chapel and what Joyce would have thought of those. In other words how much of this pantomime was grounded in anything at all.

Philippine said Goodbye and Thank You nicely, as brought up, and I did likewise. In the car going home we were both silent for a few minutes. Then she said, with a deep preliminary sigh, '*Ca, c'était surréaliste!*'

3. HOSPITALITY

Besides these larger-than-life events there have been a number of details that perhaps have contributed some of the *saveur de France* for me. I remember for instance staying in the hotel next to the Chateau de Chambord in the Loire. A winter's night with huge fires in the old hotel, a moonlight walk round the immense empty house, a cosy night followed by an early-morning stroll in weak sunshine. As we approached the lake that half-surrounds the chateau a large flock of ducks was in evidence, standing on the water. *Standing on the water?* We rubbed our eyes and looked again. Yes, there they were, all facing the same way, standing, ankle-deep. Of course, they were in fact resting on the ice that was just below the surface.

When we told our friend Paul Williams, a fellow inhabitant of southern France, about these ducks he was characteristically unimpressed: he had gone into the barn at Berdoulat, his house in the Gers, to find his neighbour's ducks equally immobile. Not understanding why they weren't flocking out into the winter morning he gave them a mild 'shoo!' but they didn't move being, after that chilly night, frozen to the floor. He rushed round to the farmer and explained the crisis. The farmer, a super-phlegmatic Basque, grunted and disappeared only to re-appear carrying a pail of hot water, This he threw across the floor of the barn instantly liberating his flock who flapped and quacked off into the winter morning. 'Lucky you had the pail' said Paul to the Basque who replied, after a long pause to find the right word for the need to have a pail on a farm, *'Indispensable.'*

Chambord is altogether weird. Francois Premier built it (not personally) starting in 1519 and it wasn't finished until 1547, after his death. It is absolutely huge and must consist of about a million tons of stone, but it was built on a marsh. Can *folie de grandeur* go any further? There are plenty of dry places in France but old Frank chose… a marsh. And he never went there. Well, to be fair, he would occasionally drop in to see how things were progressing and argue about Leonardo de Vinci's design for his staircase (always get the top man if you can.) Apparently he managed about six weeks at the place all told, always with guests he wanted to impress, and would arrive with his furniture and take it away again when he left. A very very expensive piece of trickery in the hospitality department then. When one goes there today one thinks 'Ah, the furniture was presumably all stolen at the time of the Revolution.' But no, there never really was any. It is a ghost house, in the end rather sinister.

At the other end of the spectrum from Chambord we once stayed at the most miserable hotel in Europe - well, it was in France and surely there are worse in Eastern Europe? It cost €32 for the bed, a horror beyond description, in a room illuminated so weakly that we couldn't read even with our books pressed up against the bedside lights. Dinner was at 7pm. by order of the lame elderly owner who lurched about serving it to us only too obviously desperate to get back to her own bed, presumably slightly less insalubrious than our own. We shared the dining room with an indoor plant so large that we could hardly see each other for interfering leaves and the bar was as unstocked as I had ever known a bar to be.

Walking around this dump we thought we understood the origins of the halting lady's problem: the floors were so chronically uneven that I remember trying to ascend the staircase and finding it weirdly hard because of the drunken angles of the treads; at one point I was actually going back down. For once it was their drunken angle and not my own that impeded my ascent. When we left in the morning we noticed a small sign outside that we hadn't seen on arrival '*A vendre.*' Mon Dieu, I thought, who'd buy that? The director of a horror film perhaps.

Near where we lived at Maison Garat is the village of Barcus where there are three restaurants. One

334

is rather posh, with rosettes and a proper cook and menus with things on them we'd never heard of. One is nearly always closed though we did once find it open and ate there well enough. The third is Chez Sylvain. Here an old family endeavours to keep centennial tradition going and the antiquity shows. Speaking Basque to each other, and to such of their clients as want to do the same, they serve the same food *midi et soir* 364 days of the year (*'tous les jours sauf Noel monsieur'.*) This food is not extensive in variety but it is delicious. 'Old' Sylvain looked about 70 when last seen, though he was in fact 60, and until recently he was backed up by his mother as *serveuse*. Her heart may not have been in the task (she was over eighty in about 2010) and she preferred to continue her family chores during mealtimes *in the restaurant*. At the extreme this involved doing the ironing, a task which she performed with élan, pressing large white underpants and other such intimacies in public view on the table next to where we lunched. As for Sylvain himself, when we had a noisy young man at lunch with us one day and there was much hilarity, on the way out I slipped a comment or two to *le patron* affecting apologetic indignation at the raucousness of the young. He laughed and smiled his toothless smile and then, to my utter astonishment and without explanation, said to me in English 'Spare ze rod and spoil ze child!' Where on earth had he learnt that?

In the same village of Barcus lived a digger-dumper man of the most primitive. Known as 'Pierre-the-pelle-man' in the area, at least among the English-speakers, he worked on a random basis with his ancient machine, clearing stones and trees that have blocked roads, moving earth from one place to another at the behest of local mayors, altering gardens. He came to

335

Garat to help us dig the hole for the septic tank or to put in a cattle grid or something and announced that his services would cost us €200. The day he left I was absent so I phoned his number. '*Oui*' he said when I told him I'd like to pay. '*Comme vous voulez.*' Somehow I failed to understand his address. Weeks later I found him in Chez Sylvain talking Basque to a trio of old cronies and drinking Pacharan. 'Ah, Pierre!' I intoned. '*Je vous dois €200.*' I was about to tell him that I didn't have the cash on me (he had once already refused so doubtful a method of payment as the cheque) when he got in first. '*Non non monsieur. C'est comme vous voulez.*' Over a period of a year I tried several more times and then slowly worked out that he didn't actually want to be paid, and he has not been paid to this day. In truth, some people are less in thrall to the cash nexus than others.

CHAPTER 14. SPAIN 2001 – 2016

1. QUICK

I have only been close to death three times in my life, as far as I know. The worst of these was the episode in Algeria recounted in the 'Algiers' section earlier in these memoirs. Another occasion when I was about thirty involved my first and last experience of hang-gliding. The third was a merry moment in southern Spain when I fell into quicksand.

      The hang-gliding was in retrospect ill-advised. An extravagantly courageous pal called Alan Barnes, a Yorkshireman I had met in Brazil, was playboy enough to get one of these large kites before they were at all well-known in the UK, conceivably the first chap to get one this side of the Atlantic. Like any red-blooded man he had ignored the instruction book that came with his only-theoretically-airworthy device and had decided to proceed instead on general principles. These were I think influenced by the fact that he was among other things a qualified pilot who had demonstrated new planes at air-shows, including one plane fresh in his memory that was so unusual that it proved unable to do those things that the manufacturers claimed it would do. Barnes landed it the hard way in front of thousands of spectators and was to be seen sprinting from the wreckage shortly before it exploded. He got about a hundred yards away from the ball of fire before collapsing. The surgeon who subsequently treated him was intrigued to know how he had managed to achieve such a turn of speed over such a distance encumbered by flying kit and so badly hurt that he needed sixty-three stitches in his leg. You get the picture.

He it was at any rate who invited me to the Pennines one breezy afternoon and rigged up his only-seemingly-lighter-than-air contraption. Once he had done so he stood back and looked at it for a space and then proposed, in the manner of Estragon in *Godot*, that the lighter man flirt with death first. The lighter man, by some distance, was me. I am usually the lighter man. And Barnes... well let me just say that he had played Rugby League for a professional club while still a schoolboy, sneaking off on Saturdays to get stuck in to some of the largest and toughest *sportifs* in Britain. To be fair to him I think he honestly thought that the aluminium-and-canvas monster would actually not get him airborne at all. I looked a better bet.

So it was that I put a helmet on, strapped myself to the underside of the beast and started to run, as instructed, downhill into a strong breeze with the glider above me. Below us the ground fell away fairly steeply and I was imagining, a second or two into my sprint, that I might gradually rise a little way and sort of float down the hill. But it was not to be. On the contrary: three steps into my descent I felt myself being lifted up Whoosh! Like a Hobbit being snatched by an eagle in Tolkien. The kite above me strained and pulled and I rose like a rocketing pheasant.

Now Barnes had somehow learnt one thing about steering a hang-glider and he had given me the following mantra: 'To go more slowly push the A-frame away from you; to speed up pull it towards you. You can't go wrong.' Feeling thus that my violent upward rush must constitute Going Too Fast I pushed the cross-bar, which I had been hanging on to for the first few seconds of my adventure, sharply away from my body. The effect of this was to make the kite stall and, not to become too technical, fall like a stone from the sky.

Alas by this time I was at fifty feet or more, the wind having made a real effort to get me off the ground, and Barnes, who had seen me disappear over the horizon and then reappear like a firework, now saw me disappear again from his line of sight and vanish below the horizon once more. I emitted no sound, but fell directly into a species of bog or mountain swamp of heathery softness and was at once stuck, entangled and immobilised. Seconds passed and then I heard the *whish* and thump of Barnes's boots coming through the ling. 'You OK?' he asked.

I was OK enough for him to suggest that I have 'another go.' But the cliché about bites and shyness came to my aid. 'Why don't you try it?' I cunningly asked. He seemed to feel obliged to make the attempt where I had failed. He put on the helmet and strapped himself to the A-frame. This time the adage about being bitten, or at least seeing someone else bitten, and being twice shy seemed to be working. Barnes kept the huge kite nose-down and staggered off down the slope through the thick heather. The more he accelerated the more the wind pushed the nose of the machine downwards until, in spite of Herculean efforts, my colossal friend was brought to an ignominious halt compressed, kite, head, legs and all into a small muddy space. The wind that had taken me to the heavens had forced him to plunge into the ground. I felt a moral coming on.

When we got Barnes extricated he stretched a bit and then considered his hang-glider. Many of the spars were bent and there looked to be no more flying that day. But my 'Oh well, I mean, that's it, isn't it?' effort to bring the proceedings to an end were truncated by his straightening the spars with several heaves of his

339

enormous shoulders and turning to me with the words: 'Your turn again I reckon.'

This time I did better. I flew! I simply held on to the A-frame and glided, mostly downwards admittedly but still respectably. It was wonderful. All fear left me as I sailed through the chilly Pennine breeze towards the valley. But then the internal radar we all possess began to make doubtful noises in the deeps of my mind: Where Was I Going To Land? it asked. The floor of the valley was flat, the electricity pylons some distance away from my line of flight, but there was the stream. As so often this stream was not content merely to be at the bottom of the valley, it lurked ten feet below the valley floor in a species of cutting nature had made in the Wordsworthian grass, leaving cliffs of clay on each side. The nearer of these cliffs was of course invisible to me but the further one stared me in the face. With my lack of control over the kite, but with my don't-die-just-yet radar on at full strength, I saw that I was inevitably headed at what seemed great speed for the opposing cliff-face. I shut my eyes.

The impact when it came was strange. I was dangling below the glider as I went in but most of the canvas itself went neatly onto the grass over my head as I smacked into the clay and slid very slowly down. I would have gone a lot faster but the kite held me in part and only reluctantly followed me down the vertical mud. At the bottom I had a free cold bath of course.

It took some time for Barnes to get down to me. 'Not bad' he said and we took the kite into Oldham to get the now seriously-bent frame back into shape, but the repairs seemed to be prohibitively expensive. During the evening we burnt what was probably Britain's first hang-glider. We did not make further efforts to fly.

My next and last brush with mortality, in
southern Spain, was much quicker. We were staying
near a military zone undeveloped for tourism and
generally forbidden to the public but where the beach
was nonetheless accessible to the intrepid. Our friends
Tim and Caroline Plumptre who live down there to
avoid the winter in Wiltshire and with whom we were
putting up, led us along this beach. We strolled along
admiring Africa a short distance across the Straits of
Gibraltar. The wind blew, the sun shone and on our
return journey across the sand we noticed a stream that
somehow we had crossed earlier perfectly well but now,
at this point further away from the water, seemed quite
fast-flowing although not too wide. Tim took a running
jump at it and seemed to get stuck on the further bank.
Turning to me he laughed at himself and said something
about ruining his shoes. I made one of those pseudo-
caustic comments that men share with each other to the
effect that he needed to eat and drink less if he was
going to go in for the long jump at his age. Feeling
buoyant and, surely fitter than the slightly-tubby Tim, I
trotted downstream a few yards, gathered pace and, as
expected, managed to clear the water in one rather
effortful bound. So far so good.

Then it started to happen. The sand on the far
bank where I landed, identical to the sand all around if
perhaps a little damper, simply gave way. My feet went
into it, then my shins, then my knees, then my thighs. At
this point I must have lost some of my presence of mind
because I can remember shouting 'Bloody Hell!' I
looked back at Tim who was standing transfixed but
with an expression of mild delight on his genial
countenance as he saw revenge occurring so quickly
after my sarcastic remark about his eating habits. 'Hey!'
I yelled and floundered, still sinking in what seemed to

341

be trance-like slowness but was in fact pretty fast. The water reached my waist and I was still going down as if there were nothing beneath me but very soft mud. This was because there was nothing beneath me but very soft mud. Looking up as I thrashed I saw Pauline heading down a sand-dune at a hundred miles an hour with a smile on her face. When questioned later she said that she had been engaged as she ran in four simultaneous thoughts: 1. What am I going to tell Alice and Miranda? I mean, there won't even be a *body* at this rate. 2. I'm damned if I'm going to let Lance die *this* way; it's too absurd. 3. This is going to make a good story. 4. What a pity I didn't bring my camera.

She seized my arms and pulled, I kicked and struggled as hard as I could. My descent slowed, stopped, reversed and with painful slowness I was hauled panting from the quag.

A mile away were the Roman ruins at Bologna. I wondered if the quicksand had caught any of the legionnaires who came past on their way along the coast, going to Portugal or going home to Rome. They always seem so invincible, but you can never tell the minute.

2. STEEL

I have never been so cold as the evening we spent in Toledo in January 2013. As we walked up into the old town a kind of vicarious Proustian memory came to me – not one of my own exactly but the memory of reading Laurie Lee's account of Spain during the Civil War. In direct contradiction of the sunny image promoted by and for British holidaymakers from about 1960, Lee has his readers putting on extra sweaters and turning the heating up with his bone-cracking descriptions of the temperatures in the winters of the 1930s on the Spanish *meseta*, indeed the temperatures also to be found in the intervening towns and villages where he tramped and busked and cadged and got arrested for months on end. Toledo was a hollow iceberg, with wind.

Thoughts of olive-groves, blue seas, hot earth and cooling *sangria* seemed laughable, difficult to keep in the mind in fact as we went past shops with their doors shut and I fantasized about going in to buy something just to get warm. In the bar we ate the hottest *tapas*, drank *caldo* (a hot chicken soup) and sat near the radiator.

It made me wonder about Pauline. She is a woman without fuss, an uncomplainer, and of course, as marriage involves Newtonian laws of action and reaction, this has thrown me into the position, one I much dislike, of being the fusser and complainer. So I seemed in contrast even more discontented and feeble than I was. There was a good central-heating system in our hotel bedroom and I had yearned to stay in it practically regardless of the emptiness of my stomach, though here too there were thoughts of Laurie Lee who seemed to find almost nothing to eat during his walk across Spain before he got caught up in the Civil War. Reading him makes one feel hungry as well as freezing.

But Pauline: she expressed, as I shuddered and whined in the arctic blast when we staggered from bar to bar, a *preference* for winter, for the Gothic, for storms, darkness and all such travails and tortures. I altered my whine to a groan at the thought. Pauline opens bedroom windows to 'enjoy' the wind, the rain, the chill. She loves *outside* and often tries to convert outside to inside, eating meals under trees for instance, or inside to outside by opening doors. She is, I find myself thinking, Scottish; she likes it fresh. But that

343

can't be all of it. There is a stern metal inside her, which I think is attributable paradoxically to something much softer, namely happiness. If you are happy you are not cold. If you are happy you are not afraid. And it comes from inside you and does not depend on the environment being benign. So in a non-benign situation you are protected and in Toledo the weather simply didn't affect her.

There is nothing worse than a codger congratulating himself on his spouse. He seems to be saying 'Look what I've got!' often disguised under the proclamation 'I don't deserve her!' But I believe that Pauline is a special case. Other people are often unselfish, but selfishness and unselfishness are simply not categories clearly present in her mind. Other people are avaricious or un-mercenary, but money is simply not a factor in her thinking, and I don't mean that she is romantically spendthrift or touchingly childish about cash. Others have thoughts about religion, Life and Death, but Pauline has little to say about these and remains cheerful. She is *untroubled*, she is not *committed* to being as she is, not one who *makes a thing out of it*. She has no side, no *parti-pris*, no *ideas* – I mean as in 'ideas' about Life, Humanity, the Good, What Other People Should Do - those things that clutter up our perception of the silent universe and lead to so much trouble.

I am already well beyond the bounds of good taste in describing my wife. The most splendid, wonderful and saintly people tend to reveal, in the end, the aluminium at the bottom of the pan. The spoon scrapes and you have to make an adjustment. Heaven knows, self-knowledge has the same sobering effect in my own case. But Pauline? *Others abide our judgment, Thou art free.* And I don't know why that should be or

344

why she is as she is. She has a nice older sister, a rather selfish and irresponsible older brother, another brother who seems a slightly harsh *macho*, some other sisters cheerful enough in spite of hereditary medical conditions of the direst. In that list the sisters come off better than the brothers. Is that it then? Is it just gender I am talking about here? Women surely *are* nicer, no? Well perhaps; I have known lots of nice women but none of them were so spontaneously untroubled as Pauline. You know, with most people there's usually *something*. But she doesn't do *somethings*.

That evening she rubbed my back as we walked along the hard pavements of Toledo, to help me keep warm. She chatted, made plans. The cold was cold for her too, but it didn't affect her, it didn't trouble her. She is ...what? a natural Buddhist? She comes pre-detached? It has its effect on me of course. I find myself thinking about her welfare above my own without too much effort (such a relief!) and I try to echo her detachment, but hers is the real Zen kind, in the end uncomplicated because she does not share the self-consciousnesses, recriminations and complaints of the rest of us. So I don't succeed that much in echoing. Of herself she just thinks that she's a bit wet and weak-charactered of course.

Toledo is famous for its steel. For its swords, daggers, armour. You can still get such things in the shops there. They look at you coldly from the windows of barred emporia, sabres and empty suits of steel. Enough poignards to keep an Italian vendetta going for a millennium lie in heaps, waiting to be used as paper-knives. And we say that our *metal* is what makes us strong, fierce, able to stand up for ourselves; it keeps us rigid; it strengthens. Cement-block walls and other concrete constructions have metal in them, did you know? Reinforcing their strength, supplementing the bricklayer's efforts, keeping the show on the road. We have built a few of them in France ourselves, metal rods and all.

So what is the strong material that makes up Pauline? For steel is cold. That night in the Spanish city I thought of ice, which is water re-formed so that it can be walked on, driven over, and I didn't relish the thought. But she, cheerful in the cold, was as warm as summer and as supple as water. All things to all men perhaps, but without the damned *meaning to be that* that is the lot of the rest of us.

POSTSCRIPT 2016

As I write this I am not feeling altogether well. I assume, as usual, that it's one of those anonymous vague assaults by mother nature that come to all of us, one of the thousand natural shocks that flesh is heir to that will pass without ever coming to much. But I am 70 and one or two contemporaries have died or are dying, so this could of course be It. When Laurence Sterne died his last words were 'Here It Comes!'

So what should one think about death? Well, I take it that either we won't know anything about it when it happens, or it will be an event played out along the lines of the Near-Death Experience accounts of which so many have been published in the last thirty years.

If it is the former, nothingness, then there is nothing to say. Except that life, for all its good points, may not perhaps be an unmixed blessing. Should we go with Sophocles here: 'The best thing is not to have been born'? But I still like the philosophy entertained by the concierge heroine of *The Enchanted Hedgehog*, a novel by the French writer Muriel Barbery, of 2012. This middle-aged woman and her highly-intelligent 12-year-old friend Paloma conclude separately that only some sort of touching of the infinite can make life worth it; for them it seems that moments of great art, great beauty, great communion with nature, where you are briefly outside time as you feel great emotion without any desire, are the closest we can get to the 'consonance of the universe.' This latter is the thing experienced by mystics who see, in moments of illumination, that everything is all right, that there is no need, really, for the human heart to be troubled, that all manner of things shall be well. But most of the time life tends to be a brief and undignified struggle on the darkling plain where ignorant armies clash by night. See Goya.

As I have said elsewhere in this Memoir I have experienced the mystic 'oceanic' feeling of everything being all right more than once. In bed one morning in the senior dormitory at Belmont Abbey School when I was sixteen was the first; then once in my 30s when walking my dogs in King's Park in Stirling; then three times in my 40s during Mass at the Catholic church in Callendar in Perthshire. There are doubtless plenty of good neurological comments to be made on these experiences and my brain may well, for obscure reasons, have found itself on these five occasions in exactly the condition needed to create an illusion of complete security and happiness that needs no further explanation. But then there comes the subjective rub: the knowledge of all being well that I had on these occasions was a far surer and less illusory knowledge than any other knowledge I have ever possessed or been possessed by. If you had told me at the time that I was touching or being touched by something merely neuro-chemical or psychoanalytic I would have thought the idea ridiculous. Which proves nothing of course, but may constitute a sort of stand-off.

If these 'Hedgehog' moments are mere illusion then we are doubly fooled. But what if they are foretastes of a reality to be met after death? There is quite a lot of evidence that this may be the case.

So the second possibility, the one so frequently outlined for us by accounts of the Near-Death Experience, that is to say the dark tunnel, the being of light, the life review and so on may turn out to be the way we go after death, and if so then we must do some careful thinking. Of course this would be very nice. The dead, or rather the nearly-dead, say that they have gone to a place without pain. The light there is very beautiful but doesn't hurt the eyes; all things seem to be well. This would perhaps enable one to see, as mystics have seen, that the struggles and dolours of earthly life are to be set against a bigger picture which, though incomprehensible to us, will make the odds all even.

But it might be that even in this more pleasant case much the same applies as in the case of the Nothingness that I considered first. The crucial question here is one of identity - a suitable topic on which to finish any autobiographical writing I suppose. On the 'Other Side', in the scenes of the afterlife as presented by the NDE accounts, all is indeed well but, as in the case of the first possibility (pure unconsciousness) though from another angle, all may only be well because 'I' will not really exist. There is no time over there, apparently; there is 'only one of us' (so no 'me', no 'you'); the nirvana that awaits us is a consciousness so pure that it might as well be unconsciousness: that 'n' at the beginning of the Sanskrit word *'nirvana'* has negative connotations and means 'out'; the *'vana'* may be related to 'fan' – a device for blowing air. So the word implies the 'blowing out' of a candle – *nirvana* is a place where things such as ego and desire *are not.* Behold the uses of Linguistics and the establishment of Proto-Indo-European as the mother language of, *inter alia*, Sanskrit and English. [21]

In either case (Nothingness, or a Buddhist-style 'non-Life After Death') 'Lance Butler' ceases to exist. In the second possibility, which is something similar to what we read in NDE accounts, I (he) may continue with the illusion of separate existence for a while until

---

[21] For further reflections on the matter of time I have added a PPS below, a few poems I wrote on the subject at the beginning of, ahem, this century.

the beings of light and the deceased relatives gently tell me (him) that there is another stage, some moving on to do, an ascent to a higher consciousness in which I (he) will see that all life has been a species of illusion and all separate identity only part of a greater identity.

Most people would I think prefer the idea of going on as part of a greater consciousness, especially if it is as loving and pain-free as the NDE accounts make it seem, to the blank void of immediate unconscious nothingness. Me too. But as far as 'Lance Butler' is concerned there isn't as much to choose between them as might appear.

Quite a lot of people who canvas the life-after-death possibility seem to end up as Reincarnationists, a third possibility which could well be right and which does not necessarily exclude the other two. Ian Stevenson's books on the subject, the result of many years of proper field research, look quite convincing. But if I am to be condemned to an infinite series of rather painful lives I'm not sure that I wouldn't prefer nirvana. And that's the reward in Buddhism of course – an escape from the cycle of lives, being let off at last into… well, into the nothingness, more or less.

I am inclined to think that the NDE material, supported as it is by a multitude of channelling, past-life, healing and other 'spiritual' accounts, may be the more likely of the first two possibilities as outlined. Proof of continued consciousness may never be totally convincing, but there are some small, unspectacular elements that keep on being repeated in the NDE accounts that make me take them quite seriously. One is the feeling experienced by people on the other side that they are free of pain. They nearly all say that they are glad to get away from the slings and arrows, the natural shocks, the hurting body. And then they *all* say, even less expectedly, that when conversing with a being of light or a deceased relative their words are not really words, involve no movement of the lips, and are in fact a form of telepathy. Now why would *every* NDE subject *invent* those same details? 1. No pain. 2. Telepathic communication. And, to add another example already mentioned, they all say that the beautiful light over there is very strong but doesn't hurt their eyes. What are the chances of such a very widespread coincidence of narratives if it's all just made up?

There is no need to regret life if we remember, with Hardy, that it is only ever a 'series of seemings.' Trying to *catch* life is a very common undertaking among us: we build solid houses or families, amass money or trophies or friends, take photographs, write memoirs. But nobody who thinks about it for a moment can seriously think that life has really been *caught* by any of these things. We say 'I'll love you forever', or 'this is a perpetual annuity', or 'Shakespeare is not for an age but for all time'…. but such things do not ultimately wash. This is not just because your house will not last forever, or that you will certainly not live in it forever, though those are already quite good arguments against permanent catching; it is also because there is no *now* in which you ever actually *have* anything. Remember Proust on 'possessing' a woman: 'possession in which, after all, nothing is really possessed' ('*la possession ou, d'ailleurs, on ne possède rien*') or think of Derrida on '*la présence*' which is, according to his excellent argument, the one thing that is never… present.

Time and space are not real; life is uncatchable; the past only patchily available; the future *not here*. There is, truly, *no life*. Only stories, only the wind formed into words. These things I have shored against

351

my ruins. Beckett's 'unspeakable home', if ever we reach it, will be bereft of even the words that would tell the story of what I could imagine to have been my life.

PPS. FIVE POEMS

EXAMINATION OF CONSCIENCE

Separate inspections of our lives
Lay their dark arms about the pasts we've made
Explaining this and auscultating that,
Imagining the backward rush of tide.

But life's in front, it isn't what we were.
That day you kicked the dog, the day you lied
About the stolen pen, are surely not
Escapable by reminiscent shame;

They stand before you as a newly-styled
Occasion to forget and ride the wave.
Our elegant excuses don't convince
Even ourselves, nor others in the field.

Confession's not about the past but hope.
It asks us to resolve to sin *no more*
As with resolve we muster to attempt
The empty future with an armoured heart.

The dark arms hold us, letting nothing slip
But secretly we feel the soft contempt
Of pondering the past. The actor looking back
Remembers only who was in the Rep,

His lines elude him. But when sudden roles
Unplayed are offered him, an altered case:
You see his eyes enlarge, his shining mouth
Open already for the unknown lines.

We struggle slowly to the foreign shore
To find it quite familiar and warm.
The music plays as it has played before
And on the beach we estimate the past.

But though the waters passed us, seem behind,
They wash beyond the isthmus, just as fair;
Their necessary transience need not blight
Our happy views, Pacific in their width.

There lies the sea my mariners! You're right,
Tomorrow's battle trumps all bye-gone wars,
You've not arrived, you're only on the way:
Don't mutter about tonnage, watch the stars!

HERE

Getting the cash before the evening out
Is not a prior or preliminary act
To acts that follow. It's the act itself.
The night that drags along thereafter only *seems*
To be the thing prepared for; it's no more
The act than's the decision to begin.

Whatever we expect is just as *here*
In expectation as in so-called fact.
We cannot be or not be as we like -
We do and are not done to as we think.

Packing explosives teenage martyrs fail
To notice that their crucial time is now;
The paradise for which they here prepare
Is going on around them as they load.
What better meeting could there be with God
Than thinking you'll be dying in a tick

354

With all your mind jampacked with fear and hope?
Why this is paradise nor are they out of it;
The scraps of flesh they turn to aren't *the thing*
Any more than that last view of photographs
They catch in passing cafes as they go:
The snaps that Ahmed took in London rain
When he went over to complete his course.

Preparatory comments always fail:
'Before I start' the tyro speaker grins,
As if when speaking he'd not started to.
The problem is with time: Now's never Now,
But seems to be as long as you don't look.

Here is the paradox: it's never here.
The countries that are named in Proust survive
Just as ideas of a present tense
While what he saw in Venice or beside
The sea at Balbec steadily recedes
Waiting to be named or re-record
Its present hopelessly in perfect art.

Hope not! Don't *wait*! Just notice what you can;
Your 'life' is just imagination fixed
Between two expectations, neither real.

MOMENTUM

There is no thing that's peaceful. If you wait
Time undertakes a circle after all,
Going and going without chance of stop.
Our promising new sofas never will
- All web and cushions underpinning weight -
Permit us rest as promised. There's no mind
Or insect, silver lode, moraine or fire
Could ever catch itself into a *still*.

Again the bloody spring comes round; in veins
The cat's blood readies for the next assault.
New juice in barley rises in the stalks
Only for harvesters to make it beer.
Invisible, the walnuts brace for thrust
To take their small hard greenness into brown,
Their hard brown dryness to the wire rack
That brings them their destruction and men cakes.

No waiting will bring satisfaction then,
No action leaves us at a final pause.
You may as well abandon *ending up*
And let the absent-minded moment hang
If hang it will though, mostly, busy man,
Unlike the yellow butterflies in spring,
Who do not rest but don't expect too much
And make us think we're static as they move,
Expects the second second after next.

The package holiday invests in sand
Unmoving on the glossy shore, the glass
(Time flowing smoothly through the narrow pass)
Is made irrelevant these lovely days.
The implication of the palm is clear:
Your purposes are less dynamic here.
This holy vision luminously guys
The touched-up silence of the summer blue.

And where's the need for other things at all?
What's wrong with doing nothing in the sun?
The sandflies' answer will be short and sharp;
However good you feel the climbing pain
Of sitting still too long will help direct
Your thoughts to other shores 'more comfortable'
Where, *rich enough*, you'd ever be at ease.
But that's delusion as all fish can tell –

Moving forever in the moving seas.

What's worth it's worth it only for the time;
No other prospects, carefully watched, allow
The distant blue to come to here and now
Or golden evenings *fix* their perfect tones.
It's watercolours that we live in, not
Oils or acrylic or more fixed veneer.

A small screw-ended light-bulb in the trash
Invites contempt but also some respect:
The cut you're careful not to let it give
Lies in the metamorphosis of glass.
'Don't waste your time' they say; they mean that life
Will endlessly provide more time to waste
While on the fiction that 'it came to pass'
We meditate serenely while in haste.

It's meant to be like that. No stops. The one
Condition of existence is unchanging change.
Go on. There is no going to one side.
Go on! The stillness is, if anywhere, within,
Where nothing is – only your grain of self
Unsuffocating in the rush of time.

There's no thing that is peaceful – should not be.
Each slight reaction in the movement gauges
What's always going on behind the air.
Our open-topped existence carries on,
Bumping and rushing, looking forward more
The more the second jumps. The open door
Leads on to doors more open. Here and there
The detail of the past is what presages
Futures imperfect which in turn
Look back at every turning of the stair.

GETTING RELIGION

Getting religion is like falling in love,
You find more things to smile at, choke off fear,
Like people, cease to mind the rain. A peopled
World, replacing robots, plastic, systems, cold
Unmeaning, bubbles before you to invite
Belief that now, at last, you've learnt the trick
Not to slow down but simply *dance with* time.

In every atom, papercup, ringbinder, bird
Some spirit moves, unknowable but bright,
Taking the horror from the depths of stuff,
Making the deep one light, the red one green.

Inside this country it is always spring,
The spring inside the hailstones crying out,
Not to deny the winter but to leave
Irrelevant the coldness and the harsh.

Behind the grimy window smiles the Tao,
Beyond the rubbish heap some blue god leaps,
Above the gutter sings the nearby star.
One need not concentrate on differences

Yet differences there are. I do not fear,
For instance, changes in the heart of God.
The love that moves the world can go on moving
Within me or without me, it should care,

While were you to abandon this warm house
It would be left without too many things:
Hearth, garden, garages and stream,
Windows, cello music, apple trees.

HERCULANEUM 2000 AD

Coming here now, much later, on a tour,
My red and ochre walls have lost a lot.
The corners of mosaic floors have dusted up
And pigeon-shit spots marble at my feet.

I cared most deeply, when a girl, then (then!)
For these clean rooms, the detail on a wall,
Fresh paint, clean tables, several simple acts.
The house was spare; now nothing's here at all.

This broken place and all that's come to fill
My quiet domestic in the aeons since -
The hot invasion, the cold burial,
The excavation and the tourist trade -

Seem to have left deposits furlongs thick
Across the past, though it's as yesterday
That I remember how it was we died.
My birthday. I expected a surprise.

Since then (the tons of scalding mud, the screams)
I have been back to earth a dozen times.
Each time I have pursued the gods I knew,
The body's chimes, the soul of passing themes.

Now only, Japanese, and grouped in squads
By guides with numbered batons to conduct
Our way through my old town, my family
And friends do tourist duty in the heat.

They do not see what I see, never knew
The me I had then nor could sympathise
With that glad girl I was. I don't expect
Great art, great meaning, great faith or great love.

In fact I'm happy that my mother's face
Presents a general pity for the dead.
I only see in shocking waves of pain
The personal disaster of that day.

We are not as we were, we need not be.
Again the paintings beckon and the dust,
Taking me back to Roman life as lived,
Reminds me what I was – and what was not.

Between the sea and the engulfing mud,
Like creatures now extinct but still displayed
In illustrations in old travel books,
We perished as a species without point.

I've been a sailor wanting last of all
To go beyond Gibraltar, seek the west,
A lover for whom all love was gathered up
In purposeless desire of here and now.

I was a soldier who would be a king
And died at Acre in the dusty heat
Fighting for arms and honour, God and flag;
I cannot now remember what it meant.

I was Chatterton and his nursemaid too,
Destroyed by visions of romantic death.
Now, seeing the still-bright gold-foil of my walls,
I cannot tell what purposes I had.

Given another dozen lives I'd spend
Each single one here cleaning quiet rooms.
All other paths lead nowhere – only this
Fulfils the pointless destiny of man.

What is there after all to do when, hot,
A million tons of mud undoes your work?
Why, nothing but to start the cleaning up,
Put things in order, light the stove again.

Perhaps that is the reason that I'm now,
On my first holiday from Osaka,
Abroad and silent, happy just to see
The newly-tidied place where life went past.

APPENDIX

As promised in footnote 1 early in these memoirs, I quote here a passage that expresses what was good about the British Empire.

From Arthur Grimble's A PATTERN OF ISLANDS (1952)

[This is a description of life in the Gilbert and Ellice Islands during the late colonial period and the situation of the workers who supported much of the economy of the islands by working for the British Phosphate Company, later the government-owned British Phosphate Commissioners. Grimble went to the central Pacific in 1915 and worked in the relatively new Protectorate there; he came to love the place and was in turn much loved. LB]

'The Company recruited its Gilbert and Ellice workers under indenture for two years' service, in drafts of two or three hundred at a time. One third of every draft was made up of married men who were allowed their wives and children with them; the rest were *roronga* or bachelors. Living conditions on Ocean Island were excellent for married and single workers alike. The recruit ships were handsome vessels of 6,000 tons or more with covered decks and spacious 'tween decks admirably fitted for their purpose. The young men flocked to the recruiting tables.

The company... was justly proud of its record as a thoughtful employer; I do not suppose its care for the welfare of native labourers has often been equalled or ever bettered in any other part of the British Empire.

One way or another, the Gilbert and Ellice Islanders had to be prepared, in a world from which they could not remain forever segregated, for the shock of new ideas and disturbing influences from outside. Fate could not have given them a kindlier or more profitable teacher. Missionaries had brought them schools, the British administration had assured them protection in their homes, and they had learned from trading ships something about the value of their goods to the white man; but it remained for the phosphate industry alone to endow them as a nation, from 1900 onwards, with a sense of their own personal value to the world at large. From Ocean Island they got a working knowledge of Europeans in the mass, a standard of the manual skills needed to compete with the demands of civilisation, and real opportunities of learning and exploiting such skills. What the Company and later the Commissioners gave them was, in effect, a kind of university where, in a happy indigenous environment, they could graduate from the state of Neolithic fisherfolk into beings with a technique and a morale sufficient for their survival under the inevitably increasing pressure of modern cultures. If the Gilbertese have outlived today [we might say 'survived'], without loss of their national élan vital, the disintegrating effects of the Japanese invasion of 1942 followed by the American occupation of 1943, this miracle is greatly due to the new interest values, standing for a bridge of hope into the future, which the phosphate enterprise built up in them over the first forty years of the century.'

[Grimble was an imperial administrator. He devoted himself to his islands for several decades with only tenuous support from London or Delhi or Australia. He was poorly paid, often ill and spent periods of up to five *years* separated from his beloved wife and children while he battled on to serve the Gilbertese in their own interests. An example of this last point was that he and his predecessors put an end to the vicious inter-tribal conflicts that had beset the Pacific islands from time immemorial, and they did so without bloodshed or, indeed, troops. His respect and love for the islanders stands out on every page of his book. Their peaceful life, and peaceful transition to the modern world as described above, contrasts with Grimble's own terrible illnesses and trials. His description of going home to England with his family on furlough is hair-raisingly horrible, but he never complains. We are near to sainthood here, and at all events a million light-years from the cliché of the colonial exploiter and bully. LB]